The Life & Times of Norman Travers

As told to Cathy Buckle

Published in 2010 by Catherine Buckle
cbuckle@zol.co.zw   www.cathybuckle.com

Publisher: Catherine Buckle
Editor: Allen Radford
Designer: Jacqui Taylor-Radford
fraserdesign@zol.co.zw
Photographs: Luis Manso Preto; Travers family albums;
Wikipaedia Commons, Denise Lues

Reproduction: Tien Wah Press, Singapore
Printing and binding: Tien Wah Press, Singapore

ISBN 978-1-904289-70-8

ACKNOWLEDGEMENTS BY NORMAN TRAVERS

Trying to write a book is, I found, more than difficult - and my memory is not what it used to be! But I can honestly say that, without Cathy Buckle's tireless help, guidance and hard work, you would have nothing to read. Of course Gilly, always my right-hand man, kept my flagging mind on the task. Also, my family - Barbara, John and Simon - helped. Then, David Hamilton and several other old friends whose memories and thoughts are much clearer than mine, added to this book.

The excellent drawings and etchings done by Anne Knott, Sharon Alberts and Margaret Shattock deserve praise and my grateful thanks.

Of course, other people must not be left out. Many of our African staff, such as Murambiwa, Elijah and Mattheus, who were loyal and wonderful people both with animals and the formation of the game park, are very special.

Lastly, thanks to our very special animals - what wonderful friends you all were.

Norman Travers
February 2010

AUTHOR'S ACKNOWLEDGEMENTS

For the notes, chats and many hours of recordings, I am indebted to Jane Matthews, David Hamilton, Bob Knott, Richard Thornycroft, Tony Mitchell, Bill Bedford, Mark Milbank, Howard Matthews and John Clatworthy.

To the Travers family, who happily answered my endless stream of questions and volunteered long-forgotten memories (good and bad), thank you: Barbara, Simon, John and Judy. Being geographically closest, John and Judy bore the brunt of my questioning and their time, input, support and enthusiasm was invaluable.

To Sheila Ware, whose book about Wedza, 'Winter Cricket', was indispensable and who kindly gave permission for the inclusion of numerous extracts from it. Thanks, also, to Phil Gray and Richard Thornycroft for permission to include extracts from their books and to Nicholas Duncan, Fettes Falconer, Morgan Chokwenda, Gareth Hassall and Tim Landsberg for providing anecdotes. Special thanks to Anne, Sharon and Margaret for the time, effort and love you put into your drawings - they help bring the adventure to life.

Special thanks to Ian Murphy, for his invaluable advice with regards production.

Lastly, to Norman and Gill for welcoming me into their home, for telling me the story of their wonderful life-long adventure, for making me laugh and for endless cups of tea and home-made biscuits. What a time we had, thank you.

Cathy Buckle
Marondera
February 2010

FOREWORD

I feel it a privilege to have been asked to write the foreword to Norman Travers' autobiography. Very sadly Norman died before the book's publication: I hope it will be read by many people for it not only gives a lively account of his own very active life and involvement in his country's affairs, but also a most interesting picture of life in what was then still Southern Rhodesia.

My husband, Christopher Soames, had been appointed as Governor in December 1979 in the run up to elections and Zimbabwe's independence, and he and I met Norman and Gill Travers through mutual friends - Ian and April Piercy who live at Ruwa about half an hour from Harare (then still Salisbury). Coincidentally I had already met their daughter, Barbara, who was a trained nurse working in England, and who looked after my mother on several occasions.

My husband very quickly came to know and esteem Norman, and valued his views and advice on a number of matters. He particularly admired Norman's fair and unprejudiced opinions, and his acceptance with optimism for the future of his country.

We all became friends, and we enjoyed our visits to the Travers' Imire Game Park, and particularly an expedition we made with them to Inyanga (Nyanga) very soon after the ceasefire in December 1979.

I am so glad not to have lost touch with such good friends met in exciting and indeed, historic, circumstances.

Lady Mary Soames
London, England.
14 April 2010

Norman's mother - Amelia Agnes Travers

Mrs Travers (Manageress)
Castcliff Hotel
Weihaiwei

Norman's father - Norman (Meckiffe) Travers

6

Norman at seven years old

Chapter 1

FROM SIBERIAN TIGERS
TO MONKEY SKIN LOIN CLOTHS
China to Africa 1921 - 1941

"Oh Norman! Go round to the kitchen; we can't have blood all over the carpet!"

This is one of my earliest memories of Mum - always practical and sensible, even after I'd crashed my bike, smashed my nose and arrived on the front doorstep dripping blood. Mum was tough. She had to be, bringing up a child on her own in China in the 1920s.

My mother, Amelia Agnes Travers, was forty-five years old when I was born on 10 October 1921. Her first husband had died in 1918 and they'd had one daughter, Margaret, my half-sister, who was twenty years older than me. Mum married again but it didn't last long and she'd already divorced my father by the time I was born. Mum was a partner in the Eastcliffe Hotel in Wei Hai Wei, Shantung Province, North China. Pregnant and on her own, she went to stay with her brother, my Uncle Tommy, when her time was near and, as a result, I was born in Korea.

Mum kept a record of my early milestones in a padded hardcover album entitled Baby's Record Book. Here are sepia photographs of her in a long floral dress, hat and closed shoes and my father in uniform: long jacket, wide belt and trousers caught in puttees (long strips of cloth wound spirally round the leg from ankle to knee for protection and support). In his right hand Dad carried a stick, something I later learned was a trademark of British officers who always carried a stick, both for defence and to steady themselves.

The Eastcliffe Hotel in Wei-Hai Wei

When I was two, Mum recorded in the baby album that my favourite toys were a small wheelbarrow and a gun. At three, in a space reserved for 'stunts,' Mum wrote: "Very fond of catching crabs and 'pop-fish' - in fact any 'creepy crawlies' out of the sea."

My early years were spent with Mum in Wei Hai, as it is now called, where the hotels were closed in winter but open and full all through the summer. Wei Hai was a summer resort not only for foreigners, from Hong Kong and Shanghai, but also a station for the British China Fleet. During the summer months all the British ships were based in Wei Hai - the submarine mother-ship, aircraft carriers and cruisers. The British would hold shipboard parties for the children during the holidays and it was all a great adventure. Visions of HMS Hermes and Eagle still flood my memories.

I was sent to the China Inland Mission School in Chefoo, (now Yantai) when I was six. It was a boarding school and Mum could only see me occasionally during term time. Memories of Chefoo are hazy but I do remember being confirmed. We had to wade out into the sea where the priest blessed us then ducked our heads under water. A strange experience for a little boy. I also remember having my appendix taken out whilst at school in Chefoo. Mum was coming to visit but I'd been gated for a week for some misdemeanour or other and so, in a panic, I pretended to be sick. As the school had just had an appendix scare, they whipped out my appendix anyway and the doctor said he couldn't understand why there was nothing wrong with it! Good old Mum was very sympathetic!

I didn't meet my father until I was six or seven years old and have very few memories of him. Dad was an officer in the Chinese Customs and he supervised workers unloading ships His name was originally Norman Meckiffe but he changed his surname to Travers in 1920 when he was trying to get into the acting world. Travers, he thought, was a more appropriate stage name! I didn't see Dad often but when I did he always gave me presents, one of which was a racing car that I can still picture. I went to stay with him once, in Shanghai, and we watched the Japanese planes bombing the outskirts of the city.

In the winter school holidays I sometimes went to stay with my Uncle Tommy and Aunty Rae and their three children at Puckhin House in Korea. My uncle ran a gold mine there and my memories are of snow and more snow! Uncle Tommy was an outgoing, cheerful man who enjoyed duck shooting and was a great hunter. The house was full of tiger skins and hunting trophies and for a long time I had a photo of him with two Siberian tigers lying at his feet. I loved listening to Uncle Tommy's hunting stories and perhaps I inherited my love of hunting and wildlife from him.

Folded neatly into her baby album, Mum kept a letter I had written to her from Korea in 1929. A typical boarding-school-type letter, written in pencil on hand-drawn lines, it records animals and hunting achievements that obviously impressed me even at that age:

Hakochin, Korea, April 19, 1929

Dear Mother,

How are you? I'm very well.
Our little baby bird is ded now. Tomorrow we are going for a very nice picknik at Suirbon, and two cars are going and they are Uncle Tommy and Dr Ewers. Mr Cooper has came the other day. Uncle Tommy, Mr Cooper and Aunty Rae went hunting and they got some snipe and teal duck, all-together they made 20.
We have seven parakeets now... Thank you so much for your lovely letter.

Your dear son, Norman.

When I was about eight, Mum gave me a Daisy air gun for Christmas with instructions that I should try not to shoot humans with it, just birds. I couldn't hit a thing until I met a British soldier who hit half a dozen sparrows in no time and taught me the basics, which stood me in good stead the rest of my hunting days. Another great ambition was to have my own boat, a punt, but Mum wouldn't allow it until I could swim half a mile in the sea. This I managed when I was eight and, from then on, swimming, fishing and boating became second nature to me. I recall an exciting moment when some Chinese fishermen came in with a giant jellyfish, which was some three feet in diameter and considered a great delicacy. Another recollection is of a beautiful Remembrance Day feast, when the Chinese sailed small rafts with red paper sails into the sunset, from the harbour, to honour their dead.

In 1933 I left China, by sea for England, to attend senior school. It was a scary time for a lonely colonial boy. The next four years were spent at Tonbridge, a well-known public school in Kent. As a scholar I did not shine and most of my reports seem to say: "If he tried harder he would do better!"

I remember being caned six of the best by the House Master, a strict disciplinarian, and getting the same from prefects. I don't think it did me much harm! We played a lot of sport *viz.* rugby, rowing, boxing, squash and cricket.

During the last years of school I kept an aquarium in my study, full of little fish such as sticklebacks, newts and other creatures. Once I was spied on by two prefects (as my housemaster suspected I was up to some mischief) but,

sadly for them, all I had was a bottle containing fish and other creatures that I'd caught for the aquarium. While still at school I also went to some nearby stables to be taught horsemanship. On about the second lesson I fell off, landing on my tail and couldn't walk for a week. Horse riding, I decided, wasn't for me!

Mum came over from China one school holiday. It must've been quite a journey for her on the Trans-Siberian railway, all along the east coast of Russia, and then by sea to England. Most other school holidays in England were spent with my sister Margaret, who we called Flip, and her husband Frank Chubb. Flip was very outgoing and full of fun and Frank was a quietly spoken, likeable gentleman and we had many happy adventures together.

On leaving school in 1939 I tried, through a friend of Flip's, to get a job tea-planting in Ceylon. Nothing came of that, but when a job as learner assistant, on a tobacco farm in Southern Rhodesia, was offered I jumped at it. Unfortunately, it had to wait as war broke out and all shipping was cancelled, so I went to live with my godfather, Charles Hopwood, a solicitor, in London. He was a super man and I remember thinking that he must've played a lot of rugby as he had cauliflower ears - quite an achievement and cause for some admiration! Charles was a very outgoing, strong man whom I greatly admired and he gave me a job in his office, which was not for me at all: sitting on a high stool studying books in the foggy, rainy days of November in London. I thought, then, that I might as well join up and, so, went to the nearest recruiting office but was told that the army was full, except for the Pioneer Corps. This didn't appeal so I went to a Guards recruiting office where the tough Sergeant said, "Fine, you're tall enough, sign here!"

I said, "Only for the duration of the war."

He looked at me with a stern face from under his peaked cap. "My boy, you initially join the Guards for at least seven years."

I walked away, positive that the war would only last six or eight months!

Then, from out of the blue, a passage to Cape Town came up and off I went on my delayed trip to Southern Rhodesia. What a lovely trip! I was eighteen years old and feeling very grown up as I set off. On my first night in the bar I ordered a drink and the bar-steward said, "Don't pay, sign a slip and you'll get a bill in Cape Town."

So it was I learnt my first lesson on how to be foolish!

On arrival in Cape Town I found that I had used up all my cash on my bar account (and tips) on the ship and was, consequently, completely broke. Luckily, however, I still had my train ticket to Rhodesia and, after selling off a few odd things, had enough to pay for my first few meals on the train. We stopped at occasional towns in South Africa, but never for long, just chugging along, day and night. The journey from Cape Town to Southern

Rhodesia took five days. When we crossed the border, at Plumtree, we changed over to a Rhodesian train. These were coal-driven and, unlike today, all the crew were white people, including the engine-driver, stoker and stewards. I was fascinated by the open countryside and by some of the farms, which seemed to be enormous. There were not many farmhouses and miles and miles of bushveld and, because it was December and well into the rainy season, everything was lush and green. There were some telephone poles but, as yet, no electricity lines. The train passed through many African villages where people were still dressed in animal skins. Loincloths, made out of monkey skins, were worn by men and many of the women were bare-breasted. We passed through several small settlements with tin-roof buildings and I noticed that there were very few motor cars to be seen. On the first night of the journey after Plumtree, the dinner bell went but, being broke, I stayed put until the steward came and asked what the trouble was. I explained my problem and further explained that I was a new immigrant. He responded "Leave it to me!" and, for the next two days, a tray of food arrived at every meal - all on the house! What super people these Rhodesians are, I thought.

On arriving at Marandellas, my destination, I asked how to get to the Scott family at Welton Farm. A man suggested I stayed at the hotel for the night and said he would contact Dr Leggate who would pick me up and take me to Welton. I didn't go to the Hotel, as I had no money, and slept on a bench at the railway station! The next morning I briefly looked around and the first thing I saw was the Marandellas Hotel, topped with a tin roof and later learnt it was a very friendly place:

"Mr and Mrs Plint ran the old Marandellas Hotel with it's always-open bar - probably the most friendly place in the village!" (A Fragment of Time)

There were a couple of Indian shops, one owned by a Mr Shingadia, who ran a type of general dealer store, selling a bit of everything (apparently at wholesale prices) for re-selling at farm stores. The town looked very small but I didn't stray far from the hotel and soon my lift arrived and we set out for Welton Farm.

Dr Leggate was the government doctor in Marandellas and used to travel around the farms, visiting people who needed to see him. He went to Wedza once a week to treat patients at the clinic. The journey with Dr Leggate gave me my first sight of the countryside near Marandellas and Wedza - gently sloping green hills and lovely bush and farms all along the road. The roads were all gravel, sandy in patches - of course in those days all the grading was done by oxen pulling a grader. Not a lot of bush clearing had been done except for small acreages of maize and tobacco. People planted their mealies only when the rainy season was well established and so the plants were still only a few inches high. I noticed a lot of ex-army and navy names on the signboards we passed; major this, colonel that and captain such-and-such. In a book about the district, published many years later, this military concentration was also noted:

"The South Marandellas community, because of its large compliment of former Army and Navy officers, was often referred to as 'The War Lords', the chief of whom, as far as I remember, were said to be Charles English, Bill Nash and Herbert MacIlwaine." (A Fragment of Time)

Later I would discover that Major MacIlwaine, who lived in the area, was a great one for bringing out settlers to Rhodesia. We travelled out on what is now the Watershed Road, turned left at Major Chomely's farm and went 15-20kms until we reached Welton.

Frank and Margaret Scott and their three children owned Welton farm and were a wonderfully friendly family. We lived in rondavels with thatched roofs, had no electricity and used paraffin lamps at night. I had an iron bed and a chair and water came from a well, wound up in a bucket on the end of a rope. Bath time, in the evenings, was organised by an African worker who arrived with a tin bath and one hot and one cold four-gallon tin of water. When I had finished bathing the whole caboodle was carted away to the next rondavel. Sometimes when the tin bath sprang a leak it was patched with some sort of tar, which did the job very well, except that it made the water quite dirty and you could end up dirtier than before you started! The four-gallon square petrol tin was the universal container for carrying water, petrol and paraffin and, later, even being used for roofing of chicken houses. The tins came in pairs, in cases made of half-inch thick wood and these were also very useful, being converted into tables, bookcases and all manner of other household furniture. So life began for me on Welton, where I was the Learner Assistant, for which I received no pay but was fed. Who could ask for anything more as an eighteen year old.

Frank Scott was born Rhodesian and his wife Margaret had come out from England. Frank was a typical Rhodesian farmer: tough but fair and hard-working. We used oxen for ploughing and hauling wagons. I remember so well getting my lunch basket and climbing up onto the wagon and going out with the gang. We would reap tobacco all morning and then come back in the afternoon, tie the tobacco on sticks and load it into the barns. I was very much a learner assistant and was shown what had to be done and then just went and got on with it, sometimes doing the jobs and other times supervising. A lot of the African workers had come from Malawi and we communicated by speaking *Chilapalapa* (a pidgin language of mixed English, Shona and Ndebele words). They were simple, hard-working people and I found them very good blokes to work with - at the weekends they seemed to get very drunk on their local beer!

One day, with the help of a couple of the lads, I killed a python that had swallowed a buck. I knew no better in those days, thinking that all snakes were dangerous. We brought it back to the barns for everyone to see. A few hours later our dogs kept barking near the barns. I went to investigate and found the python alive and striking at anyone who came near!

Even at this early stage I was intrigued with wildlife and studying things like birds. I shot quite a few and one of the most extraordinary things I found (behind the eye of a Lizard Buzzard) was an infestation of live worms. I've no idea what they were and should have followed this up with some professional bird people, but never did.

Our weekends were often spent at neighbouring farms - arriving in Frank's rather clapped-out old Ford truck. Tennis was usually the order of the day. Once a month we went to the local rifle range at Wedza where shooting with .303 rifles took place.

Norman and Flip with a duiker on Imire

I remember once leaving the barns and had just got to the Watershed Road when I came across a boy, about my age, on an open wagon being led by sixteen trek-oxen. His name was John Smith, which seemed odd because he was an Afrikaner! There was an Afrikaans community in Wedza but we didn't seem to mix much, the British and the Afrikaners. John Smith would later become one of the biggest landowners in Wedza.

At that time I didn't really know much about the kind of life earlier farmers had lived but found out, many years later, about farming in the area just before the First World War, in what were then nostalgically called 'the good old days':

"Every farmer in beginning his farming career had to sleep under a bucksail and gradually build himself pole-and-dagga huts and eventually, after years, build, mainly by himself, a brick house.

Nearly all of us started by growing thirty acres of tobacco, with only two barns. Many would say why start farming on such a small scale?

Being up to fifty miles from the railhead, it took three days by wagon with sixteen oxen to get to Marandellas, a day to Salisbury, if you were lucky enough to catch a goods train, and three more days to get back home. Therefore we seldom went into Salisbury more than twice a year. It took a month out of each year to transport produce to Marandellas." (Winter Cricket)

The writer of these memoirs was Dennis Collins, an old Wedza man who'd been farming in the area since 1911. Dennis described how their lives were kept free from boredom by "…tackling snakes, leopards, lions, wild dogs and level-crossings with wild trains." Collins knew what he was talking about too, once having confronted and chased off a leopard with a *knobkerrie* (round-headed walking stick) and once being dragged along by a train when the spare wheel of his car got caught by the engine of the locomotive! Our lives were far more sedate and we occupied ourselves with tennis parties and shooting trips, which were commonplace outings of the late 1930s.

We had some wonderful characters in the Wedza community. Monty Laurie, who owned Numwa Farm, was one. Monty was a remittance man and, being the bad egg of his family in England, was sent out to Rhodesia with enough money to buy his food, drink and also a farm. He kept asking his family for more money until his father sent out his sister to make a report. Monty got hold of the senior herdsmen from a neighbouring farm, whose cattle numbered thousands. He told the herdsmen he would tip them handsomely if, during the week of his sister's visit, they would drive their many herds past his house.

Can you picture Monty sitting on his verandah as herds of beautiful cattle walked past, saying to his sister: "If only I had £500/- to buy some good bulls, think of the lovely calves there would be!"

His plan obviously worked as the report from his sister was favourable!

Years later Monty ended up working for Hugh Baker and one of his first jobs was to reap tobacco. He was sent off with his packed lunch, thermos of tea and work gang by Hugh and he returned in the afternoon saying, "Aah, it's been a great day, we've reaped a lot of tobacco and done really well."

Just then Hugh Baker's neighbour phoned and said, "Hey you! What's going on, you reaped a whole barn of tobacco off my farm today."

Monty had spent the day reaping someone else's crop!

The last we heard of Monty was that his parents had died and he had inherited their estate in England. There was a title too, Duke I think it was. However, Monty didn't last long and died about nine months later - probably due to too much booze!

Another amazing character in the area was Captain Priest. He wrote two or three bird books and that was his real passion in life. There was a story, in the 1940s, that Captain Priest had gone to Moçambique and tried to prove to the authorities that German submarines were refuelling off the coast. No one believed him and he gave up in disgust. However, years later, while we were holidaying off Vilancoulos in Moçambique, I felt the islands would've been the perfect place for this purpose and that, probably, the captain had been right. Priest had a little farm in Wedza, which he sold later when he retired to a cottage somewhere in the lowveld. There he tamed crocodiles in the nearby river by feeding them meat regularly. After a while he could call them and they would lazily emerge for their meal, a feat up until then not thought possible.

Captain Strawbridge, a naval man, was another character in those early days. He and his wife had retired from England and bought a farm in Wedza. Strawbridge told wonderful tales of serving on gunboats in the 1930s, on the Yangtse River in China, and his stories always thrilled me.

There were several families of long-standing in Wedza. The Seagers, whose son, Tony, joined the RAF as a fighter pilot, Major Chomley's son, who became a pilot in the RAF and was tragically killed, and Anne Scorror's son, Tom, who also joined the air force and was killed in action. Then there were the Darroll's, whose son Bob joined the RAF as a bomber pilot. Bob was a thin, rather tall, good-looking fellow who was a great friend. Shortly before he left for the war, Bob and I went in his father's truck to an area south of Wedza Mountain - now called the Ziambe Purchase Area. It was my first taste of the wild Rhodesian bush. The area bordered the Sabi River and there were a lot of crocodiles and hippo. There was plenty of game including sable, kudu and eland - what a paradise it was! The trip sparked my love for the bush and animals, and for wild Africa. However, I knew this would have to wait because, by now, so many young men were joining up that I saw no reason why I shouldn't also get involved. In 1941 I joined the army of Southern Rhodesia. My thinking was that the sooner I could help to get the war over and done with, the sooner I could return.

One of the few things Mum managed to bring out of China was a tapestry that she'd made in C.A.C. Camp, Yangchaw. All of her friends and fellow inmates in the camp had signed their names on a piece of white linen, which Mum had then embroidered over in coloured threads while maintaining the original handwriting of the owners.

Chapter 2

WAR
Africa to Europe 1941 - 1946

My war started at boot camp in Bulawayo in 1941, progressed to KG VI barracks and then to the Royal Artillery in Salisbury, where I was under the command of Major MacIlwaine. This was the same Major Mac who had served in the First World War and later farmed in the Wedza district. During my training I met up with a chap called Wells Kerr, who came from Wankie, where his father was a doctor at the colliery. Wells and I enjoyed the same things: rugby, squash and even boxing. Our guns were 3.7 Howitzers which dated from the days of the colonial wars in Afghanistan. They were affectionately known as screw guns, presumably because you could take them apart quickly to load onto mules. Major Mac made up a little song about the screw guns, which we all joined in on but now I can only remember the first two lines:

"We all love screw guns

The screw guns they all love us…."

We did a lot of drill, played plenty of sport and did plenty of drinking in the local pubs. I bought a second-hand MG car, for £50/-, and a few friends and I decided to spend our leave at Victoria Falls. The car blew up sixty miles down the road but we caught a train to the Falls and had a wonderful time anyway!

In 1942 a draft of some sixty men, including twelve of us from the Artillery, were sent to England to be commissioned. We sailed from Cape Town and were given the job of guarding about thirty or forty British prisoners with long sentences for offences such as desertion. This was our first contact with the dregs of humanity, as many of them were.

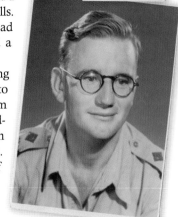

When we arrived in England some of us opted to become officers in an anti-tank OCTU. We then spent six months in Ilkley, Yorkshire, where many local families opened their hearts and homes to us; I think these young colonials with their bush hats appealed to them! We became very fit - often playing a game of rugby and then, after a shower, would join the others on a night march over the moors! The reality of war first hit hard shortly after we were commissioned when RM Sharpe, a popular member of our group of six Rhodesians, was killed on a motorcycle whilst on manoeuvres - it was a sad day for us all.

Wells Kerr and I were first posted to a light infantry regiment, which was not to our taste. Light infantrymen are usually physically small and tended to march at double the normal pace. Then we were drafted and boarded a ship sailing for the Middle East. It was a quiet journey until we passed Gibraltar, when our convoy was attacked by German planes using radio-controlled bombs. A neighbouring troopship loaded with American troops was hit and I believe a lot drowned. We landed in Tunis just as the North African campaign ended.

Sitting in a transit camp doing nothing, Wells and I looked around to see which unit would like us. Wells, whose full Christian name was Wellsley, always had a smile on his face and was very cheerful. First we went to Popski's Private Army but when they found out we had no war experience they turned us down. Popski was Polish and had led a small group miles behind the German lines during the desert war. He had lost an eye and half an arm but still went on to lead his men in Italy, with great success.

Turned away by Popski, we went to a mountain artillery mess as they used the dear old 3.7 which we had trained on. But Wells and I backed off after being asked if we played polo, which was not our scene! Eventually we landed in Italy, near Naples, where once again we sat doing nothing. Here Wells and I set off for Bari, on the East Coast, where we tried to join a parachute regiment. Wells suggested that I took the medical exam first - in case I failed! I took off my glasses and went in. The MD turned out to be a Rhodesian doctor and, after I'd passed all the other tests, he asked, "Don't you wear glasses?"

"No!" I lied firmly.

"Fine, then read this card of letters."

I failed, of course, and so Wells and I went back to Naples. On the way we also tried to join a commando regiment.

At last, and much to our joy, we were posted to a famous anti-tank regiment: the Worcestershire Yeomanry, with whom we went through the rest of the war. Shortly after we joined, the CO called us in and said, "What's this, the Commando Regiment have accepted you? I am tearing this up and here you stay!"

So our war began, in reserve, at Cassino. Trying to be wise after the event I often wondered why our Generals had to sacrifice so many men on Cassino - couldn't it have been by-passed and engaged with heavy artillery only? Maybe that's why I am not a General - my plan might not have worked either!

The anti-tank weapons we used were invented by the Americans and were called Tank Destroyers, or M10s. Our first ones were a three-inch naval gun mounted on a Sherman tank - the gun mounted on an open turret with light armour - two machine guns for good measure. They were fast and the gun quite deadly against houses, pill boxes and so on. My tank was a Honey tank with a two-pounder and machine guns. It was fast and manoeuvrable and, later on, they took off the turret leaving the machine guns. The later version of the M10 had a seventeen-pounder mounted in place of the three-inch. We were 13 corps troops allocated at first with the 8th Army and we served with some very fine British regiments, including a Guards regiment, Irish Fusiliers and many others.

I clearly remember one little affray when we were supporting an infantry attack on a small town. The infantry had to cross a large open area and a young infantryman came up to me and said, "I want your tanks to come with us."

"We are your anti-tank defence, not tanks," I replied.

"You are windy!" he said.

"Right, I'll come on condition your men climb onto my M10s and you first clear a mine-free route and we'll go at 30mph as opposed to a walking pace."

He glared at me and walked away. Nothing more was heard of the affair and I thanked my lucky stars that we didn't have to carry out my suggestion or we would all have been pushing up daisies!

Once we were sited on a rise overlooking a valley dotted with a few farmhouses. Our instructions were not to give our positions away by using the M10s firepower. Watching some Generals at a farmhouse some six hundred yards away with my binoculars, I couldn't resist borrowing a sniper rifle from some infantry guys nearby. I watched a German walk across to an outside toilet and close the door. After waiting a few seconds I fired a shot through the door and out rushed the soldier clutching his trousers! I was laughing so much that I couldn't fire again, so good luck to him!

I had my first encounter with American troops when we were told to support them in an attack on a hill. Years later my nephew, Howard Matthews, recalled how I'd told him, with a mixture of humour and scorn, what had happened:

"Norman's anti-tank group with American made MT's, with a three-inch naval gun on the front, was assigned to support an American attack of a hill. Norman walked in for the briefing to find flamboyant Americans with huge lit cigars making bold plans. The artillery barrage was due to start at 3.00 am and the advance on the hill at 5.00 am. At 3.00 am the world shook with unexpected clamour as the artillery roared away with vigour. On the command to advance they found the hill had been blown to pieces without killing a single enemy but causing very awkward pot-holed territory for his tanks to progress across. The Germans knew the American style and had fired several proactive rounds in the night and then withdrawn. On his return to his regiment Norman took back stories of the correct way to flatten the enemy!"

War is mostly boredom with odd moments of wetting one's pants from fear, something I found out on the 13 July 1944. A couple of days before, our troop of anti-tank guns were sent to support the infantry, which was a bit stupid because there were no roads and no means of getting close enough to the infantry. While we were there we were shelled and one of my M10s was blown up. In the meantime I had walked up to where the infantry platoon was based to find out what was going on. I got there to find they'd been shelled and the majority of the men were dead. Shortly after this we were sent to Tegoleto. One realised afterwards the stupidity of the command to base us right next to an artillery unit, which would invite reprisals from the Germans. This they proceeded to do and it led to another tank being blown up. We tried to get the other tanks (and what was left of the artillery battery) out of range and, in doing so, I found a man burning and screaming in the tank that had been hit and trying to get out. I hauled him out and was later awarded the Military Cross for the affair.

From Tegoleto we went on to Florence and arrived at the Arno River where we took up positions on the south bank. Florence had been declared an open city, so the Ponte Vecchio, famous for its bridge of shops built over the river, had survived. The war started again two days later in the northern suburbs. Meanwhile, a troop of Canadian tanks had discovered an Italian winery and liberated its contents, which gave us demijohns of excellent Vermouth for days!

An amusing thing happened one day when we were pulled out of the line and sent twenty miles back for repairs and maintenance. We were near a forward aerodrome used by an American squadron of fighter planes - called Lightnings, or twin fuselage single-seaters. I went on my motorcycle to see them and one of the pilots offered me a flight. "One of the planes has had its radio taken out so, with a squeeze, you can come."

I was delighted and suggested we fly over the area occupied by the Germans. We flew off at high speed and, after zooming all over the sky, we landed. What a relief! I felt sick as a dog and, after thanking them, declared, "Thank God I'm in tanks and not aeroplanes!"

We ended spending the winter of 1944-1945 in the Apennine Mountains, completely snowed in, while the war came to a standstill as far as we were concerned. The infantry, poor devils, still did patrols. Wells and I asked our CO if we could have some leave. He agreed to one month but ordered, with dire warning, "Be back on time."

So off we went. We hitch-hiked to Rome where we met a South African pilot who was flying to Cairo and organised ourselves a lift. In Cairo, at the Officers Club, we met a Rhodesian pilot flying a Dakota to Salisbury in Rhodesia, via Khartoum and Nairobi. It was a very bumpy trip but who cares, we were going home! Then followed two wonderful weeks in Rhodesia where I met a sister of Wells Kerr - Valerie - and fell head over heels in love with her. A romance, sadly, that only lasted until shortly after the war.

Wells and I hitch-hiked back from Rhodesia the same way we had come. It took us about a week. We arrived to find the regiment had moved to the Po Valley and we got there just in time for an 'O' Group with the battery commander. He welcomed us with the words:"Thank God you are here! Now, tomorrow at 6.00am you move off - here are the maps."

Quite a rude awakening for two weary men still dreaming of Castle Lager and Rhodesia!

I often wonder if our dash to Rhodesia and back wasn't a record for such a short break from the war.

We didn't see much more action after this, apart from taking prisoners and a bit of fishing in the River Po. I have to admit, with reluctance, that our method consisted of the use of Teller mines (German anti-tank mines) from the back of a boat.

Not fair, I agree, but the fish tasted delicious nonetheless. Especially after monotonous rations of bully beef!

When the war ended we went to Austria and were there for six months before being sent home to Rhodesia. Our battery was billeted in a little village where our CO, Major John Williams, took over a guest-hof, or pub, as our Officers' Mess. The owners were a delightful Austrian couple and the man had a typical German Bismark moustache, on which he put guards at night to keep it trim. His wife was a plump frau with a lovely smile and their widowed daughter lived with them - her husband had disappeared in Russia. During my travels in Italy I had acquired a split-cane trout rod and reel, a double-barrelled 16-bore shotgun and a lightweight hunting rifle, all of which made me well equipped for Austria. I soon met up with an Austrian gamekeeper, who had been wounded at Cassino and invalided out of the army. I told him that we had probably been shooting at each other! We became good friends and had many a good weekend hunting deer and trout fishing.

One day I was fishing in a river and caught half a dozen small trout, which were very welcome in our mess. I had found using grasshoppers to be far more successful than flies. A Colonel, from some horsey regiment, came wading down the river and asked after my catch. "What luck?" he enquired.

"Quite a few Sir," I replied.

"What fly?" he asked.

When I told him that I was using grasshoppers he strode off in high dudgeon, puffing and snorting. Silly ass!

One of our first official tasks when we arrived in Austria, was searching all the buildings in a village that had been occupied by the Germans and I found this suspicious looking box. I broke it open and it was full of money - obviously used to pay the soldiers. I was toying with the idea of tucking it away so we'd have a bit of cash to go out and celebrate with the boys but, just then, one of my senior officers came in and saw what we'd found. It was closed up and he took it away. About a month later I heard that several of our chaps were going on leave and being given pocketfuls of money. I went to the CO and said that Wells Kerr and I were due for some leave and we'd like to go down to Venice.

"Fine," he said. "No problem."

"By the way," I said, "we need some money."

"Oh no," he said. "I'm afraid that's nearly all finished."

I got a bit rough and exclaimed. "Look, you don't want the story about the box of money to get around do you?!"

Immediately he relented and said that he'd find us some money. In due course we received a pocketful of money each and went off happily to Venice.

Rainbow trout

22

Whilst we were there we took some lovely American nurses on a gondola cruise down the Grand Canal. It was all great fun but, to my lasting shame, it ended in an undignified farewell as I had to urgently dodge down an alleyway, bursting for a pee!

Norman and Wells in Venice

Based near us in Austria, there was a Russian Cossack cavalry division who had fought with the Germans. One day they disappeared and I had happened to be at the local railway station, Klaggenfiert, and saw British soldiers driving them into railway trucks. The poor sods were wailing and pleading not to be sent away and an odd shot was heard as one of them committed suicide. Apparently the British government had given in to a demand from the Russians to have them sent back to Russia. Sent back to what? Certain death for many of them and a big black mark goes to Britain for doing so.

In my troop was a regular soldier who had experience with horses and he rounded up a few half-starved horses that had been left behind by the Russians, together with all the necessary riding equipment. After a few weeks of good feeding, he produced them for us officers to ride. Apparently I was the only horseman amongst us - what a joke that was. Our man brought me a very bedraggled grey which I looked at with scorn. He said that it was a Russian General's horse so I mounted it and nearly got my nose broken when he came to life! We had a lot of fun and falls but, before long, it was time to go back to Rhodesia, where we were officially demobbed. I ended the war as a Lieutenant and was given a gift of a bicycle. Otherwise, like all troopies, we also received a suit, shirt and a pair of shoes (none of which were very attractive) but it gave me great pleasure to walk out as a free man!

Some time later I read, with amusement and nostalgia, an account by a friend who had also served in the war and realised just what a constricted period we had been through. It made me value my freedom even more:

"(1943) …applied for permission to draw some money out of my Army Savings Account… In those days we were subjected to compulsory saving and had to put away two shillings a day out of the five we earned." (A Fragment of Time)

Not long after my return to Rhodesia my mother arrived, having been released from a Japanese prisoner-of-war camp in China where she had been interred for the duration of the war.

This was the first time I had seen Mum for many years - probably since I'd been at school. I knew she was a prisoner-of-war and had been in a concentration camp in China. I'd read it in the papers, of course, but didn't know much about what had gone on or any of the details. At the end of the war, when Mum was freed, she left China and joined up with my Aunty Rae in Durban. I could see that she had suffered a lot in the concentration camp. Her fingernails were split and her hands calloused and there were other physical signs of her ordeal but we didn't talk about it too much. I learnt that Mum had been in the concentration camp since 1942, when the Japanese came into the war, and, although there were other people in the camp, she had had no contact at all with any of her relations. Mentally, Mum was as bright as ever but I remember our reunion being quite a difficult time. I didn't know what to expect or how I thought Mum would be after her experience and was very surprised to see her looking so sprightly. I learnt that she had been a leading light in the POW camp, looking after people who needed help and taking care of children. She talked about how desperately hungry the local Chinese people, living around the camp, had been and how they came selling fruit and vegetables in exchange for rings, jewellery or any other valuables on offer.

One of the few things Mum managed to bring out of China was a tapestry that she'd made in C.A.C. Camp, Yangchaw. All of her friends and fellow inmates in the camp had signed their names on a piece of white linen, which Mum had then embroidered over in coloured threads while maintaining the original handwriting of the owners. When they were all released from the POW camp, by the Americans, in 1945, Mum got the American chaps and a few British ones to sign the tapestry as well, providing a fascinating record of her time spent there. Many years later, with the tapestry hanging on the wall of our home on Imire, a guest recognised the name of the prison camp embroidered onto the tapestry.

"I'm sure that's the same camp my parents were interred in," he said.

On closer inspection of the tapestry he shouted in exclamation when he found his own mother's name embroidered into the cloth. What a small world!

In 1947 King George came to Rhodesia, where an investiture took place and my mother and I attended. I was formally decorated with the Military Cross and remember my mother being very proud - at least as proud as I was.

MILITARY CROSS CITATION

Lieutenant Norman Meckiffe Travers (267803)
Royal Regiment of Artillery.

*At Tegoleto on 13th July 1944, Lt Travers was in command of 'B' Troop
of an Anti-tank Battery in support of a British Infantry Brigade.
The Troop came under sudden and intense artillery concentration.
One M.10 and two Field Battery wagons were set alight
as well as the spinney in which they were placed.
Lt Travers, with great coolness, organised the evacuation of the Troop
as well as the vehicles belonging to the Field Battery, saving not only
the remainder of his M.10's but also the Field Wagons
and ammunition required by the Field Battery
who were in action on the flank.
He returned alone to the spinney and entered
the blazing M.10 extricating a seriously wounded member
of the crew in danger of being burnt alive.
Throughout this time, the spinney was being heavily shelled.
This action not only saved lives but a number of costly vehicles and also
ammunition required by the Field Battery who were in action nearby.
He has at all times shown himself a first class leader and has been
an inspiration to his men and has shown the utmost disregard
for his own safety in performing his duty.*

Chapter Three

COURTING FROM A HOSPITAL BED
1946 – 1950

With the war over, my life began in Rhodesia and I applied to the government for an ex-serviceman's farm. I was turned down and told I had to do another year as a learner assistant with Frank Scott, which I did. In 1946 the government tried to persuade me to go to Karoi, where a new farming area had been opened up, but I was only interested in Wedza. First I asked for the Ziambe Purchase area as I had such good memories of my visit there with Bob Darroll in 1940. My choice was turned down as Ziambe was earmarked for African development and so I applied for Imire. At the time it was vacant, virgin crownland, and was an outspan. This was a designated area of land between fifty acres and three thousand acres in size, where cattle could stay the night when they were being walked from one place to another. Perhaps this was how the farm had got the name 'Imire,' which means 'waiting place' and is derived from the Shona word *mirai*, meaning to wait. The government were reluctant to give me Imire as it had a lot of granite kopjes and vleis on its acreage with no fencing, not much arable land and no running water. I persisted, however, and was eventually successful.

I was lent £2000/- as working capital and, with my own £200/-, that was all the financing I had to build a tobacco farm from virgin bush! My first job was to hire a brick-maker to make 100,000 bricks for the first tobacco barns. Then a house for myself (made of pole and dagga) was constructed with floors of brick smeared with mud from anthills, which, when dry and polished, made an excellent floor. My home was very simple and I employed a cook who soon learned how to feed me! I shot the odd steenbuck and guinea fowl for meat and ate lots of mealie meal porridge - very sustaining!

Getting started on Imire wasn't difficult thanks to the help of Frank Scott who sent over his tractor and ploughed up my first twenty acres. In those days a beginner like me had no chance of owning a tractor and so I operated with trek oxen to pull wagons and even to build dams. My first vehicle was a Willys Jeep and, because I couldn't afford a tractor, I even did some of my first ploughing with the jeep, towing a two-disc harrow - and very good it was too!

Local labour was in short supply in these early days and so we sub-contracted from Wenela, taking men on for two years at a time. Wenela was a South African company recruiting labour from Angola, Northern Rhodesia and Zambia for the gold mines in South Africa. These men were usually emaciated and thin and had no knowledge of farming at all but, after a while, they turned out to be good workers. After their two years on the farms they went off to work in the South African mines. I gave new workers three days to settle in and build their huts, which were made from bush poles and thatched with grass. They were given 14lbs of mealie meal, ground-nuts and beans with a ration of meat once a week and soon gained strength and put on weight. They enjoyed the weekends drinking home-brewed beer and drumming and dancing. I enjoyed listening to them and their customs varied according to whichever country they had come from. One group of recruited workers, who came from Angola, I couldn't make out at all. The foreman showed them where to build their pole and dagga houses and showed them how to do it but they just built little bee-hive shaped dwellings. They cut small branches which they bent round into domes and covered the whole thing with thatching grass. Later we discovered that this was the traditional way of house building where they came from, and pole and dagga huts were something very new to them.

Like everyone else I made a lot of mistakes but learnt as I went along. Thanks to my time with Frank Scott I knew about growing tobacco; how to plough lands and build barns and how to cure the leaves. In those days we worked on the reaped tobacco in grass sheds next to the barns. The tobacco was tied in bunches and flicked over onto *mateppes* (sticks about four feet long and an inch and a half in diameter). The loaded *mateppes* were then lifted up and hung from the tiers in the barns, spaced about nine inches apart. Imire had a variety of local trees, but not in abundance, so when lands were stumped for crops the timber was used for curing tobacco. So my next priority was planting gum trees which, being quick growing, supplied wood for the tobacco furnaces as well as roofing poles for huts and some farm buildings. In the beginning I only grew tobacco and a bit of maize as food for the labour force. I found out very quickly that the secret of good crops was good ploughing. If you didn't do good ploughing, you didn't get a good crop. It was that simple.

Very soon I started taking on assistants to work on Imire, usually people younger than myself who needed work, and it was an arrangement that suited me very well. The youngsters learnt the trade, and did the hard work, and many went on to become very good farmers themselves. We built a couple of cottages where the young assistants could live on the property and be independent in their own right. One of my first assistants was my good friend, Wells Kerr. After the war he'd taken a job in Salisbury but didn't enjoy it very much and decided to go farming. He came and worked on Imire around 1948 and we did well together. Later, Wells married Winnie Reid Roland, whose family were big names in the tobacco world, and bought his own farm in Sipolilo.

Our own Wedza community started to thrive in 1948 when Frank Scott donated some land on Sheffield Farm, which he owned at the time, for the purpose of building a country club. It was quite a big area, two hundred and forty-five acres in fact, which included a kopje and a fair amount of land all around. I was twenty-seven at the time, not married and involved myself in the project from the beginning. All the farmers in the area contributed different things; we made the bricks from antheaps, which were dug out on site, hired a builder and built the clubhouse.

The Club Minutes books recorded some fascinating early details and the Wedza Club notes, from the Wedza Gazette, provide amusing memories:

"In November 1948 the membership fee for the Club was fixed at £2.50 for ladies and £5.00 for men….

The first workers at the Club were employed for £2/- and 30s per month each respectively as Caretaker and general worker….

At the 27 May 1949 meeting… D Collins explained how the cricket club expenses had exceeded £50/-….

At the July 22 meeting the parlous state of the accounts and finances was discussed!…

(1963) Bert Hilliard has taken over the offer of a bottle of whisky for the player who, driving off the 9th tee, can hit the old ESC pole on the fairway without a bounce. Witnesses will, of course, be called for and caddies do not fall into this category."

(Winter Cricket)

The Wedza Club was a very important development for the district. Straight away it became a focal point where people got together. It was very much a family place and, within a few years, there were tennis courts, a squash court, swimming pool and even a golf course. All over Rhodesia these country clubs sprang up and played a very important part in uniting the farming community. Prior to the development of country clubs, the farmers had their own little circle of friends - usually within walking or riding distance - but the clubs united entire districts.

The Wedza Club

Not long after this my own romantic endeavours began in earnest! In 1949 I set my sights on a lovely girl in Marandellas named Gill. She was very popular and so, winning her affections was to be a tricky business. Her parents were Howard and Janet Smetham, both charming people and very involved in local affairs - particularly in the horsey world. This was not my scene but became a hurdle to be jumped!

I first saw Gill knocking about in Marandellas and then, one day while driving to Salisbury, I saw her on a horse, riding along the fence-line of a farm which bordered the main road. I waved at her and she waved back.

"At least I'm making some headway!" I thought.

The next time I saw Gill was at a tennis party on Val Blundell's farm, which was next door to Imire. I could see Gill was a good tennis player and thought I'd better build a tennis court on Imire, which I did in record time - two or three days in fact! I picked a level patch outside the house, graded it, smoothed it over, packed it with anthill soil, watered it and rolled it. The next step, of course, was to hold a tennis party. These usually started at about two -thirty in the afternoon and, after the games, there were drinks and snacks before everyone went home. We were very prim and proper in those days so staying on into the evening wasn't done. Not long after the tennis party I had another encounter with Gill, this time at a dinner dance one Saturday night. It went on into the early hours and I got to know Gill a little better.

Gill Smetham was seven years younger than me and, while I'd been preparing to go and fight in the Second World War, she had been living in Cheshire, England with her parents and younger sister, Jane. Born in Rhodesia, Gill had gone to school in England when her father joined the Royal Air Force. The family had experienced great tragedy, losing both of their first children, Barbara and John, in the same year: Barbara from a poisonous spider bite and John after a bout of diphtheria. In 1941, as the war intensified in Europe, Gill's father decided it would be best for the family to return to Rhodesia and, so, Janet Smetham with her two young daughters, Gill aged twelve and Jane aged four, set out by sea from England. The events of that journey would stay with the two sisters for the rest of their lives, as Gill recalls:

"The ship, The City of Nagpur, was mainly carrying women and children who were getting away from the war. The ship should have been travelling in a convoy but the captain said he had good luck and so we set out alone. We were told to sleep in our clothes, not to wander around at night and to put all our most precious possessions in a small bag which we could take quickly in an emergency. Jane and I shared the top bunk in the cabin while Mum slept below. In the middle of the night the ship was hit by a torpedo. Two sailors were killed, the engine room took a direct hit and the ship started going down.

Mum and Jane and I stood on the top deck waiting to get into a lifeboat but it was chaotic as some of the lifeboats had been damaged by the torpedo. 'Oh Mum, look at all these lovely stars,' Jane said, but the beauty of the clear night sky was over-shadowed by the sound of the suction which was pulling the ship down into the cold sea. Climbing down the swaying rope ladders in the black of night was a terrifying experience which I have never forgotten. We were very cramped in our lifeboat and I remember being perched on the edge with huge waves rolling all around us. All the women took oars and helped row in order to get away from the ship, which was sinking fast and went down in twenty-five minutes.

Twenty-four hours later we were rescued from our lifeboats by a British battle-ship, which had taken a long time to arrive, after initially being given incorrect co-ordinates. Not long after this, when we were safely aboard the battleship, we saw something emerging from the water. It was a submarine. In fact, the very German destroyer whose torpedo had sunk The City of Nagpur. The German captain came on deck and called out. 'When you get back to England, give my regards to Churchill.' Words I have never forgotten all my life."

Mother and daughters were delivered safely back to England and set out again for South Africa some time later on a ship travelling in convoy. Gill finished school in Rhodesia and went back to England. Jane describes this time as the period when her sister was equipped for life:

"Gill went to the Monkey Club, a finishing school in Knightsbridge, where she learnt cooking, flower arranging and all those other 'girly things'. She was presented at Court, before King George VI, in 1948. At that time daughters of Commonwealth people were regularly presented at these garden parties, after which Gill was prepared for whatever came her way!"

In between courting Gill, my work continued on the farm and, because Imire was very dry, with no running streams, dam building was essential. I built my first dam with trek oxen and dam scoops and it has stood the test of time, still holding water sixty years later. I never dreamed that one day I'd have crocodiles and hippos in those same little farm dams; but that was all to come in the years ahead. A little while later I bought a D4 Caterpillar tractor at a reasonable price, as it was ex-army stock. We built several dams with it, over the years, and the dams paid for themselves over and over again, supporting irrigation schemes on both tobacco range and pasture. My poor old D4 sadly had to be put down eventually, except for the engine, which we mounted on a trailer and used as an irrigation pump for many years; in fact the latest irrigation unit installed on Imire, in 2009, was called D4!

We stocked our dams with various species of bream and bass. My first attempt with bass was fifty spotted bass fingerlings imported from South Africa. A river fish, which, I later discovered, grew to about 2lbs and then disappeared without ever breeding. One lives and learns! Florida bass, however, were very successful. I think 2lbs was the biggest hooked and they gave lots of fun and good eating - to this day. Nilotica bream also did well and grew up to 12lbs - but these big ones were bagged mostly by spear fishermen.

The dams weren't only good for irrigation and fishing, as I soon discovered during my on-going romantic endeavours. Gill's sister Jane remembers some of her earlier visits to Imire:

"In 1949 Gill and I would go out to Imire at a time when Norman's house was still a little rondavel. Norman had lots of friends and we would go in his jeep, driving straight up the kopje. We would all have to sit in the front and on the bonnet so our combined weight would prevent the jeep from tipping over!

Norman used to take Gilly out on a little rowboat, on one of the dams he had built, and would sing to her 'Cruising down the river on a Sunday afternoon!'

It was so romantic and Norman was wonderful to her. I thought he was fabulous, rough but tender and they just adored each other."

In April 1950, I passed up a rugby game and went on a baboon shoot organised by the Native Commissioner in the Wedza Reserve. We were some thirty miles inside the reserve and I was walking ahead of a good friend of mine, who was not very experienced with guns. He was using an old hammer shotgun which caught on a bush and went off accidentally. Luckily I was only a few yards ahead and took the shot in my shoulder. 'Why luckily?' you might ask. Well, if I had been ten yards or so ahead then the spread of shot would have killed me!

Right there on the mountain where it happened, friends applied pads to my shoulder in an effort to stop the bleeding. I walked down to the truck, still bleeding profusely, and we raced off to the Wedza Clinic where an African orderly, Marshall, undoubtedly saved my life by stitching up the artery. I needed hospital treatment as my whole shoulder had been virtually shot off and so we rushed to Marandellas, stopping in at Imire to see Wells Kerr who was working for me at the time. Medical staff in Marandellas took one look and said they couldn't handle the problem and sent me directly to Salisbury. I was operated on by Mr Trevor Jones who took a couple of inches off my humerus bone, leaving my right arm permanently shorter by two inches and unable to be lifted above my waist. I was hospitalised and in plaster for some weeks but, to my great joy, Gill came to visit but I had to pour eau de cologne all over my arm as the smell was a bit high!

After a week or two I persuaded a friendly nurse, Pete Nielsen's sister, to put a bolster in my bed to bluff the matron. My car was outside and, dressed in my pyjamas and dressing gown, I took Gill to a hotdog stand and then on a drive up Salisbury Kopje for a little romance! I must have been seriously love-struck because I don't remember a third person being in the car! But Gill's sister Jane does and tells how she was there in the back seat:

"Gilly took me along to the hospital to see Norman. I was still a schoolgirl at the time and there he was, just the same as he is today. Same naughty little quips and defying the nurses at every turn!

I remember Norman taking Gilly out, escaping from the hospital, wearing only his pyjamas, and going on a drive up the kopje, with me in the back seat. I'm sure the hospital staff must have been looking for him but he didn't seem to be at all concerned!"

Eau de cologne and night-time car escapes in pyjamas - what a way to conduct a romance, but it seemed to work, thank goodness. When I had recovered, I went back to work on the farm. I could no longer play much sport but still tried tennis with my left arm and could manage rather feeble golf. Luckily I could still fire my shotgun and rifle by using a pad on my shoulder. Funnily enough when I had a chest X-ray, over fifty years later, a strange and perfectly white circle was visible on my lungs. It was one of the pellets left over from being shot in 1950! Closer inspection showed another two pellets in the same region.

On the 28 December 1950 Gill and I were married in Salisbury and her sister Jane, again, remembers the day clearly:

"Norman and Gilly had a wonderful wedding at the Salisbury Cathedral and even though I was only thirteen, I came out of school and was one of their bridesmaids. This was followed by a huge reception attended by about five hundred people at the Meikles Hotel. When it came time for them to leave, a few of these huge chaps picked up the car completely, all four wheels off the ground, and I can remember Gilly's face very clearly. A picture of fear and anticipation at what was going to happen next."

The adventure was, in fact, just beginning.

Norman and Gill's wedding.

33

Chapter Four

BIG GAME, BIG FISH, BABIES
AND A BUFFALO CALF
1950 - 1960

Shortly before our first child was born, I received a request for work from a chap in Inyanga. David Hamilton and I had a mutual friend in Gerry von Memerty who recommended that David come to Imire and see if I had any work going. David clearly remembers his approach to me in 1951:

"My application for a job as a tobacco assistant (and Norman's response) rather indicates the direction of his priorities. My own position, at the time, was Government Conservation Officer at Inyanga and I was very keen on trout fishing in my spare time. Upon the recommendation of Gerry, I paid Norman a visit on Imire, met Gill and generally discussed the possibilities of employment with him. Norman offered me the position and said, 'If you want the job let me know by Saturday. 'From Inyanga I sent a telegram to him saying: 'Accept position. Start 1st October. However, trout fishing season begins 1st October. Suggest we meet Inyanga and I begin work 7th October.'

Norman's reply, also by telegram, read: 'Meet you Troutbeck 1st October!'"

A life-long friendship with David Hamilton was to follow. We not only worked together but also went on countless hunting and fishing trips and, later, spent holidays together with our families. We also had many adventures with Gerry von Memerty whom I'd known for many years. Gerry was of Polish stock, his father having coming to Africa in the early 1900s. The youngest of four children, Gerry was too young to join up for the Second World War and so, as a very young man,went whaling in the Antarctic. In between seasons he was a life-saver on the beaches of Durban and spent a year contract-hunting near the Sena Sugar Estates in Moçambique, providing meat for the labour force. I first met Gerry in the 1940s when Bill Swanson asked me to look out for the youngster, who was at a loose end. I was having trouble getting enough farm workers at that time and, as Gerry had just done a stint with the Native Department in Gokwe, he said he thought he could recruit labour for Imire in Gokwe. He set off in a clapped-out old truck and I didn't see him again for a month. When Gerry got back to Imire the truck was laden with biltong, tusks and two old African men - so much for recruiting a vibrant, young workforce!

Gill produced our first child, a daughter (Barbara), on 22 November 1951 and what a joy she was. Gill's sister Jane described Barbara as "the perfect little girl, enchanting and angelic."

David Hamilton had been working with me for three months by then, and recalls the circumstances surrounding his observation of Barbara's christening a few months later in January 1952. I'd sent David to collect a grading gang in Buhera but, due to incessantly heavy rain, the lorry kept getting stuck. After spending two nights in trouble, one sheltering under the lorry and another in an African hut, David borrowed a bicycle and rode the fifty miles back to Imire. He arrived on the farm just in time for the christening but, as he remembers, not very stylishly:

"Bobby and Eileen Stirrup, dressed to the nines, actually passed me cycling back to Imire and splashed me with their little Austin. I had arrived back at Imire whilst the select Wedza community was arriving for Barbara's christening. Consequently, due to my muddiness, Gerry and I got thoroughly tight in my bachelor quarters."

David soon got the hang of things when it came to working for me, including the need for regular fishing:

"On a typical afternoon, during the tobacco curing days, I would be preparing for a long and tedious evening filling barns and tying tobacco in the shed. Along would come Norman, in his truck, at about 4.30pm. 'How's it going?' he'd ask.

'Well, we've filled one and are beginning on number two.'

'Grab a rod, the flying ants are out,' Norman would say.

'But what about these barns?'

'Oh!' A long pause and then he'd say, 'They can look after themselves. The senior barn-worker knows the ropes.'

And this is how it would continue, for at least a couple of evenings a week!

He would, also, periodically break the monotony of a day's work.

'Don't I want to go to a certain dam in the TTL after breakfast and net some Tilapia?' he'd ask, or 'Off to old Jack Collins for some black bass. Coming?' Or, on one occasion, it was a trip to Lake MacIlwaine for some small tiger fish. The latter lived in the dams on Imire for a couple of years but, following a very cold snap, they all appeared dead on the surface. Some as large as 1kg."

In between fishing, time went by and I, fortunately, grew good crops of tobacco, which enabled me to expand. In 1951, I bought Numwa Farm for £10,000/-. Numwa was across the road from Imire and proved a real bonus as it had the Chenikwa River running through it. Then, in 1952, I bought Eldoret.

It was a thousand acres on the same side of the road as Imire and had Numwa School on it. These were good years for tobacco and in that same year I won the Field Cup in what was called the Five-Year farming Competition, for gaining the highest marks for tobacco over five consecutive years.

I loved experimenting with new ideas - a lot, of course, were unsuccessful. Tobacco was cured, traditionally, in barns with furnaces fuelled by wood. As time went on wood obtained from stumping and clearing the bush became short, so I went in for steam curing. I bought two large loco-boilers, which went through lagged pipes to the barns and to a large radiator with a fan. It was an ingenious contraption but, alas, sometimes ended in disaster - especially when an attendant fell asleep and the fire went out!

However, in-between the demands of growing tobacco, it was hunting and fishing that remained the favourite pastimes. In the 1950s we had an aluminium rowboat, about eight feet long, with a seat at the back and a thwart (rower's seat) across the middle. The boat held three people at most; in fact even three was crowding it. We used to tie it to the roof of the car and take it on most of our trips. The boat wasn't heavy and two could easily carry it. We had a little 5hp outboard motor, which we put to use - why row when you can use an outboard!

I went on one fishing trip with Nigel Thornycroft, who was a neighbour and close friend. Nigel had spent most of his youth and early days in Norfolk (England) where his passion was shooting, which he'd do at least twice a week. Nigel had been a prisoner-of-war for five years in Germany during World War II and, because he always tried to escape, he ended up in a high-security prison. He was thin but tough and went on to become a fine Wedza farmer. On this occasion Nigel and I went down to the Hunyani River, on the border with Moçambique, in my trusty old Ford truck. We camped by a mile-long pool near an African village where the fishing was excellent. I shot a large crocodile, which the locals said had killed several people and the bangles we found in its stomach backed this up. This croc seldom lay still on its sandbank and kept going into the water and coming out again every few minutes. It was strange behaviour and, again, we discovered the reason after I'd shot it. The croc had an old wound which led into his stomach. When he lay on the sand the flies would harass him and when he went in the water the small fish must have done the same and driven him crazy.

We caught some big vundu (catfish), which were up to 80lbs in weight, but the locals said these were babies! They told us an interesting story about these big fish. The villagers built little palisades in the water in order to protect the women when they were collecting water. "Because of the crocs?" I asked. Their answer was affirmative but not only for crocs. Apparently, just before the rains, the vundu had been known to take small children and, if you've ever looked into the maw of an eighty-pounder, you could definitely believe this.

There was a coloured professional hunter living near the Hunyani River, just inside the Moçambique border. His wife was the daughter of Chief Japoto - the local Chief. Chief Japoto used native hunters to shoot problem elephants and I told him I wanted to shoot a buffalo - never having done so before. My rifle was a 7mm Mauser and our friend the professional hunter said I was mad but, if I wanted a buffalo, he would show me a tree near the water. I was to sit in the tree and then, during the night, when the buff walked below me to drink, I could fire and then remain safely in the tree until dawn. I turned down his suggestion and he commented, "You Englishmen are crazy!"

I tried hunting buffalo in the bush, after this, with no luck and, following a few frights, I began to appreciate the merits of his suggestion.

Other fishing excursions were to the Inyanga area, where I caught a few 4lb trout in the Gairezi River. I helped in the founding of the Gairezi Fishing Club, under the leadership of Major MacIlwaine, who I found was an ardent fisherman. This was the same Major Mac who had played rugby for the British Army before the First World War and had then been my commanding officer in Salisbury, in 1941, during the Second World War. Nowadays fishermen mainly release their fish but, in our day, we ate them all.

Hunting at home, around the farms, was mostly for duck, guinea fowl and francolin in their respective seasons. David Hamilton was part of this group, as he recalls:

"The Chiota Pan Shoot became an annual event of two or three days, around Christmas or New Year. The privileged guns were John Bedford (Lord and Master), Norman Travers, Nigel Thornycroft, Geoff Maitland and, lo and behold, myself! I had the good fortune to own a very old 4x4 Landrover - the only such vehicle available amongst the gun-happy crowd of Christmas 1952."

Gerry von Memerty had enormous experience of hunting (and the bush) and I always thought of him as a real bushman who loved the outdoors. He always used to make his own shorts out of kudu or buffalo skin. I'm sure this was to do with his background in Poland and Germany where they wore leather trousers (*lederhosen*). I went on my first proper buffalo hunt with Gerry in Gokwe, where he had permission from the Native Commissioner to shoot two buffalo. After a long days walk, stalking a small herd of bulls (commonly called dagga boys due to their fondness for lying in cool mud, or dagga), we came upon them asleep under a tree, but in very open ground. I had to take my shot at about fifty yards with Gerry's 404. A cloud of dust arose as the buff stampeded away. Then, from out the blur and commotion, one came straight at us, limping badly. After another two shots, he fell, to my delight. However, examining the animal when we reached it, our tracker said. "That wasn't the bull you shot at!" and pointed out that the damaged leg was, in fact, from an old bullet wound. We went back to the tree and, sure enough, there was blood spoor leading off. Briskly we followed it, with Gerry behind issuing instructions. "Don't look at the spoor - leave that to your tracker. Carefully watch the left, as the wounded animal can easily ambush us. I'll watch the right-hand side."

It was a lesson well taken because, after about a mile, on an anthill a few yards ahead of us, stood the buffalo. I raised my rifle but he slumped over dead before I could fire. The lesson learnt was this: after wounding a buffalo which has disappeared, sit down and have a smoke for at least ten minutes. Your life could depend on it!

Organising a hunting trip depended on what the 'bag' would consist of. Sometimes it entailed a fortnight away for elephant and buffalo, together with impala, kudu and waterbuck. We had to take a 50kg bag of salt, mealie meal for the staff, some tinned fruit, curry powder and, of course, a couple of cases of beer for ourselves. Not forgetting, also, the guns. A .458 rifle for big game and a light 7mm rifle and shotgun along with a small pair of powerful binoculars. A tin of Red Cross supplies contained such essentials as anti-malaria tablets, laxatives, bandages and lint. Another necessity was my 4x4 Toyota with tow ropes, jack, tools and a forty-four gallon drum of diesel. We also took a block and tackle to hang up dead game and also to pull us out of trouble when stuck! Clothes were easy: a couple of pairs of shorts and two bush jackets (with four big pockets) and loops for holding cartridges.

With everything prepared we'd set off the 400kms odd, from the farm to the Zambezi Valley, accompanied by my trusty tracker, Elijah, a cook and four or five general workers. When we reached National Parks offices, beyond Marangora, we would pick up a National Parks tracker and off we went, well-laden, to meet up with our two or three co-hunters in our designated camp, which consisted of a couple of rondavels and a long drop. We always took fishing tackle for hunting camps on the Zambezi. A light rod for bream and a stronger one for the tiger. For bait we had a small drum of worms which had to be hung in the shade from greased wire to keep the ants off.

Sam Marnie came on many hunts with us in the 1950s but never hunted himself. Sam was always the self-appointed Camp Commandant and looked after the meat and the biltong. Dealing with the meat was always a priority - nothing must be wasted. The meat was cut into strips for biltong, salted, seasoned with pepper and put on racks in the shade. The racks were made of wires strung out between trees, sticks were laid across the wires to make a table-like surface and the meat was laid out on the racks and dried in the sun. The whole time we were in camp we'd be making biltong otherwise we'd have to take back wet meat which wasn't ideal and would be very heavy. While the meat was drying we used to put little fires all around the racks and had a watchman to guard. Other animals did still try to snatch a bit but were chased off. The meat, of course, was to take back to the farm as rations for the workers - and very popular it was too. Our staff also had their own sacks of dried intestines (and other choice pieces to their liking) for themselves. We tried to make use of all the meat and dried and salted the skins for sale or to make *riempies* back on the farm. We'd go down with a five or seven tonne lorry so we could bring back quite a weight of stuff. The dried meat from one elephant alone would have been in the region of about 500lbs.

David Hamilton has clear memories of his first hunting trip with me:

"My very first trip into the Zambezi Valley was with Norman and we went to Kanyemba, where Chief Chipoto reigned. Norman knew about every aspect that the valley could offer, including a night at Mashumbe Pools in a boat spotting dozens of crocodile's eyes. We went on a hairy boat ride (rowing) up past the Red Cliffs in search of bream but none were found and, I remember, the nights were always filled with shouts and crashing undergrowth, bellowings and drums as locals tried to keep hippo and elephant out of their crops."

Life wasn't all hunting and fishing in the 1950s. It was also about developments in the district, friends and relations and our own growing family. It was also about coming to terms with what we'd all been through in the World War and how differently people had been affected by it. My sister Flip and her husband, Frank Chubb, came out to Rhodesia and we built them a house on Imire. Frank had been through a tough time in the prisoner-of-war camps. He and Flip and their son, Christopher, had been interned in Hong Kong, which was known to have had the worst camps. Christopher Chubb, my nephew (and a very young boy at the time), later told me little snippets of what he remembered of Hong Kong during the war. Christopher recalls:

"One day there was an almighty noise and planes screaming around the top of the Peak and apparently we were at war. Then our house got hit and everything was very dusty. When all the booms and bangs ended (it was Christmas Day) we went to

Norman and friend at a Zambesi hunting camp

share a house with another family (the Langstons). They had a large garden in which they dug a ditch and set up a cubby house for us to play in. This later became a toilet with a boom gate set into the hedge. My next recollection was walking down the Peak and seeing dead soldiers and a pile of bent rifles."

What Christopher remembered was actually the battle for Hong Kong, as his friend Peter Langston explains:

"After the surrender of Hong Kong on Christmas Day 1941 we left the Peak where we were billeted on Boxing Day and returned to our house. Mr and Mrs Chubb and Christopher, Mr and Mrs Blake and Carolyn, Mrs Hobbins and Michael came with us as their homes had been blitzed. The battle for Hong Kong lasted eighteen days during which time the defending army (made up of British, Canadian and Indian troops together with volunteers) were hopelessly outnumbered by the battle-hardened Japanese troops. The Prime Minister of England urged the Allied Forces to continue fighting as long as possible but went on record as saying. 'They have not the slightest chance.' This is now the title of an excellent blow-by-blow account of the tragic battle, where the Japanese soldiers carried out unspeakable atrocities not only on Allied Troops but on the civilian population as well. Probably the worst atrocity took place at St Stevens College, Stanley, which had been turned into a hospital. The Japs murdered all the patients, doctors and nurses with the exception of one nurse, who hid underneath the dead body of a soldier."

The families were then kept under house arrest for a month while the Japanese found a place to intern them. Peter Langston described how they used the time to try and hide some of their more precious possessions:

"My mother gathered together all the valuables she could to hide in or around the grounds of the house. (These valuables also included an old Bible which Mum had given to me in 1930 which I, in turn, gave to my grandson Mark in 2009).

Hiding places included the chimney, under the floor-boards and in holes dug in the garden.

On the 24 January 1942 we were ordered to assemble in Statue Square, in the city of Hong Kong. We had a wait of about three hours, during which time we were searched, which was a very nerve-wracking time for my mother. She had sewn jewellery into a teddy bear that I was carrying under my arm."

Howard, Norman, Gill, Gaga, Janet and Barbara in Marandellas

My young nephew Christopher, four at the time, describes how his Mum (my sister Flip) dealt with saving essential items:

"My mother said she sewed into my overcoat, to take with us, every conceivable utensil she could find. Cutlery, mugs, scissors etc.."

Interned at Stanley Prison, Christopher remembers mud-ball fights, collecting fighting spiders (*gum se mau*) and throwing stones across a ravine. He remembers two visits to the hospital; once to have a tooth pulled (when the home-made chloroform made him vomit) and the second time to have a large worm removed. He had memories of his parents which made me realise what a tough time they'd all had, including my mother, although she'd been in a different camp:

"At first I used to wander round collecting cigarette butts for my father's pipe. He refused to accept this filthy stuff but, after a while, he relented and asked me to go out and find more. These he ground up with pine cones for his tobacco.

The camp kitchen was in a small block just past the temple. We'd have to go there after the morning hooter let us out and it was always a case of first in, first served. Once I was instructed to run for it as soon as the hooter went off but I stubbed my toe running down the path. Result: no 'food' for the day. Food was always a sort of gristly/watery stew but, on occasions, my mother used to rustle up a delicious bubble-and-squeak from leftovers for a special meal. I cannot remember ever feeling hungry but, by later accounts, food was at lower than starvation levels most of the time, and I never saw a banana until we left in 1945.

A while later my father, mother and I were walked out of the camp, with a large group of others, to the Stanley jetty and then onto a smelly freighter or motorised junk. We were all kept in the hold and only allowed out once it was dark. We arrived at a new camp in Kowloon, just below the hills and the edge of town. Then, unexpectedly, there were great shouts of jubilation in the middle of the night. It was the end of the war and the Japs had lost! Immediately, Peter and I went over the wire to explore Kowloon and visit the soldier's camp at Shamshuipo. We also climbed over the hill and had a look at the Jap planes at Kai Tak, all in their protective bunkers. Then we were released and housed in a large block down the road. Here I had my first bath and I remember having to ask my mother what to do!"

When Frank and Flip arrived in Rhodesia they didn't have anything. All the valuables and jewellery that they'd hidden in their garden in Hong Kong, at the start of the war, were gone; someone had got there before them and stolen it all. We decided that it must be a family trait because, throughout our history, we've consistently lost things!

Frank was mechanically-minded and helped out on Imire but then, sadly, after five years or so, he had a heart attack and died and Flip went back to England. My other links to China and Korea were also weakened, in the early 1950s, when Uncle Tommy died. After the war he and Aunty Rae and her sister, Aunt Winna, came out to South Africa and set up home in

Durban. They had come out on a visit to Imire, with my mother, in the early days and had stayed with me before my marriage, when I was still living in a pole and dagga house. Then I also received news about my Dad. Apparently he'd retired to Canada and turned to religion in his later years. We were all very disappointed when he didn't come over to our wedding but, as it was, my mother was against his coming. I have always regretted that Dad and I didn't communicate later in our lives because, when the news of his death came, it was too late to do anything about it.

We spent a lot of time in the 1950s with my great friend Bob Darroll. Bob had come back to Rhodesia after the war and worked on his father's farm for a while and in 1947 I'd been his best man when he married Brenda. Sadly, just a few years later, Brenda died and Bob was broken-hearted. Gill and I did what we could to comfort him and help him through his anguish. Later Bob met and married Lorna, an Australian girl, and they emigrated to the Antipodes and settled there. Bob seemed to become very distracted in later years and I think his experiences of flying bombers over Germany had affected him. He always seemed to have these flights on his mind and on his conscience. I felt sorry for him because I'd never had those sorts of experiences, so it doesn't worry me. I could see Bob went through his own little hell in trying to come to terms with his past.

Gill's parents were very much in our lives as we built up Imire and were busy having children (or at least Gilly was) in the 1950s. Her father, Howard Smetham, was a great character. He'd been in the cavalry in the First World War and, in fact, had participated in the very last cavalry charge. One day I asked him. "Surely you weren't riding horses into those machine guns?"

He replied,"We weren't as stupid as that! We went round the back to the flank of the Germans and charged where there weren't any machine guns!"

Howard had also served in the Royal Air Force in the Second World War, in an administrative and logistical position. He had an OBE and an MC for his wartime service and went on to become involved in building up a great legacy for Marandellas, which would benefit Gill and I half a century later. Mrs Dorothy Borradaile Bell, wife of the Anglican Rector of Marandellas, had conceived the idea of a retirement home for pensioners in the town and Howard Smetham was involved from early on. Mrs Bell recalls how tough life was for pensioners and how the Borradaile Trust began:

"You couldn't get a room in Marandellas in 1950 for under £8/- a month, most were £10/- and the Old Age Pension was £15/- a month.

On 16 March 1951 Mr Howard Smetham joined the Committee.

I wore out many pairs of shoes hunting around Salisbury and begging for money and some of the big shops gave me £25/-, £50/- and so on. My relationship with the Chairman (Howard Smetham) was this: I was expected to sniff out possible sources of revenue and then he went in for the kill if I couldn't manage it. And, my word, he was magnificent! For a whole year we worked on Meikles without result. At last Mr Smetham went and saw the Managing Director and said. 'I've come about the Borradaile Trust.'

'Yes, let me see, I have heard about it,' said the Managing Director and got out his cheque book. 'I'll write you out a cheque for £100/-.'

'I beg your pardon,' said Mr. Smetham. 'A cheque for £100/-? Good gracious, the people we are begging for are the people who made Meikles. You ought to give us a cottage, at least, and it will cost you £1000/-.' With that he picked up his hat and walked out. We received a cheque from Meikles for £1000/- a fortnight later!"

While the Smethams were involved in developing Borradaile Trust in Marandellas, I became involved with others in Wedza by helping with renovations to the Inoro St Cross Church. The Church itself was built way before my time, 1910 or earlier, on what was thought to be Inoro Farm, which at the time was owned by the BSAP. Reverend Simpson, who was based at a Mission twelve miles north of Marandellas, used to walk thirty-two miles from Marandellas to Numwa, where there was a little post office and butchery. Apparently he used to carry a dagger in his sock for protection against leopards and sable bulls - a fat lot of use that would have been! The Reverend, with the help of a few local people, moulded the bricks and built the church himself and christenings, marriages and services were held every other month before the building was even completed.

My input to Inoro St Cross Church came some time in the early 1950s, not long after I'd bought Numwa Farm. It was then that a land survey showed that the church wasn't on Inoro Farm, but actually on Numwa! I donated the land to the Anglican Church, so that it would be in their name, and later built a small hut for Sunday school. Many people in the district became involved in renovating the church and it contained pews, stained glass windows, an altar and featured a font built by Andries Rabie. Andries was another Wedza character and a meticulous farmer who paid attention to every detail. I remember visiting his farm once, lit my pipe and threw the match on the ground near the grading shed. Andries bent down, picked up my match and put it in his pocket!

Many years later I heard from Tim Landsberg, son of Roy Landsberg who had sold me Numwa farm. Tim had many happy memories of his early life on Numwa in the 1950s and 1960s, as he writes:

"Norman had a film projector and periodically we used to watch black and white films of the time in one of the two rondavels that Norman lived in. My father and Norman had a lot to do with each other, because both were tobacco growers and all farmers helped each other. Making a living out of growing tobacco was not easy because, among other reasons, Wedza was not a good tobacco district. In the end Norman survived the business and my parents did not, so Norman bought Numwa.

The major interest for my elder brother, Joe, and me was the bush, and Numwa was superb. Imire and Numwa are located on what was called the Bridge Road from Marandellas, simply because it had two bridges on it. 42kms from Marandellas you reached the turnoff, on the left, to Imire, and 43.5kms from Marandellas, on the right, you reached the turnoff to Numwa. Just before you reached the house at Numwa, after passing the tobacco barns and grading shed on the left, there was the most magnificent avenue of 'gum trees', as we called them. Eucalyptus, of course. If my memory serves me correctly it was about 100m long, the trees were huge and leaned inwards to form a complete canopy. We all loved the 'avenue' as we called it, and it was well known in the district. It was also something of a favourite spot for snakes and, on one occasion, as I sprinted down the avenue I had to leap over a very large black mamba, which lay across the road.

Joe and I walked Numwa many times, and in particular we used to go to Castle Rock, the beautiful kopje located on the banks of the Chenikwa River. Castle Rock was a haven for dassies, there were plenty of guinea fowl in the area and, rumour had it, a leopard lived there but we never saw it.

The centre of the world then was the Wedza Club, located across the Chenikwa River on a section of land owned by Frank Scott, whose farm also bordered Numwa. To this day you can see the massive gum-pole beams stretching right across the club house roof which were installed by my father. That club house was the scene of many a riotous party and those familiar with the heyday of the district would remember names like Seager, McDonald, Rutherford, Darrel, Brundel, Scott, de la Harpe, von Memerty, Thornycroft, Stirrup, Partridge and many others."

Tim Landsberg was right about the people and there were many I thought of as great "characters" who started out in Wedza, including the Hamner brothers. Bill and Charles Hamner first opened up a farm in Wedza south but

decided it was for the birds and so they rode by horse through the Sabi until they got to Melsetter (a journey of a good 320kms or so). The Hamner brothers were from a well-off family and later went on to buy eighty thousand acres of land in Inyanga, paying one shilling and ten pence per acre. They split the land between them and Charles developed the Inyanga Downs area, with Major MacIlwaine, while Bill settled further north towards the Gairezi River and Mozambique.

In 1953 Gill gave birth to our second child, John, and his early claim to fame came when he won the baby of the year competition in Marandellas. Gill remembers how it happened:

Norman, Barbara, Gill and John   44

"I had gone shopping in Marandellas and had taken John with me. I met a friend from the garden club and she said I should take John along to the Baby Show. I didn't know anything about it and wasn't prepared but I tidied him up a bit and entered him into the competition. A little later I was delighted when I heard the announcer calling out that John Travers was the winner of the Baby Show!"

In 1955 I bought Welton Farm, which was below Numwa. Welton was three thousand acres and the original farm where I'd learnt the business, as an assistant under Frank Scott, before and after the War. The Chenikwa River ran through a part of Welton and Castle Kopje is located there - a place which would become so important to Imire in the years ahead. I had some great young assistants working for me in the 1950s. Before long we developed a subdivision on Imire, called Kurima, where David Hamilton built a house and lived and where the tobacco barns were located. Ant Wyrley Birch came as an assistant for a while and he was a super chap who later went on to be the grounds-man of a big school in England. Skip Francis was another youngster who came and worked for me. He was a terribly nice young fellow and a keen sportsman and, although he

Norman and Gill aboard The Queen Mary

had a withered arm, it didn't seem to hamper him at all. Jack England worked on Imire in the early 1950s, a few years after he first arrived in Rhodesia. He was an excellent chap; quiet, well-spoken and who played a big part in the Wedza community. Jack later went on to marry Margaret in the Inoro St Cross Church. Margaret was given away by Gill's father (Howard Smetham) and the wedding reception was held in Gilly's beautiful garden on Imire. Jack went on to become a well-known cattle breeder and tobacco farmer in the district and a judge in ploughing competitions.

Our third child, Simon, was born in 1957 and was a quiet, shy little boy but destined to be the brainy one in the family! Gilly and I had a break from farming and babies towards the end of the decade and went on a long holiday to the USA, travelling by sea on the Queen Mary. Coincidentally the purser was Fergus Gillmore, an uncle of David Hamilton. He looked after us very well and we sat at his table making many friends on the journey. One couple invited us to their luxury holiday home (it only had twelve bedrooms!) on Long Island. We met up with Bill van Ess, Aunty Rae's son, and his wife in New York and also a cousin of mine who I knew well from Korea days. Then we travelled across the States by train, which was a great experience.

We visited Aunty Rae and her sister Winnifred and, in San Francisco, we stayed with my Godfather, Uncle Chris. One day he took us to Fisherman's Wharf, a famous seafood restaurant. A menu about three feet square was produced! With eyes boggling I asked the waiter for his advice. He said, "South African crayfish tails have just arrived."

What a let down!

Then we went on to Las Vegas where the floor shows were dazzling and the gambling was all set to empty your pocket. Yosemite Valley was a superb sight, together with the Grand Canyon where some red Indians did a war dance - feathers and tomahawks and all. Then, to our amazement, they changed into jeans and got into their cars and drove away. Tourism ideas for the future!

On to Louisiana, which we loved. Wonderful food and music. After touring the tobacco states we spent a week in Florida and tried some game fishing. We caught a lot, mainly bonito. After one day's fishing I pleaded with the leader. "Please take over, I'm exhausted."

"You paid, you catch!" he replied.

All the fish were released, except for a shark, which he shot.

Once back in Rhodesia, politics became more and more of a hot topic and David Hamilton relates how I stirred the pot in Wedza!

"Towards the end of the 1950s, 'majority rule' became the most controversial political issue of the decade. A referendum had recently been held and narrowly won, thus ensuring that within fifteen years there would be an African majority in the House of Assembly and, in all probability, a government controlled by the majority. This created opposition from the growing number of right-wingers and also the non-committal floating voters. Into this tense situation and as the Chairman of the Wedza Farmers' Association, Norman Travers decided to throw down the gauntlet and invite Herbert Chitepo, a lawyer and leading African politician, to the very next Farmers' Association meeting. He wanted an indication of what Mr Chitepo, as a responsible politician, foresaw when it came to the land question, along with the future of commercial farming and its effect upon the existing white farmers.

All hell broke loose at the very thought of a black man entering the sacred portals of the Wedza Country Club, let alone having a drink at the bar afterwards! Many would have, no doubt, been weakened by the onslaught. Not our Norman! Compromise, yes.

"We will hold the meeting on the Club verandah then."

But give up the idea - never!

So Herbert Chitepo came and spoke, giving a modicum of hope to some and a 'never in a thousand years' attitude to others."

The Hamiltons, Gill and I had become firm friends by then and, toward the end of the decade, we holidayed together on a houseboat called The Pelican, which we shared with the Bedfords. It was a big iron boat with a chug-chug engine and we'd go across from Kariba town to where the Sanyati River flowed into the newly-built and rapidly-filling lake, camp in a sheltered place on the shoreline and fish. Out fishing one day, we came across Bets and Peter Haarhoff, who were sitting on top of a drowned but floating Baobab tree. They were doing very well because bream, sheltering under the tree's shadow, made for easy pickings!

One day we heard this thunder of hooves and a herd of buffalo came rushing past. We assumed they were being chased by lions and, after the dust had settled, we heard this calf bellowing. David and I jumped off the boat and went ashore and, sure enough, in an open space there were lion tracks and then we found this little buffalo calf alone, with wounds on its shoulder. I said to David. 'Look, I've only got one arm that's any use, you've got two, so you dive in and grab it while I keep an eye out for the lions.'

David obliged! He grabbed the buffalo and then we carried it back to the boat. It was only a little chap, perhaps two months old. We put him on board and because we didn't have any fresh milk, made up a bottle of powdered milk - fixing up a teat made from a plastic bag. We fed him on the small island where we were parked and he became very friendly. He would come to us when we returned to the island, to drink the milk we fed him twice a day, and seemed to be doing well. At the end of our holiday we put the little chap on the boat and went across the lake. Doing the right thing, I went to National Parks and told them about the baby buffalo. They were very surprised and said that I couldn't take it back to Wedza but that they would look after it, which they did. Regrettably, I heard that the little buffalo died about six months later - I think from the wounds inflicted by the lions. Little did I know at the time that I would indeed have buffalo on my farm in Wedza before long - and all sorts of other animals too.

47

Chapter Five

ANTHONY AND CLEOPATRA
1960 - 1970

In May 1960 our family was complete with the birth of Alastair, our fourth child and third son. Barbara, our first born (and the only girl), was already nine years old and often felt in charge of the pack when she was home from boarding school:

"My earliest memories are of Nurse, a wonderful coloured lady who was our full time carer. Nurse lived in a room attached to the house and was a very strong character. She told us what to do, looked after us and organised our clothes for us: the boys had bloomers and I had little tops and pants or dresses that Mum made. As young children we had all our meals with Nurse - that's the way things were done in those days. Mum would come and kiss us good night, smelling beautiful and wearing gorgeous gowns, before she and Dad went off for dinner parties in Marandellas.

John and I were close and would play in the sandpit together but I can remember being very jealous of Simon, once pouring a whole bag of salt into his pram! However, being the baby of the family, we all just adored Alastair. Because I was the eldest, I can remember being in trouble and getting whacked if the boys weren't wearing their hats, or if things weren't quite right.

Boarding school was tough and we'd only see our parents once in three months, at half-term. When I was about nine I got my first horse, Noddy, who I absolutely loved. Dad hated riding but I can remember going riding on the farm in the holidays with Mum and John, whose horse was called Silver Heels."

With the children away at boarding school we always tried to spend as much time together as a family when they were home. The December holidays were busy times on the farm, with tobacco and maize to attend to, but in the late 1950s and early 1960s we used to have joint Christmas parties with the Seagers, whose children were about the same age as ours. One year we'd have it at our house and the next year with the Seagers. The parties were very entertaining.

The men put on dinner jackets, the ladies wore long dresses and we'd have a big Christmas dinner together and, afterwards, we'd play games. Some of the games were great fun and we'd have teams playing against each other. One of the games was the Matchbox Game where you had a matchbox on your nose and, with hands behind your back, you had to pass the matchbox from nose to nose along the teams. Another favourite was a game called 'Are you there, Moriarty?' One person from each team was blindfolded and lay on the floor opposite the other so that, with outstretched arms, they could just touch their opponents fingertips. The interrogator had a rolled up newspaper and would call out, 'Are you there, Moriarty?' A whispered reply would come, 'I'm here,' as the opponent tried to dodge out of the way of the interrogator's whack! Pass the orange was another silly game which was amusing. Hands were tied behind your back and an orange placed between your knees. The orange had to be passed from person to person in the team without being dropped on the ground. Later, when the games were over, the kids were put to bed and the grown-ups would dance and drink till the early hours!

I had a number of young assistants working for me (and learning the trade) in the early 1960s. Steve Grinham was one, a super fellow and the life and soul of the pub in the Wedza Club. Peter Murray worked on Imire but didn't stay very long - however, I don't think it was because of the snake incident, which he later related in 'Winter Cricket':

"I was working for Norman on Imire. We were pulling seedlings from the beds and a general commotion indicated that the labour had got a fright for some reason. They wouldn't go near one of the beds and, on enquiring, I discovered that there was a small puff adder inside the seedlings. To beat the place with a weapon, in the hopes of killing it, would have provoked Norman's wrath, and those of us who aspired to work for him, never aspired to that. I picked up a nearby stick and gently probed the area until I found the offending snake. Having studied the recognised methods of retrieving snakes, I gently pressed the stick down on its head until I had it pinned to the ground and, keeping it firmly trapped, I grabbed hold of the neck, keeping the head out of danger and picked it up and deposited it in the nearby grass.

'How did you do that?' I heard Walter Hall ask, as he worked with me then. 'Easy,' I said. 'Like this.' And I repeated the exercise.

This time, however, I wasn't as careful and the serpent managed to extricate itself and tried to sink its fangs into my index finger."

I won't deny that I was a hard task-master and would *shupa* my guys all the time. Peter, like my other assistants, knew that I felt there was no

Puff adder

Planting out tobacco

reason to kill a snake unless it was dangerous and in your house. Peter eventually ended up in Malawi and became a very successful tobacco farmer.

Another young assistant, at around this time, was Ian McCallum and I must admit that one of my main reasons for taking him on was that he was a very good rugby player! Ian was a popular chap, a gifted guitar player and knew all the old songs. He only lasted one season on Imire and then said he was off to university in South Africa. Later he went on to play for South Africa. In later years Ian ended up, very successfully, in the medical field.

I am never one for remembering the bad years but there are often hard times for farmers and, in the 1960s, it was the weather, politics, sanctions and instability that interfered with the smooth running of daily life. In the early days locusts had been a problem and I can remember working for Frank Scott, in the late 1930s, when huge swarms invaded the farms. The workers would go out and scoop them up in their thousands, filling sacks with the insects which were much sought after and considered a delicacy when roasted. The locust problem had subsided by the 1960s, presumably because they were controlled, with sprays, in countries to the north of us and so they never got a chance to get this far down the continent.

Droughts were an ongoing problem and we had two bad ones in a row at the beginning of the 1960s. Droughts usually meant big arguments about my overdraft with the bank manager. Friend and neighbour Nigel Thornycroft was interviewed by The Sunday Mail on 12 May 1963 and described the position we all found ourselves in:

"The situation would be bad but still not desperate if his tobacco was fetching good prices on the auction floors. So far he has sold 26,000lbs, averaging 28 pence per lb. However, average production costs are between 24 pence and 28 pence per lb."
(Winter Cricket)

I was always looking for ways to cope during droughts; digging dams and drilling boreholes were the more obvious means to this end. The Imire area was granite country, which I always thought wasn't good for boreholes but some people were lucky and did sink boreholes successfully and these made all the difference in drought years. Various people in the area were into water-divining and used a variety of peculiar methods. Some used a ball on the end of a piece of string which would start swaying from side to side if there was underground water but I thought I'd have a go with a stick. I used a forked mulberry stick which would pull down very strongly at the tip whenever water was located - so hard, in fact, that my hands would go white from the pressure of gripping the stick. I don't think I was very good at it. No-one believed me and, of course, I never found anything substantial.

I came up with another idea of getting water, after we'd gone through a spell of repeated droughts, and it turned out to be a bit of a novelty. I'd heard about a firm that was selling rain-rockets in Salisbury. Apparently they were being used quite successfully in Italy and, although the Rhodesian government was cloud-seeding to try and break the drought, you couldn't ask them to come and seed a cloud over your farm, so rain-rockets it was!

For individuals the rain-rockets were fairly expensive but, if they were successful and saved the crops, then they would more than pay for themselves. I went and bought two or three initially, took them to the farm and read the instructions. A rain-rocket was four or five foot long, five inches in diameter and had fins at the base. The rocket itself was filled with something like silver oxide in the head and had an explosive charge in it. There was a launcher, very much like a space rocket but not quite on the same scale! You lit a fuse at the bottom, the rocket went *psshhew* and up it went, a thousand or fifteen hundred feet and then it would explode inside the cloud - if you'd aimed it properly! All being well, and literally within minutes, you should see a break in the clouds where the rocket had exploded and, shortly afterwards, a shower of rain would follow.

The first time I tried a rain-rocket I was too impatient, didn't wait long enough and the cloud wasn't big enough. Aside from this the rocket, on first attempt, did everything correctly. It disappeared into the cloud, went boom and a slight mist came out of the cloud. I thought this really could work if one picked the right cloud. After a couple more attempts the final rocket worked and we had a shower but, sadly, the rain didn't land on us but on our neighbour! He complained bitterly because it rained all right, but not on his tobacco where he needed it!

We had probably about 25% success with the rain-rockets, which wasn't all that satisfactory, but it all depended on the clouds, which had to be full of rain. On one occasion a rocket gave us a nice half inch of

Burley tobacco seedling

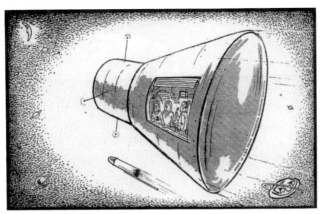

Some guy from a place called Marandellas asking if we have seen his rain rocket
(The Farmer)

rain on the tobacco crop, which paid for that rocket and some of the others that hadn't been so successful. The kids loved the rain-rockets and John remembers the excitement quite clearly:

"Dad was the first person ever to use a rain-rocket in Wedza (if not further afield) and you can imagine the excitement we had, as kids, when Dad would say. 'Look, there's a big black cloud!'

We kids would jump into the back of the truck, with the launching pad and the sacks of sand that secured it down and off we'd go. You'd almost never shoot the rocket directly overhead, or on your own farm, because the cloud would be moving at five miles an hour, or whatever, and so we'd have to shoot off to someone else's farm to launch the rocket. Dad would have to anticipate when to pull the trigger and then, whoosh, off it went!

I distinctly remember the rain-rocket that was fired over Mike Bartlett's house at low level. One day Dad and some mates got a bit sloshed at the pub and decided to have a bit of fun. They shot this rain-rocket, at about forty-five degrees, over Mike Bartlett's house where it exploded ! This was at a time when everyone was a bit sensitive to bangs and loud noises, but it was all taken in good spirit."

Our final effort with the rain-rockets was in Moçambique, when there were British patrol-boats cruising off Beira, trying to enforce sanctions. I thought at the time that my boat, with its 50hp outboard, could go quite fast and that it might be fun to take a rain-rocket out and shoot it over a patrol-boat! Luckily for me I never got to use it because, if I had, I'm sure they would have replied with a lot more than a rain-rocket!

There were of course other years when the problem for farmers wasn't too little rain but too much. In one memorable season we had seventy to eighty inches. This was a tremendous amount considering we would normally average thirty to thirty-five inches in a season. That year I can remember water literally bubbling up out of the ground on our driveway. A little stream started trickling down the drive and, walking along, I found numerous barbel (catfish) wriggling on the road. They are carnivorous scavengers and really are the most fascinating creatures; over the years I have seen many strange things where they are concerned and this movement out of water was something I knew about. The barbel actually have a spongy structure above the gills, which allows them to breathe out of water. They would come out in large numbers, flapping along in the wet grass from one dam to another. The Africans used to stand below the spillways and catch dozens of them. We were once digging the core of a dam and two or three feet down, in the clay, was a little pocket of air and inside there was a barbel - alive. The hole was moist, but not wet and the barbel must have hibernated there for what? Months, years - who knows? How did it feed itself? Was it breathing air? How long can they hibernate - so many questions! Once, I was in the tin boat, the Pelican, with the Hamiltons and we were just coming into the Sanyati Gorge to try some fishing when we saw a seething mass of barbel, probably fifty metres long. The fish were obviously migrating up the Sanyati. There had been heavy rains upstream and the barbel were heading there - presumably to breed. What extraordinary creatures!

Back to the weather though, the farmers' constant topic of discussion; there were the years when ice fell from the sky! I can remember having very bad hail-storms some years and once, got into big trouble with one of my neighbours. I had sent up a rain-rocket and, not long after, had a very angry phone call from him to say he'd just had a hell of a hail-storm as a result of my rocket! I wasn't very popular! Sometimes we had such bad storms they would wipe out our entire tobacco crop. The ground would be literally blanketed with hail-stones afterwards with the crop completely shredded. We tried to recover what we could by ratooning. You use a sharp knife and cut what remains of the main stem at a diagonal about two to three inches from the ground. A sucker will come up and then another and, after a fortnight or so, you remove all the suckers - but one, and grow the plant through. I learnt that you could ratoon a crop and, if you handled it properly, you could get a fairly decent harvest. You had to watch out for spreading disease of course, like mosaic, so the knife had to be dipped into a tin of disinfectant before you cut each stem.

In-between droughts and other natural calamities, I indulged my passion for fishing. I even went on a couple of the tiger fishing competitions in

Kariba, in the early days of the event. In 1962 our team consisted of Peter Hudson, Peter Worsley-Worswick, Tony Seager and I and we won the Tiger Tournament! After going up once more I said count me out.

I enjoyed the fishing and being with a bunch of guys on a boat but I wasn't very enthusiastic about the competitive side of it all. It became too intense for my liking. Every year the number of boats seemed to double and all these professionals would go up long 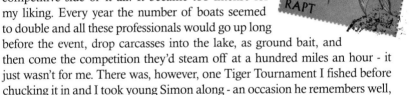 before the event, drop carcasses into the lake, as ground bait, and then come the competition they'd steam off at a hundred miles an hour - it just wasn't for me. There was, however, one Tiger Tournament I fished before chucking it in and I took young Simon along - an occasion he remembers well, although it was more because of my bad temper than for the fishing:

"Dad had invited me to go with him to the Tiger Tournament when I was ten or eleven and I had a broken finger, which was in plaster. Dad had a 50hp motor and he thought he was one of the heavies in his little dory with his fifty horse engine. We took off, going flat out, in the usual race for the best fishing spots in the Sanyati Gorge when my hat flew off. Dad was livid because we had to turn back to try and find my hat - that was the end of being first to the Gorge!

In fact that wasn't the only time I had trouble with Dad when we were fishing. I remember once going with him and Brian Curtis and, while we were fishing somewhere, I got a triple fish-hook stuck in my cheek. Dad said his knife was too dirty to cut the hook out then and there, so I had this damned lure hanging out of my cheek all day until we went home and Dad cut it out!"

A more leisurely pace of fishing suited me and I loved sea-fishing. My first trip to Moçambique was in a double-winged aircraft flown by Jack Malloch, who was flying up fish from that country. We flew over the Pungwe Flats and could see great herds of game, sadly there are none there today. Then followed some exciting fishing with plenty that got away!

My good friend David Hamilton was with me on many fishing trips and remembers some of the more amusing, and hair-raising, encounters we had:

"Norman always did things in a BIG way. His aims were always big, his achievements were invariably big and the only aspect of life that remained in moderate proportions was Norman's ability to actually save money. To Norman, money was there to be spent - in a big way too! Very seldom was anything conventional. Big game also meant big fish to him and, in this sense then, it was Norman's ultimate ambition to land a billfish - such as marlin, which he never achieved. The nearest he came to this ambition only happened twice.

On the first occasion we were out on the seven-mile reef off Bazaruto. Norman was fully-armed with a 140 reel, 125lb line and a short, sturdy boot rod; a harness and rod bucket strapped to him (not the rod bucket on the seat which is the luxury job) and he suddenly exclaimed he was onto a monster. Judging by all the exertion, grunts and groans, he surely was.

After half an hour of heavy toing and froing it became obvious that the fish was, undoubtedly, a grouper attempting to head for a coral cavern. Norman relaxed for a minute, flexed his weary arms and hands and allowed the leather strap around his shoulders to take the weight. Groupers of 400 - 500lbs are not uncommon in these waters. Suddenly, with a mighty pull, the leather strap broke and away overboard went rod, reel, line and all. After a moment taken to recover from the shock Norman's only comment was. 'Well I suppose these things are sent to try us!'

On the second occasion four of us were in the boat and had, again, sailed out from Bazaruto. One 300lb hammerhead shark had already been landed after an hour-long fight, when, once again, Norman was onto something big. Away went his line and it was obviously a very large fish. The line screamed out and the fish remained on the surface.

12.00pm: It must be a marlin and it must jump soon.

3.30pm: No sign of the fish; still just as strong and still pulling out line. We take turns pouring water over the reel to keep it cool.

4.30pm: Norman is absolutely exhausted. We are still pouring water on the reel and the fish is slowing down. It comes close to the boat.

'It doesn't look very big?' says I.

'It does you know, looks just as big as the shark,' says Norman.

'It is another hammerhead!' I exclaim. 'But why has it fought for so many hours?'

The answer was not long in arriving. The fish had been hooked in the tail, hence the four hour thirty minute battle! Billfish eluded Norman then and continued to elude him evermore!"

I seemed to be good at catching sharks. There was one epic battle, which left me fighting the fish while David fought the storm, (with some frustration), as he recalls:

"Norman and I set sail in my catamaran from the beach in a heavy sea and a good south-easterly wind. I raised only the jib sail and Norman immediately busied himself with baiting his hook. Needle and cotton and total concentration! The sea became more and more ominous.

"Norman, I don't like the look of these waves!'

No response, head down and total concentration. A little while later I tried again.

'You know these bloody waves are beginning to worry me Norman.'

No response and Norman had now dropped the completed bonefish bait into the sea - in order to inspect the trim of the bait! Satisfied, at last, Norman allowed the bait to flow out from the reel until it was some twenty or thirty yards behind the catamaran. He then leant back and said. 'Good Lord, is this where we are? How's it going?'

Norman eventually hooked a shark and, after an epic struggle, I got the boat, shark and him into shallow water, whereupon he leapt off the boat and began to play the shark toward the shore. Suddenly the line parted. The shark lay motionless for twenty minutes until, eventually, both Norman and shark drifted back into their respective habitats, to lick their wounds and contemplate the future."

As soon as our children were old enough, probably from six years old onwards, they came on these holidays with us. Their love of the wild and the sea and the bush stemmed from these happy days. Barbara remembers them as wonderful times when she discovered the difference between talking and doing:

"We went to Moçambique, most years, in the August school holidays. We would go for three weeks, driving down, often breaking down on the way, and we always started in Beira where we went to Johnny's and had Portuguese food. Then we'd go down to Vilancoulos and go across to the islands on a dhow, taking all our food and we'd have the most wonderful holiday. We often went with the Hamiltons and the dynamic of the two families was wonderful. The Hamiltons were the talkers and we were the doers. With the Hamiltons we'd sit around talking for hours, which Dad didn't like very much, and so he'd go off fishing. When we saw Dad coming back we'd all jump up and run around the beach collecting crabs and being 'doers'."

Barbara was right about the fishing, which I did at every opportunity. In Beira fishing from the shore beyond the lighthouse was very productive. I became sold on shore-fishing one morning at high-tide, after I caught a 50lb kingfish, along with some others. We always kept our fish in those days - no returns like today! We would drive to Vilancoulos where we could hire a boat for three weeks. It had a crew and was fully provisioned, including a dozen live chickens, and off we went to stay on Paradise Island under tents. Paradise Island was originally a penal colony of the Portuguese and the ruins of the foundations can still be seen there. We caught lots of fish from the boat and plenty of crayfish when goggling. There were beautiful coral gardens with their hosts of brilliant fish. Goggling off the reefs we mainly caught crayfish and the biggest I remember, fed about six of us. What a meal!

We had many a happy holiday on Bazaruto Island with not only the Hamiltons but Brian and Babs Curtis and their children, Steve Grinham and others too. Bazaruto was a long island with inland lakes teaming with birdlife and also crocodiles. They must've survived when the islands were part of the mainland thousands of years ago. In the lagoon facing the sea, on the southern side, there was a large flock of flamingoes. The lagoon also provided us with delicious crabs when the tide came in. The kids loved it, swimming, goggling and fishing - what a magic life it was. Flamingoes at sunrise on the sand-spits; catching edible crabs on the incoming tide in the bay; cooking the crayfish we had caught over an open fire. One day I brought in a conch shellfish and cooked it for hours, telling the children this was a delicacy in the United States. It was as tough as boot-leather, and they all laughed at me - the suckers!

My son John will remember once returning from goggling through a gap in the reef. I had taken them all out on the tide to show the kids some sharks. To our dismay there were dozens of them so we hastened back into the lagoon and lazily swam back towards shore. I glanced behind me at John, and saw a thresher shark following him. I motioned to him to look behind.

He took one look and passed me, breaking all Olympic swimming records! I gave an underwater shout and the shark disappeared. Thresher sharks aren't man-eaters - or so they say!

It was, of course, an encounter that John would never forget, even though the details he remembers are slightly different:

"We were at northern Baz, Roy MacIlwaine was with us and I was probably eleven or twelve. Dad had enough faith in our pluck, to goggle us out beyond the reef and into the deep blue sea. Looking down at a 70 degree angle you could see everything! It was absolutely fantastic but I literally clung to Dad. I think Roy and I were trembling with fear and excitement the whole time, especially when we came across a black-tipped shark and then a thresher shark. When we were on our way back to shore, which was probably about two hundred metres away, and swimming at quite a pace, we suddenly saw a shark fin pass us at full speed. Realising that this shark had already passed Dad was absolutely terrifying and we then swam at full tilt, landing on the beach at terrific speed, throwing goggles off with our hearts absolutely pounding. Dad had given us the adventure of a lifetime, goggling in the big blue sea, something I will never forget."

On another occasion, when luckily the family were safely ashore, Brian Curtis, David Hamilton and I sailed from Bazaruto Island. Our intended destination was Beira and we left Bazaruto in David's catamaran. It had twin floats and a sail, but no cabin. We had enough food for two days, a demijohn of very bitter wine and some water. On the first day we were going strong until we passed Inhassoro, when the wind died out and we just drifted until the evening. Then a north wind got up so our captain, David, said, "No-go for Beira, we'll head back to Inhassoro."

So we broached the demijohn of wine and looked out at the lights of the

Gill, Alistair, Simon and Barbara on the beach at Bazaruto

village in the distance. Suddenly the lights in Inhassoro village all went out! There must have been a power cut and so we sailed briskly along, singing old drunken songs until, with a crunch, we cruised up the beach. After walking for about half an hour we found the hotel and, the next morning, flew to Beira with a Portuguese pilot named da Silva. There we found our families still gazing wistfully (I hope!) out to sea, expecting us at any time.

The idyllic life we had on these wonderful holidays and on the farm, and all over Rhodesia, was interrupted in the sixties when politics stepped in. For the people of Wedza a chap called Winston Field was very much at the forefront of the community. Winston had come to Rhodesia as a young man, starting out as I did (a learner-assistant on a tobacco farm) and went on to become a very successful tobacco farmer on Karimba Farm, in Wedza. Winston was always very keen on encouraging immigrants to come and settle in Rhodesia. And as far back as 1954 he'd introduced a scheme to bring Italian families out to Karimba Farm. He would bring out these poor farmers, build them a couple of barns and a house, give them some of his land and then teach them how to grow tobacco and maize. One of his sons eventually went on to marry the daughter of one of the Italian families. Winston's ideas were fine but, after a few years, the immigrants learnt that there was no way they could make money with a couple of barns and a small acreage of tobacco, it had to be bigger. After a while they would leave Winston and start up on their own, in all sorts of other businesses. Winston himself was very much an Englishman, a meticulous farmer and deep thinker who went into politics, winning a seat in Parliament in 1957 and becoming Prime Minister in 1962. I was never keen on getting actively involved in politics but, in 1963, I went to Bulawayo with David Hamilton. Writing in 'Winter Cricket' David describes what we heard:

"Friend or not, those against Winston Field were firm in their conviction. Norman Travers and myself attended Whitehead's last congress in Bulawayo - in 1963 - where Whitehead stated: 'I believe that in fifteen years time we will have majority rule in Rhodesia. We must begin to prepare for it now. Abolish discrimination; build up the African middle class. Allow African leadership in all spheres of private and government sectors, and begin an integrated education programme.' He was right on the date - within fifteen years! With hindsight, what a pity this forward-thinking policy was never allowed to flourish. It was swept aside by the tidal wave of 'never in our lifetime' and then, after the 'night of the long knives' against Winston Field, came Ian Smith, the Ironman."

On 11 November 1965 Ian Smith declared UDI and it wasn't long before farmers began to feel the effects and had to adapt. Being interviewed in the Rhodesian Tobacco Journal some time later, I was asked if UDI had been a blessing in disguise, to which I replied. "Without any doubt; it has forced us to farm more economically without the golden handshake we used to

get every year from tobacco. UDI only helped push us to diversify into cattle, to move it along that little bit faster."

On Imire, mixed-farming led me into all sorts of new practices. We went in for pastures, not only on the tobacco lands but also for dairy, which we started with Friesland cows. I developed a thirty acre patch of dryland and vlei and turned it into an irrigated pasture. I imported seed from the UK including rye grass, silver leaf clover, New Zealand white clover and other English grasses and legumes. These did remarkably well, particularly the clovers, but all needed heavy watering during the dry winter months. The clovers supplied nitrogen to the soil and, from time to time, we had to undertake heavy liming. To produce good growth the ph of the soil had to be watched closely and, for this, I relied on the expert testing and advice provided by John Clatworthy. The specialists encouraged new ideas and experimentation and were always on hand to tell us what we needed to add to the soil to get maximum benefit. John was the Senior Pasture Research Officer in the Department of Research and Specialist Services, based at Grasslands Research Station on the Watershed Road, and describes our early attempts:

"Several farmers in the Wedza area (eg. Bob Rutherford) and elsewhere (eg. Harvey Milner and Ben Norton) grew very successful vlei pastures and I'm sure they all followed the same general pattern. We mainly used clovers, typically the European white clover (Trifolium repens) and Kenya white clover (T. semipilosum). We also planted legumes as they withstood heavy grazing well and used several local grasses, such as Torpedo grass (Panicum repens) and Nile grass (Acroceras macrum), as well as the European ryegrasses (Lolium spp.). The pastures needed quite careful management…"

Years later we would find that the strips of legumes, that I had planted as an experiment, had spread all over Imire and provided valuable grazing for both domestic and game animals, thus making this one of my more successful ventures! While developing and refining the vlei pastures, I read an article on mobile dairies in the UK which appealed to me. Why walk the cow twice a day to the milking parlour when you could milk them on the pasture! Makes sense doesn't it? So I imported my first milking bail and it came up by Gascoignes. It consisted of a trailer containing three milking stalls, a diesel engine and milk cooler. The whole contraption was towed by a tractor, with a small trailer, which transported the milk to the main farm buildings and into the main cooler. It looked good so I asked a local firm, Colnie and Maddoc, to make me a duplicate so we could milk five cows at a time. So, with a tractor and small trailer, we milked our cows in situ for a while! In the early days a transport firm, Elcombes, transported our milk daily to town. However, when they closed this service, dairy farming didn't appeal anymore because our work became much harder.

We dug pits for silage in the tobacco pastures in order to self-feed the dairy cows. We rotated the lands; one year we grew tobacco and the next we put down Rhodes grass and, the following year, we had a beautiful pasture. I didn't believe in making silage and having to cart it out and dump it, it was expensive and so I started the on-site silage pit. We made a wooden frame, that the cows could feed though, fitted it over the silage pit and, every day or so, we'd move it forward and it worked fine. The machinery I bought to make the silage was imported from Europe. It consisted of a big endless conveyor belt with a mower at the bottom. You pulled it along with a tractor and mowed the grass, which went up the conveyor belt and into a trailer. Once the trailer was full it was taken to the silage pit, spread out and covered with molasses. Then we'd run a tractor over it to consolidate the cut grass and, by then, the next tractor would be coming in with a load. It was a good way to make cheap silage for feeding - and when you're a farmer everything is based on economics.

The next idea to get more out of the farm came when Alan Savory started us on the hundred acre paddock scheme. The idea was that you put one hundred cows on one hundred acres, grazed it fairly heavily for a few days and then moved all the cows into the next hundred acre paddock. When I was asked, by the Rhodesia Tobacco Journal, how I was getting on with mixed-farming I had just started on the Savory system and was very enthusiastic:

"The Savory system has really opened our eyes. We looked at cattle first and thought we had the answer to management. Of course it's no good having animals without grass. Now you look at the grass first and the animal follows - the better the grass the better the animal. We are all getting down to far higher grazing capacities on our veld and pastures and all because of the management which we didn't have before. I used to run a beast to eight acres now we are running a beast to four..."

There were disadvantages, too, because of the cost involved in the extra fencing and then there was also the problem of providing a water supply in each hundred acre field. So, while Savory's idea did make sense, it was often very difficult in practice.

Another new idea came when I decided to try and develop a maize crop on Imire vlei land. Vleis are swampy wetlands leading to water courses where the soil is heavy clay and the vegetation sour and unpalatable to grazers - both cattle and game. The only time the vleis could be used for grazing was if you burnt off the grass in the spring with, or just before, the first rains, otherwise the rest of the year it was unutilised, unproductive land. I ploughed up my first vleis when they were dry enough to get a tractor in, around June/July during winter. The soil needed lots of lime to build up the ph and then I built up ridges as high as I could: about fourteen inches high. The high ridges were essential because the vleis would become waterlogged when the rains came. We planted the maize on the ridges, starting them off with irrigation, getting the plants going before the rains started. By the time the rains came in earnest the maize had sprouted quite a few inches and were well away. The plants put down taproots to get to the underlying vlei water and their lateral roots in the ridges held them firm. A good top dressing with Ammonium Nitrate and the maize grew beautifully. Some of our yields reached up to forty bags an acre, which was much better than our dryland maize where we would be lucky to get fifteen or twenty bags to the acre.

After these early successes I was encouraged to really develop our vleis and found that we could grow maize on the same vlei land for two or three years in a row. We put contours right through the vleis before they were ridged and this helped with the drainage and reduced siltation. The average sand-veld farms in the area had up to 50% of the land covered with vleis or semi vleis and because this was unutilised land it was worth looking at any new possibilities. After holding one or two field days a few other farmers became interested in the idea of vlei maize and followed our example.

I had some great assistants during these difficult years of sanctions, including Richard Moore, a very quiet man who was mad about birds and ornithology. Alec Barby came as a tobacco company assistant for a season. The tobacco companies were developing other African countries where they could start growing tobacco in opposition to us. They would send these youngsters out to growers like me, we'd teach them the ropes and then they'd go off and set up in other countries. The tobacco company would pay me to teach the youngster and they paid the chap's wages too - it was a very favourable arrangement. Basil Rowlands also came as a company assistant to learn the ropes. He was a terribly nice fellow, a keen rugby player.

Kim Muir was a great assistant in these difficult years. Before he came to me he'd been sheep farming in Natal. I was building up a sheep flock at the time and had decided to go in for wool and, therefore, Kim was the ideal assistant. I bought these beautiful Merino/Suffolk rams, put them in with the Black Headed Persian ewes and Kim undertook the shearing. We sent the wool down to South Africa and were very disappointed when it was down-graded because of the hair in it. My sheep experiment faded very quickly once I realised that the wool had to be completely free of hair to get good prices and that I'd have to change all of my breeding ewes and start again!

Some time in the mid-sixties, when we were trying new farming ventures, and when John was still a young teenager, he and his friend Richard Thornycroft, from the next-door farm, had a close encounter, which Richard will never forget:

"John and I had been out guinea fowl shooting, when I was about twelve. Our parents were very strict about guns, mine particularly. After we got home to Imire (where I was a guest for the night) Norman told John and I to go and clean the guns and put them away and told us that, while we were there, we should give all the guns an oily wipe-

over. There were a couple of Luger pistols in his gun cabinet and as I was wiping one over, "bang" it went off! The bullet went straight through the study wall and into the kitchen. John was standing next to me but I can remember being more petrified about what Norman was going to tell my Dad, than about what had just happened.

Norman came into the room and I think he was quite shocked and, for a change, didn't even tear a strip off us. I think he realised that he was partly in the wrong for having a loaded weapon. In retrospect, perhaps he kept the gun loaded for security reasons but, at the time, he just looked at me and said. 'Let that be a lesson to you.'

I couldn't believe it because Norman was incredibly strict with his kids. I can remember him from when I was five years old and I used to go over there and play with John and Barbara. He would give us a hiding at the drop of a hat if we did something out of line. He was also a great kidder and very jovial and good for a laugh but if we did something wrong he let us know about it. He even used to put boxing gloves on John and I and let us have a go at each other. Luckily no one was hurt in the accidental discharge, when I shot a hole through the study wall, and I will always remember it as an occasion when I saw a gentle side to Norman and I've never forgotten it. He never did tell my Dad, either!"

I didn't retell that story but, for years after, we all retold the story of what happened to Richard's Dad, Nigel Thornycroft, when we were on a hunting trip once. My nephew, Howard Matthews, has heard me tell the story and relates the first part:

"It was at one of the lower Zambezi hunting camps when you had a bag and National Parks allowed bystanders to have a pot-shot occasionally. An afternoon was spent guinea fowl shooting. Nigel and Corona Thornycroft were left at the lower Rukomechi while Norman and hangers-on were to drive further up and walk downwards to meet them.

After a long walk down, Nigel and Corona were found in much the same place as they had been left, with Nigel stretched out under a shady tree but he now had grazes on his forehead, face and all down his body. Corona told us that they had been walking around a patch of bush earlier, when Nigel said. 'Flush the birds from that side, Dar!' Corona came round the bush to find Nigel entangled in the horns of a buffalo with his legs around its neck. She took his shotgun and fired two shots of No. 6 birdshot into the buffalo's hide. It put its head up in amazement, which allowed Nigel time to slither away. He then took the gun and blasted four to six shots, at point blank range, into its skull and finally killed it."

That isn't quite the end of the story, as the whole of Wedza gradually discovered in the years ahead! Nigel sustained a couple of broken ribs and knew that he wasn't going to be doing much hunting or walking around after that. He was lying under the big shady tree and said to Corona. "Dar," (he always called her 'Dar'; short for darling, I presume), "Dar, remember that Egyptian goose nest we found with the eggs in it? Why not go and get me some eggs and I'll try and hatch them here in my sleeping bag while I'm off my feet."

Sure enough two of the eggs did hatch later on when they were back on their farm, Merryhill, in Wedza. They called the two geese Anthony and Cleopatra! In those days we'd never even seen Egyptian geese in Wedza before but Anthony and Cleopatra thrived. They went off to breed on one the dams and formed the basis of the whole Egyptian goose population of the Wedza district.

Not long after this, our various new ventures, combined with UDI, began to show positive effects - these being mixed-farming and diversification and, in our district, another plus was the formation of WADS, the Wedza Agricultural Development Scheme. David Hamilton explains:

"After UDI the Wedza farming community discussed the effect that sanctions would have on the district. There was no fuel for conservation staff to visit farms, no contouring, no transport for fertiliser and selling crops etc.. So WADS began. The area was divided into five communities all having the same approximate number of farms."

In our area a group of farmers got together, visited each other's farms and learned from each other. It was all linked to productivity and, every couple of months, we'd have a field day and discuss successes, failures and problems and learn from each other's mistakes. Mark Milbank, new to the area, describes how he met me and then benefitted from WADS:

"I first met Norman soon after I arrived in Wedza from South Africa and moved onto Chirume Farm in 1967. I was introduced to him by my father-in-law, Rick Holme, who had himself only recently arrived in Wedza.

'This bunch here is very different,' he told me. 'Discussions at farmers' meetings are at a very intelligent level and the meetings are always very well-attended. One of the leaders seems to be a guy called Norman Travers - you should meet him.'

And I did.

Typically, my then wife, Fran, and I were immediately asked to dinner and introduced to a number of other Wedza farming families. After dinner we played bridge and I experienced, for the first time, Norman's unique brand of bidding. I had always thought bridge to be a very serious game - but not after you've played with Norman! He backed his hunches, roared with laughter when they failed and made the game a lot of fun for us all.

I was frequently grateful for Norman's help and advice over the best way to feed cattle in winter, how to manage the grazing, what sort of things to buy on the sales and a hundred and one other problems relating to cattle farming in Wedza. He was often the host on Imire of what became known as WADS - a discussion group amongst farmers to help resolve mutual problems."

As well as being practical, WADS also provided an opportunity for a social gathering and we had an amazing variety of people in the district that did all manner of amazing things. There was even one chap, a Scotsman, Fred Sandeman, who farmed in the south of Wedza, who made and played bagpipes. Writing in 'Winter Cricket', his wife Peggy explains:

"Fred Sandeman was famous in Rhodesia for being the only bagpipe maker in Africa. Some rare exhibits, such as ivory pipes, are now in the Edinburgh Museum. Fred trained the Churchill Pipe Band and played the New Year in at Wedza Club for many years."

As the 1960s drew to a close, in November 1968, I was to have one last major adventure in Moçambique, which had the district and the country talking. The story became known as 'lost at sea!'

For those who aren't familiar with the account and to avoid any embellishments, or, more likely, lapses of memory that accrue over time it is repeated here, with kind permission, as told by myself in 'Winter Cricket':

"Three of us, Peter Worsley-Worswick, Charles Jobson and I, set off for Beira in Peter's truck, towing his boat, on Wednesday morning, the 6th of November. On Thursday we launched the boat successfully into the surf and proceeded to Beira harbour where, after numerous delays, we got the permission of the port captain to proceed to Santa Carolina, 140 miles south. We left in fairly choppy weather at about midday. At sundown, with the seas rising, we decided to make for shelter for the night and reached a small fishing village where we spent a comfortable night and bought an extra five gallons of petrol for emergencies. We also consumed several beers to combat the rather ferocious mosquitoes. We reached Santa Carolina for lunch on Friday after a very pleasant trip.

Saturday we spent fishing in quite heavy seas north of Bazaruto Island. We did not catch anything big but nonetheless had a pleasant day.

On Sunday, we again went out in calmer and sunnier weather conditions and had good fishing, catching a hammerhead shark of about 200lbs and a ragged tooth shark of about 600lbs and a number of smaller fish. The larger shark we were unable to get into the boat because of the size, so we roped it to the stern to tow back.

Our efforts with the sharks were to give ourselves the knowledge and experience for the prime target, which was, of course, marlin.

The weather was still fine but with a rising sea and low clouds forming up on the southern horizon when we set off for home about 4.00pm. However, we were slowed by rough seas. By 5.30pm we were within two miles of Santa Carolina when our engine overheated. After several unsuccessful attempts to get it going again we anchored and attempted to get our spare engine, a 50hp outboard, to work. By then the sea had risen alarmingly with very strong gusts of wind and rain. The outboard became completely saturated by

Bazaruto lighthouse

waves surging over the stern. We could see the lights and palm trees of Santa Carolina quite clearly, so we tried signalling with our torches but without success.

We pumped out the bilge of the boat and lay huddled and wet in the small cabin. During the night our anchors dragged on the sandy bottom and by morning we found ourselves some five miles from Santa Carolina but with our anchors now firmly gripped on a coral bottom. All Monday we stayed anchored in very stormy seas with high winds and rain. The boat took this weather extraordinarily well and very few waves actually broke over us. When they did, most of the water ran off - so pumping out the bilge was not a big task.

We had approximately three quarters of a gallon of drinking water, oranges, raisins and cake on board, so we rationed ourselves to half a glass of water per day and a handful of raisins and cake.

About 8.00pm on the Monday night, the first anchor rope broke with a loud report. The second soon followed its miserable example and away we drifted with the storm. We quickly threw out a mattress to act as a sheet anchor and attempted to make a sail from the cabin door canopy.

That night was a worrying one as we swept up the coast due north, wondering if we would be either washed ashore in the high waves or turned over on one of the many sandbars that spread out to sea along the Sabi mouth, fifty miles to the north.

Being continually wet and cold made us feel miserable but our morale was good and conversation, perhaps not very witty, did flow.

The next day, though still stormy and constantly raining, found us in blue water out of sight of land. This was a great relief, as a drifting boat close along this coast is always in danger of grounding on sandbanks. We kept ourselves busy by making another sail from a sack, a rudder from planks and trying to get either of the engines working.

By Wednesday afternoon, we were sailing, or rather dragging ourselves steadily northwards with our makeshift sails - but what the coastal currents were doing to us was anyone's guess. We saw neither ships nor planes, though by now we realised or rather hoped, someone would be looking for us. The sea grew considerably calmer as the wind dropped and we had high hopes of sunshine on Thursday, to dry out the engines and get ourselves back to civilization.

At 8.00pm on Wednesday we spotted the lights of a ship on the horizon and, after frantic SOS signals with our torches, we saw an answering flash. Our troubles were over and the Swedish ship, Elgaren, picked us up, both boat and bodies, and filled us with lovely cold beer, schnapps and food, until we happily fell asleep. For the record, we were picked up about thirty five miles from land and about eighty miles north of Bazaruto." *(Winter Cricket)*

There are a few other details that I remember but did not put in print. During one of our conversations, in those long days at sea, I said. "At the mouth of the Sabi River there are many sandbanks, way out to sea, and these are breeding grounds for sharks so we should tie ourselves together and prepare for a long swim."

Peter turned this idea down!

Then, to cheer them up, I said that often at shipwrecks the fattest person would have to give themselves up for the good of his friends. Charlie Jobson (the fattest) wouldn't speak to me for hours!

The morning after being picked up we asked the captain to drop us off in Beira.

"Not a hope," he said. "We're sailing to Lourenço Marques. But come and meet my passengers."

These were five American widows and we enjoyed our few days with them in Lourenço Marques. The captain refused our offer to pay salvage - what a man! We left him in Lourenço Marques and eventually arrived home.

Being lost at sea naturally affected the whole family and Gilly had the ordeal of telling the children and waiting and worrying at home on Imire for the five days we were missing. John was fifteen at the time:

"I was at boarding school at Peterhouse. Mum pitched up at school and told me Dad had been missing for two days. I was devastated at the thought that my beloved father was lost at sea. It was a very, very traumatic time and nothing worked at school until the news came that Dad had been found and was safe."

An article in The Rhodesia Herald on 15 November 1968 added a couple more details:

"The disappearance of their eighteen foot boat led to a massive search along the Moçambique coast, including numerous launches and search aircraft of both the Portuguese and Rhodesian Air Forces."

David Hamilton, not with us at the time, was later told how the others fared on our 'lost at sea' adventure:

"After their three-night ordeal when Norman, Peter Worsley-Worswick and Charles Jobson were lost at sea off the Moçambique coast, I happened to meet Peter and he told me of their extremely frightening experience.

'You know, you could not find a better bloke than Travers to be stranded with in the middle of the Indian Ocean,' said Peter. 'He was the eternal optimist. He always reckoned that the weather would soon clear up and then we could dry the engine out and get it going again.'

When dawn broke on the first morning and there was not a sign of land anywhere, Jobson and Peter were somewhat apprehensive, not so Norman. 'Thank God for this,' said Norman. 'Now we won't find ourselves overturned on a shoal or smashed up on a rocky, or even a sandy, shore.'

'You know,' said Peter. 'He never seemed to feel the bloody cold and wet, or, if he did, he never mentioned it. On the last day, when the sun was beginning to shine again and we were about to be rescued by a liner, Norman suggested that we just get our map location and a course for either Beira or Inhassoro from the liner's navigator, dry the engine out and make our own way to port!'

He was, understandably, out-voted!"

A year after being lost at sea I was in trouble one last time with the coastal authorities in Beira. This time my son Simon was with me and remembers what happened:

"We were in Beira for four or five days with the Curtis family. We had taken down the dory and, even though the weather was terrible, Dad was desperate to go out fishing. After about three days of sitting around, Dad became determined to go out in the boat and so we went to the Yacht Club in Beira, where we used to launch from. The harbour master said no boats were allowed to go out, it was too rough. Dad and Brian ignored him and, with Paddy and I to help, we launched the boat and went out. There were huge waves breaking over us and a plane buzzed us, indicating that we had to go back. When we got back the harbour master was furious and started shouting at Dad until Dad told him he was Norman Travers.

Shaking his head in disbelief that this could be the same man who had been lost at sea, the harbour master and Dad ended up being great mates, sharing a demijohn of wine together and getting quite sozzled!"

John, Barbara, Alastair and Simon

Norman, Barbara, Gilly, Gaga, Janet holding Alastair, and Simon

Chapter Six

A JACKAL ON THE FISHING LINE!
1970 - 1972

David Wrench was working as my assistant on Imire at the start of the seventies, when political tensions were high, the bush war was intensifying and morale was generally low. David was a little short fellow and, as with many short people, he was quite stroppy! He was a conscientious and hard-working chap and I felt more than happy leaving the farm in his safe hands to go on my increasingly dwindling hunting trips. Gill would come on these trips too, whenever she could, not for the hunting but because she loved the bush, the walks and the birds. When Gill came along everything was much more organised, particularly the camp, menus and meals. This was not the case when Gill couldn't come along and David Hamilton remembers one particular occasion when the food was, apparently, well below acceptable standards:

"A memorable camp meal came one evening after a long hunt. Roasted guinea fowl was on the menu. After a brief inspection Gerry whispered, 'Aaargh - it's rotten man.'

I inspected the bird and said, 'Hell, we can't eat that.'

Norman poked his nose right into the gutted bird's belly looked at us and asked plaintively, 'What's wrong, it's just right!'

He obviously liked a high bird!"

I think that was the exception rather than the rule. The usual case concerning camp meals is described, by me, in an issue of our local Wedza Gazette:

"Meals are scarce. Usually no breakfast, a cold lunch of guinea fowl anytime from noon to 4.00pm and a large supper at night, following our ration of one bottle of beer each. We have a varied diet of buffalo steak, marrow bones, warthog cooked in clay, chops and stews and, with Gerry in charge, most of this is in the form of strong curries! I must not forget the fresh bream fillets on toast, surely the finest sundowner snack you can have."

When I couldn't get away from Imire and go to the Valley, I'd make the most of hunting in the neighbourhood. There were always people who wanted to come along. Mark Milbank remembers with nostalgia, these local excursions:

"One of Norman's main loves was shooting - be it birds, buck or big game. I loved bird-shooting too and, not long after I arrived, about five or six of us agreed to meet

every Tuesday in the winter months, on different farms, to chase guinea fowl and francolin. Norman's farm, Imire, was the one we shot on regularly, as well as on Merryhill, Scorror, Ashlyns and Chirume. We never got a lot of birds but the walks through those Wedza farms were a delight."

My love of hunting was often the cause of controversy, both at home and further afield. I always believed that ethical hunting was definitely a good form of utilisation. Many of our wild areas, like the Zambezi Valley, without hunting concessions, would be a target for land settlement. Hunting also brought in much needed money for National Parks.

Criticism about my love of hunting even came from my own daughter, Barbara, who was particularly opposed to it:

"I can remember having conversations with my father and saying that hunting wasn't right. Dad and I fought about it a lot, he used to say I knew nothing and was being stupid and it wasn't until I had my own son that I understood. When you're a hunter you learn about the bush, the animals, the environment and you fall in love with your prey. Because Dad was a major hunter it was obvious that he would, in time, become a great conservationist."

In our local Wedza Gazette I tried explaining it once:

"There is not space in this article to go into the reasons of why we go shooting. There are many reasons and, I will admit, a great many strong arguments against it; but I would like to say this, that the life one leads on a shooting trip is, to my mind, an experience which is impossible to get anywhere else. The excitement of the Rhodesian lowveld with its animals and birds is always fascinatingly beautiful, often comic and, of course, sometimes sad."

The boys didn't feel the same way and, when John was a teenager, I took him on his first buffalo hunt. We had a long hot day following the spoor but eventually we found the herd. John recalls what happened:

"It was blistering hot and we were all exhausted and, being my first hunt, the adrenalin was pumping. Being so experienced Dad took me up to a big lone tree and pointed and, sure enough, there was my first buffalo bull - only about fifty metres away. Dad was my back-up and I kept whispering. 'You are going to back me up, aren't you?'

With his reassurance my confidence returned. I stood up and took a shot. Dad did a follow-up shot and with that support the kill was a success."

John started out at Springvale School, which had been founded by Robert Grinham, only a few years earlier. When John went there the headmaster was JM Paterson, whose son, Chris, would go on to be a wonderful supporter of Peterhouse and friend of ours. John wasn't a gifted scholar but did well at sports: 1st eleven cricket and rugby at Peterhouse school, in Marandellas. In spite of running into a lot of scrapes he went on to become a prefect. Some years later we were in the bush, together again on a buffalo hunt, and this time Judy Hamilton was with us. The pair were, by then, engaged to be married and Judy remembers the hunt very well, as this is when she first learnt of her prospective father-in-law's temper:

"I remember one buffalo hunt very clearly, when John and I were engaged, and it was the first time I'd been out on a hunt with Norman. We'd spent the entire time looking for these buffalo, had walked miles and it was boiling hot when we finally found them. First, we heard the ox-peckers and so we belly-crawled in. It was very dusty and I remember Norman crawling over all these wag-'n-bietjie (wait-a-bit) thorns but then, at last there was this huge herd of buffalo in front of us. Suddenly, I had a fit of coughing and couldn't stop. I was stuffing my hat in my mouth but that didn't help and Norman was absolutely seething mad and glared ferociously at me. He was so angry that his glasses misted over but the more he glared at me the more I coughed and, of course, the buffalo took off. Norman turned round and said, very coldly, 'Look what you've done!'

I think he was sure I'd deliberately chased the buffalo away!"

The following year I took Simon on his first buffalo hunt, no girls along this time! We did a big stalk, following the spoor of some animals and eventually got right into thick bush where we came across two buffalo bulls. I whispered to Simon. "There you are, there's an old dagga boy, take him."

Simon shot the bull and it went down immediately. When we went up to examine the animal I told Simon that he had a magnificent trophy. Instead of the horns measuring the usual fifteen to twenty inches across, I think they were more than forty, very worn but with a very thick boss. It was good hunting and a prime example of a perfect trophy from a buffalo near the end of his days, who maybe had a year left in him. Simon had done really well but I don't think hunting was really for him. He liked bird shooting and fishing but not really hunting.

Before the war put a stop to our hunting, Gerry, David and I had a few more memorable hunts, which were always filled with excitement along with humour, as David recalls:

"We camped the night by the dry, sandy, Sesame River and could hear lions grunting nearby and so set a plan in action: go out in the Landrover, shoot a small grysbok, tow the corpse round about in the hope of attracting a lion.

For some unknown reason I had a 9/0 deep sea fishing reel and line with me. We attached the fishing line to the grysbok carcass and I hung the reel next to my sleeping bag and set the ratchet.

At some unearthly hour in the night Gerry called out. 'Dave, Dave, the ratchet is ratcheting!' We woke Norman and all armed ourselves, breathless in anticipation. We turned on the hunting lamp and…a lion? No! A very small jackal was tugging away at the grysbok corpse and we all returned to bed, leaving the jackal to his feast!"

Just as this became a much-repeated story, the story of Gerry and the puff adder was

Helmeted guinea fowl and chicks

equally often told. It didn't happen when we were hunting in some remote area, which was just as well. The way the story was told to me was that Gerry had picked up the snake and was posing with it when the damn thing bit him. Peter Murray, who witnessed the event, relates the facts:

"We repaired to the bar and endeavoured to take on board as much alcohol as we could in the time available. At some stage the Club attendant came into the bar to report that there was a big puff adder behind the entrance door. On moving the door closed, there lay a king-sized snake and someone was about to dispatch it with the brick that held the door open when Gerry demanded that we all stand back whilst he removed the serpent. With brick in hand he gingerly attempted to pin its head to the floor. This snake was wide awake, however, and lunged at the object approaching him and sank its fangs into Gerry's index finger."

Someone managed to administer anti-venom and someone else applied a tourniquet but the next morning, remembering that Peter was experienced because he'd been bitten by a puff adder when he worked for me on Imire, Gerry arrived at Peter's farm and exposed the bite. Peter continues:

"He unwrapped his hand and to my horror I saw this dreadfully swollen blue/black mitt with bits of skin peeling off.

'When you got bitten, did your hand look like this?' Gerry asked.

'Indubitably no,' I replied and suggested that he proceed post-haste to Marandellas to see the doc. I believe it was Dr Jaffers who immediately surgically removed Gerry's finger, which had already started putrefying from gangrene. Gerry used to joke thereafter that he himself had used a meat cleaver to do the job." (Winter Cricket)

And then there was the story about the black rhino. It was questionable just who was the hunter and who the hunted in this story. The encounter left Gerry and David chuckling for years afterwards, as David describes:

"Norman is a fearless hunter with very good eyes but is deaf, very deaf. This, for sure, must have been a big disadvantage in so many ways to Norman, who remained in ignorance of a possible encounter with a startled buffalo, elephant, lion or other big game. His deafness was also a disadvantage to trackers and accompanying hunters. A case in point involved Gerry and myself stalking up a river bank while Norman, going in the same direction, was walking down in the dry river bed.

A black rhinoceros was walking in the same direction along the further bank. Norman was oblivious to the presence of the rhino and the rhino was oblivious to our presence. Gerry and I tried frantically to attract Norman's attention. For at least a hundred metres a pantomime was performed: Rhino very blind. Norman very deaf.

Gerry and I, not wanting to alarm the rhino and/or Norman, whistled, waved and shouted softly - no response. Eventually Norman emerged from the river bed, none the wiser, and the rhino carried on, equally ignorant! Deafness and blindness had the advantage of obliviousness to danger but, in general, the disadvantages outweighed the advantages."

David and I had one last trip together in the early 1970s:

"Our last hunting camp was a 'Father and Son' camp in the Chewore area just before the war reached maximum proportions. I remember filling my vehicle with sandbags just in case of landmines and it travelled along the ground almost like a fat dachshund! When we removed the bags my dear old vehicle stretched itself up corner by corner until it reached normal proportions! The two boys each shot a buffalo on this trip."

In 1971, with the bush war on our doorsteps, Bob Knott took over from David Wrench as my farm assistant on Imire. Bobby was a fine young man, quiet-spoken and very good at handling the labour force, unlike me. Bobby rarely lost his temper and provided a good counter-balance to my volatile temperament. Bobby remembers those early days as very difficult ones:

"I started working on Imire in 1971, which was a very turbulent time in the country because of the war. One of the first things I remember doing, as the farm manager, was going to the tobacco lands and saying to Norman that the way he was reaping the tobacco was archaic. He was still reaping the tobacco by putting it on the contours and then moving it to the barns and tying it there. We were working from 4.30 in the morning until 11 o'clock at night, every night, and it was just not on. I told Norman that this was out of the ark and that he had to modernise. I suggested Tilita clips, which had been invented by Tilden Edridge, a farmer in the Wedza area. With this system there were long pieces of wire with clips on them and, as the tobacco was reaped, it was put straight into the clips, which were then transported and loaded straight into the barns."

I didn't appreciate at the time what it was that Tilden Edridge had invented. Tilita Clips were rectangular wire frames about thirty two inches long and two inches wide. Laced across this were Z-shaped springs and, as you picked the leaves, you placed them in the frame and the springs held the leaves in place. The entire Tilita frame held about ninety leaves and, once filled, it was laid on a trailer for transportation to the barns. Once at the barns the Tilita clips were lifted up and hung between tiers where the drying process would begin. Edridge had been nicknamed the 'Wiry Wizard of Wedza' because he was a dedicated time and motion engineer. Observing that the tobacco was being handled too many times, with too much breakage, he came up with the idea that led to the invention, in 1958, of his famous clips. A few years later, Tilden went on to invent a mechanised batch cur-er, and said his ideas were the result of his own idle-ness! They were, nonetheless, innovations that made tobacco farmers' lives much easier. Although, as he himself writes:

"I should be classified as a very average, idle fool because my constant efforts to find ways and means of avoiding

work have been singularly unsuccessful. Not only do I find myself doing more and more work, but piling it onto my unfortunate wife also."

Despite Edridge's successes, I wasn't convinced, as Bobby found out when I returned from looking at Edridge's clips at the local farm supply store:

"Norman had a look at the Tilita Clips, grumbled and mumbled and eventually said, 'No, they are far too expensive.'

A little while later Norman arrived with Kurt machines, dumped them outside the barns and said, 'Here's modernisation, get on and do it!'"

The Kurt machines, although not as modern as Edridge's clips, would do! They'd been in use since the 1950s and were metal conduits about six feet long, angled down at the bottom, with a wheel at the base. The Kurt machine was braced against the reaper's stomach and pushed along through the rows. A string arrangement ran through the top of the conduit and, as you reaped the leaves, you twisted them into the string as you went. The strings held about ninety leaves and, when they were full, were unhooked from the conduit, loaded onto trailers, taken to the barns and hung between the tiers.

Challenging me about my long established tobacco-reaping system was one of a number of hurdles young Bobby came up against, and it was not a happy time for him, as I found out years later:

"Within three weeks of starting on Imire, I had almost had enough and Norman virtually had me in tears. I'd been told to go up to the lands where he was ploughing because there was a problem with a tractor. I took his old pick-up truck right along the headland to where the tractor was and Norman came over and was furious. He gave me a major ticking off saying the vehicle wasn't to be driven off the roads, wasn't to go onto the lands and so on. He had been a lieutenant in the tank corps in the Second World War and had a very military approach to everything. He operated by inspecting his troops (or his workers), looking for problems and things out of place and then reprimanding them! His management style was to come out in the morning and prod anyone daring to sleep in. The nickname given to him, by the African workers, was 'Umgufu' which literally means 'to prod' and that's what Norman did! He wasn't totally ruthless and once you understood that this was his system of management everything worked fine. After a while Norman and I achieved a relationship in which I grudgingly earned his respect! Because I had been trained at Gwebi Agricultural College, I was soon supervising two hundred and forty workers and I knew every single one of them by name including which section of the farm they were working on. I had a motorbike, to get around all the different sections, and most of the time I would set off before Norman, who also had a motorbike, was ready. He would follow me about but could never keep up!"

Despite the upsets that he had with me when he first came to Imire, Bob was dedicated to farming and loved his work. He was in from the beginning with both the vlei maize and the Savory system of grazing and stayed on at

Imire for five years before setting out on his own. He became a very efficient farmer himself and owner of a large dairy farm in Marandellas, which he has to this day. Later, he married Anne Sainsbury who was also very quiet but with a nice sense of humour and she obviously suited Bobby down to the ground. Anne is a gifted artist and has done lovely pictures of the bush and scenery of Imire, particularly of Castle Kopje.

Bob might have thought of me as a hard task-master and I probably was! When I asked Gill if the farm assistants came and cried on her shoulder, she laughed and said they didn't go that far but did say I was difficult to work for. She added, "But Norman, you were just being you, darling!"

I suppose I also gave the kids quite hard time - for their own good! Barbara remembers that being the first in the area to get television, was more trial than triumph:

"Dad was a very loving father but very strong and we were frightened of him. We were the first people to get TV in the district but I remember it being a terrifying time. Whenever the news came on, Dad would start with his questions: Who is that talking? Who is that man? And we were all supposed to know. He was desperate for us to be aware of what was happening in the world but it wasn't long before we all learnt to disappear at news time!"

I try not to remember the nastier things but do admit that there have been incidents, which show I'm not a saint - far from it!

8 March 1972 marked the end of an era for me - the day my Mum died. What a hard life she'd had: alone and forty five when I was born, sixty four when war broke out (followed by six years in a Japanese prisoner-of-war camp in China) and seventy at the end of the war. In 1947, Mum came to Rhodesia and watched me receive my medals from King George V1. She then moved to the country permanently and lived with us on Imire. A few years later Mum was one of the first people to move into the retirement home, Borradaile Trust, which had been started by Gill's father, Howard Smetham. She moved into the little cottage we had built for her and was happy and still very much in control of her affairs. Gill's sister, Jane, recalls one incident which summed Mum up perfectly:

"Norman's Mum was a fierce lady. I remember once she had an intruder in her cottage. She got up, grabbed him by the collar and shook him, shouting, 'What are you doing here?' The man got such a fright he took off! Mrs Travers had the courage of a lion - she had to have, after what she'd been through in her life."

Another story about Mum, that caused amusement, concerned my friend Johnny Vlismas, who ran the bottle store in Marandellas at the time. One day Johnny said to me, "You know Norman, your Mother comes in from time to time and buys a bottle of gin and I'm putting this on your account." I said that was fine. Vlismas said, "You know, she's buying rather a lot of gin lately!" (A bottle every two or three days, in fact). Mum liked her tipple alright, but she still adored her family.

Gill said she remembers how my mother almost waited outside on the doorstep of her cottage if she knew I was coming. The children all called her Gaga, as John explains:

"Gaga got her name from the grandchildren who couldn't pronounce Granny. I never remember Gaga living on Imire, it must have been before I was born, but I do remember visiting her at Borradaile Trust. When we were kids Mum and Dad used to pick Barbs and me up from school and we would often stop in and have a cup of tea with Gaga. She always had a tin of sweets or biscuits in her drawer as a special treat for her grandchildren. Gaga ruled Borradaile Trust with a rod of iron. She was an incredibly strong person and stood head and shoulders above everyone else. I remember us all anticipating and hoping we'd be getting a letter from the Queen for Gaga's hundredth birthday, but she didn't quite make it. She died in 1972 at the age of ninety seven - still quite an innings!"

Perhaps I inherited my strength from Mum and learnt leadership during the war but both qualities were to stand me in good stead as the first farm-attacks began. David Hamilton, a man with a great ability to remember names, numbers, dates, details and facts, recalls how the bush war came to Wedza and my role in the community at the time:

"Prior to the first farm-attack (that took place in Centenary, Christmas 1972) there were approximately sixty or seventy farmers and their families in Wedza who were ex-servicemen from World War II. Many were experienced leaders in their own right during their service lives and Norman was one of them. Norman had qualities that made him the automatic leader for our community of intelligent, free-thinking farmers - as well as their families and labourers - in the very traumatic years that lay ahead. Wedza was a singularly united community opposed to independent 'go it alone' attitudes. Everybody pulled together. Norman was never one to put himself forward, quite the reverse in fact, but still he was the natural choice. He is a man that thrives on pressure in a crisis and the more the odds are stacked against him the greater his determination becomes to defeat the obstacle, whatever - or whoever it may be. He possesses unflinching courage and the ability to make instant decisions which are never reckless or foolhardy, regardless of what steps he may be forced to take."

Early in the 1970s we were again in uniform, in the Police Reserve, which most able-bodied men, and women, had joined. The ranks from WWII were thrown out the window. Whether you were a colonel or a private - everyone became a police reservist and the hierarchy started from scratch. Sadly, there was a tragedy in the early training camps when the district had its first casualty, namely Tony Seager. I knew the Seager family well when I first worked for Frank Scott in the 1940s. Tony had joined the air force and was a fighter pilot during the Second World War. He survived that war but was killed in a police training exercise on Numwa Drift. He was a great enthusiast when it came to these sorts of exercises and when the other group, the so-called enemy, started attacking us, Tony rolled under a vehicle for cover. The driver of the vehicle didn't know, of course, and when he drove off, ran over Tony.

Police Reserve wasn't very arduous in those early days and I did my bit with call-ups to Mutoko, Nyamapanda, Matabeleland and even to a place near Cahora Bassa. The Police Reserve had been established by the BSAP, not for political reasons, but for security, as David Hamilton explains:

"The Police Reserve was formed to protect the farmers, their families, their labour forces and the vitally important agricultural output of each and every commercial farm. Consequently the reservists were of every political affiliation. These ranged from the extremes of 'never in our lifetime' to 'let's get around the table and talk, the sooner the better'. Norman Travers was very much middle-of-the-road. Never a member of the Rhodesian Front, he always voted in favour of any opponent to the RF and, being a realist, he knew that the final outcome must be rule by the majority. However, he also believed that any future African leader would be unlikely to destroy the commercial farmer and lose this highly-productive farming expertise."

People in the district knew about my political beliefs and my opposition to the RF. I can remember in the Wedza Club one night I nearly had a stand-up fight with my oldest friend, Gerry, over politics. I suppose my politics might have made me unpopular, I never really asked! Being popular was never important to me but one principle that I believed in, very strongly, was that of making full use of everything you had. It was something I tried to instil in all our children as they were growing up and Simon remembers the lesson well:

"Everything with Dad was that whatever you shot or caught you had to utilise fully. There was no point shooting a dove or catching a fish unless you were going to eat it. Whenever he went hunting nothing was ever wasted. The skins were all dried and brought back, the meat cut up into mountains of biltong and taken home for the workers - everything was used. When we went fishing at Baz we always used to fish on the seaward side and Dad was adamant that all the fish we caught had to be eaten or preserved. It was a helluva climb over the lighthouse hill, something like a thousand steps, and whatever we caught we had to carry back over the hill and give to Dad, so that the fish could be dried, smoked and taken back to the farm.

I remember, as a youngster, catching a little shark and Dad made me carry it all the way back, on my own. Mum would always say, 'Come along darling, I'll help you.' But Dad would say, 'No, you caught it. Carry it on your own'.

The biggest lesson that Dad taught us in life was how to utilise things. As a kid I had a scheme where I shot doves and sold them. Dad said that was fine but I could only shoot so many, in such-and-such an area, at a certain time and, after I'd sold the birds I had to give him the money! He would keep it until there was enough to buy something sensible - like a cricket bat! It was never just for fun but had to pay for itself."

On one of our last holidays to Moçambique after Barbara and John had left home and when Simon was about sixteen we witnessed a very unpleasant scene on the beach in the middle of the night. It was a sight Simon would never forget:

"The last trip we did to Moçambique was when I was about sixteen and just before the border closed. We went to Coconut Bay, down in the south, which we hadn't been to before and experienced the most horrific thing. There was a big reef in front of our chalets, and there, at about the closest point where the channel meets the coastline, three whales beached themselves. We were woken at two o'clock in the morning by the sound of their screeching and, within a very short time, a couple of hundred locals had arrived, and instead of helping the whales, had begun chopping chunks off them! Dad went berserk and picked up a stick and was trying to chase people off these poor creatures, which were still alive but absolutely stranded and helpless. The next morning we managed to get one of the whales back out into deeper water and it swam off - but it was too late for the others."

We didn't know then that our happy holidays in Moçambique would never return but, for me, a whole new life was about to begin. As the Rhodesian war gathered momentum, so did my desire to bring game animals to Imire. Everyone said I was crazy - that it couldn't be done - but I actively began to pursue my dream.

Simon and Gilly

John as a teenager

Norman, Simon, Gilly and Squinks in Moçambique

Chapter Seven

WAR AND INDEPENDENCE
1970 - 1980

For me, the Rhodesian war is a time best consigned to oblivion! However, it is still part of my history and part of all our lives. Throughout it all I was bringing game animals onto Imire and building up the game park - but that is another story, to be told a little later; first to the war. Here, my involvement in the conflict is best related by my friends, whose memories are far clearer than mine. Mark Milbank recalls how it began, for all of us, in 1972:

"When the bush war started Wedza was not, at first, directly affected and most of us farmers were called-up to serve in various capacities in areas where there was a problem. However, it wasn't long before Wedza had plenty of problems of its own. We farmers no longer went away but were kept quite busy looking after our own areas. Indeed, we were too thin on the ground to do a proper job as well as run our individual farms. Indeed, by 1972, the local Wedza police were far too busy, themselves, dealing with problems in the Wedza TTL, to be of much help to us.

Norman had always been the leader / elder statesman of the area and it was now that he showed why. He, with the help of others, such as Ian Murray, reckoned that we, as the Wedza community, should recruit our own militia and have a small force operating exclusively in the Wedza area, paid for by ourselves. Norman put the idea to the police and readily got their blessing. We farmers agreed to pay a monthly sum to finance this idea and Norman set about recruiting likely candidates. I am not sure how he was actually found, but it was not long before a young captain (who had just left the British army) was interviewed and offered the job of commanding a stick of some five young Rhodesians to operate as an anti-terrorist unit in our area. His name was Mark Collacheci and, for about two years, he and his men did a very useful job and took a lot of pressure off us farmers.

They worked very closely with the police but they were our guys and we told them what to do. To this end Norman reckoned that one of us should always be based at Wedza police camp to liaise between Mark's lot and the police. A small brick house was built in the grounds of the Wedza police camp, a radio installed and Norman was the first 'General' to help co-ordinate operations between the police, our lot and other security forces that happened to be in the area. On quiet nights, when sitting around

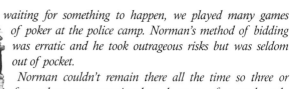

waiting for something to happen, we played many games of poker at the police camp. Norman's method of bidding was erratic and he took outrageous risks but was seldom out of pocket.

Norman couldn't remain there all the time so three or four others were appointed to do turns of a week each. I was to be one of these and we had a regular meeting every Monday morning when the new 'General' took over. These meetings were chaired by Norman and always involved a relaxed discussion of what was best to do for the safety of the community during the following week. Norman's practical, thoughtful mind nearly always got to the crux of any problem - and there were plenty of them! I am sure that the whole of the Wedza community slept more soundly in their beds knowing that there was someone of Norman's calibre looking after their interests. Wedza was the first farming area in the country to introduce this sort of self-help in those increasingly difficult times. Others followed suit and a lot of the credit for the idea was correctly given to Norman."

In these early days there were some very strange things going on - and some strange weapons about, too. Because I was involved in local security and the Police Reserve I got a call one day from the police camp. They said they'd just been sent a new weapon, which they thought was more up my street than theirs, and they wanted me to try it out. I went to the police camp and there, in a crate, was this weird three inch diameter barrel mounted onto a little chassis with what looked like wheelbarrow wheels. It came with a ramrod, little packets of gunpowder and iron and steel ball bearings. I thought it looked a bit strange, rather like something Nelson had used two hundred and fifty years ago. Someone had named this thing the 'Garden Boy' - presumably because it was mounted on wheelbarrow wheels - and so we got ready to try it out.

We put up a drum as a target about fifty yards away, read all the instructions and prepared our first shot. I rammed in the gunpowder, added the steel balls and lit the little touch fuse. Then we all stood back and BOOM! The whole thing shook and vibrated and lifted off its wheels. But the steel balls just rattled around inside.

"That's not much good," I said. "Let's try with two bags of dynamite."

We put two bags of dynamite in and repeated the whole process and, this time, it worked and made holes in the drum.

"There you are," I said. "It works - just tell your boys to use two bags of dynamite!"

I left them to it. I certainly didn't want to be involved in the use of the thing and its usefulness fizzled out shortly thereafter.

By 1975 the security situation had deteriorated even further. David Hamilton explains how farmers in the Wedza area became affected:

"Once the handover of Moçambique to Frelimo by the Portuguese had taken place, in June/July 1975, and Portuguese troops had been withdrawn back to Portugal, increased incursions by invading forces along our eastern border were intensified. First and foremost because their increased numbers had to be fed. Cattle theft became a priority and the south Wedza farmers were the first to suffer. Not just in ones and twos did the cattle disappear, but in fifties, eighties and hundreds - overnight. The cattle would be run at a fast trot throughout the night and, by pre-arrangement with the local tribesmen in the Wedza communal area, the beasts would be dispersed amongst various tribesmen and hidden during the day. A small portion of the cattle rustled would be left in the particular Tribal Trust Land as payment and encouragement for future operations. Meanwhile the nightly journey would continue; in our case, into Buhera and over the Sabi River into the newly independent country of Moçambique, eventually, to feed the gathering guerrilla army being formed there.

The Wedza farmers' reaction to the ever-increasing onslaught was initially a rather haphazard spoor follow-up by the farmer concerned with help from one or two neighbours. But after calling all reserve stick leaders together, followed by an invitation to the Wedza BSAP Member-in-Charge, a plan emerged. Norman was elected chairman of the newly-formed Wedza Action Committee. The BSAP Member-in-Charge, Inspector Pete Saunders, was asked to be included (whether he had sought permission from his superiors in Salisbury is not known) and he was full of enthusiasm for the idea. As a result, depending on which farm the cattle had been stolen from, a radio call would go out to all farmers. The nearest team of farmers, on their motorbikes, would gather at a certain point. A follow-up vehicle would be provided by the police and the follow-up would begin. A number of cattle were returned on these sorties - cattle that had been left along the route, or the remains of cattle that had been slaughtered, and some arrests were made.

Before long the Wedza Action Committee, under Norman's directive, extended its horizons beyond cattle rustling and became involved in providing support ('Bright-lighting') to the more remote farms, particularly those adjacent to the communal areas. The Wedza Action Committee also provided a presence immediately after farm attacks. Norman himself made it his duty to be first at the scene right after an incident."

Despite our best efforts at organisation and response and despite an extremely united district, sadly, there were casualties:

"After the bush war started hotting up in the early 1970s, the first death was that of André Joubert, on Chard Farm. Later we lost Simon Edridge, Alan Hill, Peter and Alastair Gilpin and several members of the police from Wedza Camp, not to mention the numerous farmworkers who lost their lives." (Winter Cricket)

The Rhodesian flag

David became the group chairman of the Marandellas Area Farmers' Association in 1977 and this automatically made him a councillor in the Rhodesia National Farmers' Union (RNFU). David put forward our Wedza Action Committee as a model:

"At our monthly meetings, each member of the council was asked to give a detailed account of the security situation in his particular area and, in mid-1977, I highlighted the steps that had been taken in Wedza and the BSAP involvement in the local scheme. At the end of the meeting one councillor stated that 'the most important item that has been brought up during this meeting is the Wedza approach to safety of the district and it should be supported by Government.'

John Strong, the President of the RNFU, said that he was attending a combined operations meeting in two days time and would recommend this approach as a priority. Which he did, and, before long, the country districts were asked to form co-ordinating committees along the lines of the Wedza Action Committee. Trucks, motorbikes and radios were provided for outlying farmers, with various other innovations, that certainly improved the security of the farming regions. Norman, deservedly, received an official honour for this valiant and selfless contribution undertaken for the safety of the Wedza farming community, as well as for the time and effort he put in for eastern Mashonaland's security."

During the 1970s I got to know the Prime Minister of Rhodesia, Ian Smith, and liked him very much, even though he knew very well that I was not a supporter of the Rhodesia Front party. Ian Smith and his wife, Janet, often came out to the farm where Gill would provide a wonderful dinner for us all. In these difficult years I also got to know some of Smith's cabinet members, these included Mark Partridge, David Smith and Dennis Norman. Peter van der Byl was another, and always a character of note. He was very 'anglicized' and had fought in the last world war in one of the Guards regiments. I remember pulling his leg, saying, 'All you blokes were good at was marching up and down outside Buckingham Palace!' He was furious, of course!

At one point I did get involved in politics and assisted an independent candidate who was standing against David Smith, the RF member for Marandellas, in a by-election. Tom Edridge was a great character, enthusiastic about life, loved gambling and clay pigeon shooting and was chairman of the Ploughing Association of Rhodesia for many years.

Tom was also a very meticulous farmer, successful and forward-thinking. I liked his politics too! He was one of the few of us who disagreed with the RF and I think he would have made a good MP.

Tom asked me to be his election agent and I had to organise meetings, gatherings and talks for him.

Ian Douglas Smith

David Smith, his opponent, was a very nice guy, besides being an old friend of ours - but he was also a powerful politician. As a result, we didn't expect Tom to win but it was quite a close election and, in the end, an interesting time. Tragically, Tom died in a car crash a few years later.

In 1977 my son, John, and I were involved in an ambush. John, by then, had been allowed to come onto the farm as he and other youngsters had been formed into a PATU unit for the district. John was a machine-gunner and had his weapon with him. He was living at the lodge on Imire, at the time, and one evening I was told by one of my guards that there'd been some firing up the road; shots had been heard. I phoned John who said he'd been informed and was busy preparing to investigate. At the time I didn't know the details, nor did I know that my son and David Hamilton's daughter, Judy, were anything more than neighbours. However, it transpired later that the whole ambush story actually began much earlier and, initially, involved another farmer altogether, as David explains:

"Nigel Thornycroft, my near neighbour, was on his way back home from a meeting at the Club, which, one understands, had ended with a couple for the road. As Nigel approached a rather reed-filled vlei, on the Numwa Road, according to his description, he saw what he could only describe as a number of fire-flies going past his windscreen and a distinctly explosive noise coming from his differential, or some such place, in the darned vehicle! It happened to be a very ancient car indeed but it really did perform with veritable alacrity under the circumstances. As it was, Nigel carried on home, had supper and went to bed - having quite forgotten about the fire-flies and explosive noise! It was later that Norman got involved, when he and a couple of security guards drove in his Peugeot truck to the lodge where John lived. John piled into the back of the truck, set up his MAG machine-gun and pointed out the place where the rifle fire had appeared to come from. They set off at about 9.30pm and drove down the Bridge Road to the Numwa Road and on down to the Chiutsa Drift - nothing.

They had turned, passing the spot where Nigel had been ambushed - for an ambush it had been - and were carrying on back towards the Bridge Road again, when all hell broke loose!"

John and I had a pretty good idea that we'd be ambushed and had made a plan, of sorts. I'd said, "I'll drive through the ambush and, fifty yards from them, slam on the brakes. By then these blokes will have run out of ammo and will have emptied their mags. Before they can reload you'll have seen where they are and can rev them."

It was a good plan but things don't always work out as expected, as David continues to explain:

"The scrub to the right of the truck erupted with rifle fire. Tracer bullets came flying in from all angles. John opened up with his MAG causing what can only be described as a pyrotechnic display. However, in the dark, John had unfortunately trained his machine gun too far forward and all his bullets were tracking through the cab of the

truck! All about eighteen inches from Norman, who could not understand what all the flashing lights were beside him! He decided to put his foot down and get the hell out of it.

A study of the Peugeot the following day revealed that only two bullets from enemy fire had actually hit the vehicle. One entering the truck an inch or so above the driver's door, missing Norman's head by about three inches. The other had hit the side of the door, travelling just behind the seat - again, an inch or so from Norman's back."

No-one from either side suffered any injuries during this distinctly melodramatic encounter, which was fortunate for everyone concerned. There is, also, a lighter side to the incident. David continues:

"As one can imagine, with the sound of rifle fire that can be heard as far away as 20kms on a still night, everyone in the district was glued to their communication radios. Nine o'clock at night and a minor war seemed to be taking place in the very heart of the district. Suddenly, the dulcet tones of a young female voice rang out.

"Wedza control, Wedza control. I am looking out the window, tracer bullets are flying out of the bush and there is a tremendous lot of shooting going on."

Who the dickens can that be, everyone wondered.

"Last caller, last caller, identify yourself please," demanded the recently appointed OC of BSAP Wedza, Inspector Kettle. "Identify yourself."

"I can still hear some firing," came the response. "I can still see car headlights down at the junction of the Numwa and Bridge Roads."

"Will you please identify yourself," repeated the voice of Kettle over the radio.

At last it came. "I am Judy Hamilton and I'm in John Travers' house, at the lodge. John and Norman have gone to see about the shots they heard earlier on. But wait, I think I can see the lights of the truck returning…"

Inspector Kettle turned to the reservist at the Wedza station. "Well, that's rather blown it for them," was his comment. Pat and myself, sitting up in bed and having a listen in to the whole saga, looked at one another in amazement.

"You know, all the time I thought it was Judy's voice!" I said.

"I did, too. In fact I'd rather hoped it was," smiled Pat.

And the whole district smiled (and probably still smile) at the thought of that particular moment of tenderness during the war of attrition that we had been enduring for so long."

While David and Pat discussed the obvious romantic escapades of John and Judy, I returned home after the ambush to tell Gill what had happened. We phoned Nigel and asked him if he'd heard all the firing. Nigel said, "Funny thing, I was coming home and just before I got to the Bridge Road I heard a few noises and bangs and thought it was my old car! Then I suddenly realised, when I saw some tracer going past the front of the windscreen, that someone was shooting at me. I went off the main road, nearly turned the car over but managed to get out of the ditch and drove home.

I asked. "But Nigel why didn't you report it?"

He replied. "Well, they didn't hit me!"

The sequel to this story came about three weeks later. One of our Wedza farmers, down in the Wye Valley, had built a huge double-story house, which was more like a fort. The family had all sorts of security gadgets and fences and things but they were still attacked. They wounded two of their attackers and, when they did a follow-up, they found the two had both died. In the pocket of one they found a diary. In the diary, on the date that we were attacked, it read: "We had a sharp contact with John and Norman."

When I heard this story, I thought. "My goodness, they know us by our first names!" I knew then, for sure, that the war was lost. It was finished and we were wasting our time. Worse was yet to come in Wedza, as David remembers:

"Shortly after the Numwa Road ambush, Peter Purcil Gilpin and his son were ambushed one evening while driving home. Sadly, both of them were killed and this stunned the district. Peter was a highly-respected cattleman and one who played an important part in the National Cattle Industry. He and his wife, Heather, had produced a large Catholic family. 'My cattle are all Catholics, too, hence their high conception rates,' he would jokingly tell us. They were a much-loved family and played a great part in district activities.

The morning after the attack, Norman organised an early follow-up, although one had little hope of apprehending the ambush gang. About eight local reservists, in two trucks, spent all day looking for spoor, questioning farm labourers and anyone else who might have witnessed the attack or the aftermath. All our operations were confined to the commercial farming area and we were specifically asked not to enter the adjacent Chiota TTL where, we were informed, the Scouts were operating.

By mid-afternoon we were all pretty tired and downhearted and one or two of us decided to investigate a house, on the other side of the fence, in Chiota. The locals became rather sullen and uncooperative. One or two members of our stick over-reacted and, suddenly, the hut was on fire. Norman immediately organised the clearing of the hut but it appeared to be empty and he suggested that we all return to the correct side of the fence.

The next minute the radio began crackling:

'I am OC of the Scouts in Chiota. What's that smoke? What are you doing in Chiota? I demand that you leave immediately…'

I don't believe that one of us would not have let fly at that authoritarian self-opinionated voice at the other end of the

Norman tries to steal Judy Hamilton's vundu!

radio, so intense was our mood. We had lost a respected and much-loved farmer. We had suffered a fruitless and frustrating day and now this overbearing voice barked at us as if we were a bunch of raw recruits - we were all itching to get on that radio. Not so, Norman. He was the very model of propriety.

'Yes, I'm afraid we did go into Chiota and I'm afraid a hut was set on fire. No real loss and certainly no-one hurt. We are now back in the commercial farming area. I hope you have more luck than we have had in catching the perpetrators.'

I, for one, was quite taken aback by Norman's conciliatory attitude. Yet, in retrospect, it was the correct one. What would have been achieved by a stand-up row? Certainly not the co-operation we so urgently needed. Norman taught us all a bit of a lesson that day."

Despite all the responsibilities and encounters that the war entailed, I always tried to keep up a pleasant routine every Friday lunchtime throughout the 1970s. Gill's father, Howard Smetham, had introduced me to a few people at the Salisbury Club and we'd meet for a few drinks, some lunch and a chat every Friday. 'The Lunch Bunch', John called us. The group included all sorts of people, from a wide range of backgrounds: Hossack, Standish-White, Ben Norton, John Wood, Clifford Du Pont, Mike Hunt, CG Tracey and, once, even the PM Ian Smith. Ken Flower, a well-known CIO operative, was a regular.

In the meantime, while I was otherwise occupied at the Club, Gill would be dropped off at the top end of First Street, with her list, and she would work her way through town, collecting shopping and doing all sorts of errands.

1977 ended with yet another attack - we heard of it, from David, whilst in high spirits:

"New Years Eve, 1977. A dance at the Wedza Club was in the throes of becoming a real party, when news of an attack on Wye Valley Farm came. A duty team, comprising regular and reserve police, were on their way to support the two elderly Mossops, who were on their own. A stick of young police reservists hastily left the Club in order to help with the follow-ups. This was the third attack on Wye Valley Farm and the Mossops were, understandably, determined not to stay there for a moment longer than was necessary. They decided to gather their belongings and move somewhere safer and not so remote - settling on their son-in-law's farm in Umvukwes.

Wye Valley certainly was remote. It lay off the Ruzawi River Valley, flanked by heavily-wooded hills to the east, south and west. The following morning, Norman, with a Police Reserve stick, arrived at the Mossop homestead and found the family in the process of packing their belongings. A quick study of the farm showed fine crops of tobacco and maize and a general picture of the most attractive situation that one could wish for in times of peace. It didn't take Norman long to make up his mind what to do. 'Get someone to take over the farm as soon as possible,' he suggested. 'Every effort should be made to carry on farming as usual.'

He held a meeting with nearby farmers to explain the benefits of this idea. He received a certain amount of support but there were, undoubtedly, elements that were all for abandoning the property. The following day, Norman and I proceeded to Salisbury with three ports of call organised: The Rhodesia Herald, to advertise for a person with an adventurous spirit to take over a remote farm with established crops of maize and tobacco; the chairman of the Land Bank, to explain the situation and persuade them to lend the running costs should a suitable farmer be found, and, finally, the Minister of Agriculture, Mr Micklem, to solicit support for decisions to keep the farm operating at all costs. The advert was placed in the Rhodesia Herald in January 1978 and read as follows:

'Situations Vacant - Exciting farming opportunity for one or two men with agricultural experience and guts. 150 acres of maize, 50 acres of tobacco abandoned by farmer due to terrorist activity. Crops are average to good. All facilities, other than labour, are available. Start immediately. Phone Wedza 2240.' "

The response from Minister Micklem was very non-committal although the Land Bank gave their support - if we could find the right man. Well we did! I managed to get in touch with Dereck Hurlstone, he arrived, liked what he saw and remained on Wye Valley Farm for two years under the most adverse security conditions imaginable. These included a farm attack, a wheat crop destroyed by fire and various ambushes and other escapades. Hurlstone survived, never complained and only left when peace arrived in 1980.

As negotiations towards ending the war gathered momentum, under the Lancaster House agreement, Gill and I were fortunate enough to become friendly with Lord Christopher Soames and his delightful wife, Mary. Other friends, Ian and April Piercey, introduced us to them. Ian was a professional hunter and ran a successful concession in the Zambezi Valley. Unhappily, due to political shenanigans, he lost the concession in the late 1980s. The Soames' arrived in the country in December 1979, with Christopher taking up the role as Governor until new elections could be held. Our daughter, Barbara, was already well-known to the Soames family and recalls how her friendship with them began and how acquaintances were renewed back in Rhodesia just before Independence:

"After nursing training, I went to England and nursed Lady Clementine Churchill, widow of Sir Winston Churchill, (and Lady Soames' mother). It was during this time that I met Lady Soames, who would quiz me about every aspect of her mother's care and all manner of other things. I would often be invited to have these wonderful five-course meals with them and their guests. It was a whole new world for me and alien to anything I'd experienced before.

When the Soames' later came to Rhodesia, we renewed contact and I invited them to have dinner with me. At the time I was twenty-eight and living on my own in a delightful little cottage in Salisbury. Two days before the dinner, the police and security men came round and checked everything out and inspected the premises and the garden and, on the night, they were everywhere. Watching every move, bodyguards and police sitting in the trees!

Mary and Christopher Soames and their son Nicholas, who was my age, arrived and it turned out to be the most traumatic and devastating dinner party I've ever had. We had a fondue outside in the garden and things went wrong from the very beginning. On lighting the fondue, oil spilled onto the table-cloth, which caught alight. Hardly was that under control when things got worse! I picked up the fondue pot but it tipped in the stand and spilled burning hot fat all over Nicholas. We had to strip him fast and, even though it wasn't funny, we were all laughing gaily as we tried to undress him. First we struggled with the shoes and trousers and then found that, even in Rhodesia's climate, he was wearing long-johns and so these, too, had to be struggled off. Luckily Nicholas wasn't hurt and his good humour saw us all through a dinner to remember!"

Not long after this, Gill and I persuaded the Soames' that we should organise a trip to Inyanga where I promised them fishing on the Gairezi River, which had only just re-opened; it had been closed to the public for a long time, because of the war. Preparations were duly made.

Christopher, Mary, their daughter - Charlotte, and the ever-present entourage of bodyguards and security men all booked in at Troutbeck, while Gill and

I went to our little cottage at Connemara. One evening, during the weekend, we were having dinner at Troutbeck with the Soames' and I'd ordered a bottle of wine. The waiter drew the cork and poured the wine for me to taste. Foolishly, I sipped it casually and announced it as 'just fine!' The waiter went around filling the glasses till Charlotte Soames suddenly exclaimed, "Daddy, this wine is corked!"

The poor waiter must have been new to the job because he started looking for a cork on the floor around our table. It gave us all quite a laugh.

Next day we went to the Gairezi River in a convoy of vehicles, which included Pookies, (mine detecting vehicles, with wide wheels and metal-detectors in wings, which covered the road), bullet-proof vehicles and a large contingent of soldiers, bodyguards and security men. When we arrived at the river, Gill

Lord and Lady Soames on their visit to the Gairezi River

and Mary decided they wanted to have a swim in a nearby pool but Mary didn't have a costume. "You go away!" Mary told the security people. "Go on, off you go! Come back in an hour!"

Having persuaded the bodyguards to give them some privacy, Mary stripped off completely and the two women slipped into the water. "Mary, an hour is almost up," Gill urged a little later. "You'd better come out and get dressed before the men get back, here, use my towel."

When we returned from our fishing, we were horrified to hear that Mary had been swimming in the nude! But, no harm had been done. We had a pleasant weekend, didn't catch any fish but the girls had a wonderful swim and a good time was had by all.

Luckily the press weren't around on that occasion. However, they did report another event we were seen at with the Soames':

"How many cigarettes are made from a bale of tobacco?" was the amusing question raised by Lord Soames, when he and Lady Soames made an unofficial visit to the tobacco floors. Lord Soames, sharing a laugh with Tony Taberer, managing director of Tabex, was shown around the floors by a personal friend, Mr Norman Travers, a tobacco farmer from Wedza and his wife Gill, and daughter Barbara." (The Rhodesia Herald)

Christopher Soames had the unpleasant and, of course, locally unpopular task of solving the political problems of Rhodesia. We became good friends and I enjoyed the occasional lunch with him - he enjoyed the odd drink and a cigar. I remember him asking me once, just prior to the 1980 election, who I thought would win.

"Muzorewa," I said.

"Oh I think Mugabe probably will," Soames responded. "What do you think?" I was shaken.

"Don't worry," he said. "All will be well."

About two months before Independence (18 April 1980) Gilly and I heard that Barbara was to be Prince Charles' official escort at an Independence reception to be held at Government House. It made us the proudest of parents and, for Barbara it was, naturally, a momentous event:

"Shortly after the disastrous dinner, Mary Soames asked if I'd like to be Prince Charles' escort at the Independence Reception and, of course, I said yes! For weeks beforehand I was trained in the protocol required and was called in, on numerous occasions, to practice where to stand, how to curtsey and never to make direct eye-contact. Mum took me to an Italian dressmaker, who made a Grecian-looking dress in grey silk - very simple but perfect for the occasion. I remember being so impressed by the Prince's vast knowledge of such a range of subjects; he even knew the names of the frogs that we heard calling. I was shocked when I realised how little I knew about my own country.

While we were all lined up for introductions I totally forgot to curtsey and Prince

Charles, standing in front of me, whispered:
'Barbara, curtsey!'
I did and so everything turned out fine. Over dinner he asked me questions about subjects I knew about, such as horses and animals, which put me at ease and it was all great fun."

The press, as might be expected, made a huge fuss of it all and our Barbara was on the front pages of many newspapers all over the world. The Rhodesia Herald described her as 'Cinderella':

"Rhodesia's own 'Cinderella' will tonight meet Prince Charming at a private reception and dinner at Government House in Salisbury.

For tall, 1.7 metre, slim, blonde, grey-eyed Miss Barbara Travers (28) tonight is one she is likely to remember for a very long time since she has been invited by the Governor, Lord Soames and his wife, to spend the evening with Prince Charles.

During an interview yesterday, Barbara, the daughter of Mr and Mrs Norman Travers, of Wedza, described herself as 'the luckiest girl in Rhodesia,' adding that it was still 'almost unbelievable' to think about meeting and spending the evening with the Prince.

What opinion had she formed of Prince Charles over the years?

'I think he is a marvellous person, very down to earth and deep-thinking.'

(Sheila White in The Rhodesia Herald. 16 April 1980)

There had been both good days and bad leading up to Independence in 1980. Perhaps I should mention that they gave me a Long Service medal and a DCM - presumably for good behaviour! The citation read:

"The award of the Meritorious Service Medal to Mr Norman Meckiffe Travers.

Since taking up his farm in Wedza in 1948, Mr Travers has been a progressive farmer and leader in community development. He is an exponent of game-farming and the conservation of game.

In the face of the terrorist war he has displayed outstanding leadership. Through his perseverance the Wedza Action Committee was established early in 1978. Under his leadership the Committee has done much to ensure the safety of the Wedza area, and experience gained has proved of immense value to other committees countering the terrorist threat elsewhere in the country. Mr Travers has given notable service to the farming community. Sir."

In 1980 I was again humbled to be recognised by my fellow farmers, as Mark Milbank relates:

"When the war finally ended we all subscribed to give Norman a 12-bore shotgun, as a gift, in recognition for what he had done for the area. It was presented to him at the Wedza Tobacco Show of 1980."

David Hamilton was present when the Wedza Co-ordinating Committee was disbanded, in 1980, and remembers the occasion well:

"The disbanding of the Wedza Co-ordinating Committee took place at the Wedza Country Club and the meeting was an extremely emotional one. It was the end of

an era, which stretched back to the beginning of the century. There was resistance to the inevitable changes, tears shed and gloom predicted. All of these emotions and yet Norman Travers, in his speech of farewell to the past and acceptance, with optimism, for the future, made possibly the best speech that he ever made. For the following twenty years Norman's predictions were justified."

Looking back on it all, thirty years later, the war is not something I like to dwell on. Some memories stick, like doing our stints in the Police Reserve - sometimes on the border of Moçambique. Once, I remember seeing a roan antelope in the middle of a mine-field. There was nothing we could do and so, sadly, it was blown up - what a waste. But I was busy during those war years, gradually building up my dream of Imire, the game park. David Hamilton says that I never once faltered:

"Norman has the most incredible optimism, refusing ever to recognise defeat as a possibility. He was determined to establish a game park on Imire, regardless of the most ominous clouds on the horizon. The establishment of a game park is no short-term operation and, right until the final months of the conflict, Norman continued to transport game of all descriptions from all ends of Rhodesia. He continued to erect his game fence, holding pens and bomas right through the war. Once the animals had been quieted down and became used to their enclosures and human handlers, he went ahead and released the game into the area fenced off for them.

It became obvious how justified Norman's confidence was once peace was declared and Independence came in 1980. Imire Game Park became an immediate attraction for both visitors to the country and locals from every walk of life: young or old, wealthy or of moderate means, all of whom had not experienced a day in the Rhodesian countryside for at least six or seven years."

Chapter Eight

A CROCODILE IN THE SWIMMING POOL
Imire ~ Early 1970s

My progression from hunting to farming wildlife followed a natural course of events. Because of my love of hunting, I felt I owed nature something back and, it became apparent that conservation of wildlife was the way to go. I don't know how long I'd dreamed of having game animals on Imire. My daughter says that she remembers me talking about it when she was little:

"Dad said that when he first started with Frank Scott in 1939, when he was living in a rondavel, he used to watch kudu and reedbuck and said that was what he wanted. His dream was to have game and cattle together on the farm. Dad always looked outside the box and the more people told him it couldn't be done, that you couldn't mix game with cattle, the more Dad was determined to do it."

All the books by old hunters, like Selous, showed animals all over the country that moved back and forth according to the natural seasons and cycles. So, it never occurred to me that there would be a problem, and there wasn't! My daughter-in-law, Judy, remembered me telling her that it was the ancient rock paintings in Wedza that inspired me to make my dream reality:

"The Bushman paintings in Markwe Caves show elephant, buffalo, giraffe, hippo, impala and kudu - all on the cave walls - proving that the animals had been there in the past. Norman said that whilst driving on Imire one spring day, when all the msasa trees were in new leaf, he could just visualise the grasslands teeming with animals."

The Markwe Caves, situated on the neighbouring Markwe Farm, are on a kopje known in Shona as *Madzimudzangara* (the spirits dwell here) and are a traditional burial place for Soswe chiefs. The stone-age paintings at these caves, were apparently visited and noted by Selous in the late 1800s. An excellent insight into the historical significance of the area was once given in the Wedza Gazette:

"Most of the sketches are of animals, of which the hunted kudu are particularly good. There is also an enormous superimposed outline of an elephant, with white tusks, and an owl on a branch with a white crescent moon behind it.

In the cave is buried the eighth Chief Soswe of the Vambire tribe; by name Chiku-ngwa Gusha Tiyai. Verbal history indicates that Chief Soswe was murdered by the

Matabele towards the end of the 19th century. The Chief is believed to have taken refuge in a cave on Markwe kopje, which is two miles from the Madzimudzangara, and upon which is the common boundary beacon of Imire, Ruware and Markwe farms. The Matabele smoked the chief to death in this cave and, when his body was pulled out, he is alleged to have developed breasts like those of a woman. This aroused much derision amongst the Matabele raiding party. It is probably not factual but merely an embellishment to ensure the tale loses nothing in the telling. After the departure of the Matabele, Chief Soswe's body was retrieved and buried in the cave containing the paintings." (WG Swanson, Wedza Gazette)

The pictorial evidence of abundant game in Wedza, as painted on the walls of Markwe Caves, was proof that Imire had once been occupied by hunter-gatherer Bushmen.

Corona Thornycoft did a count of human and animal paintings on twenty-two sites in the area, which included Imire and a few other sites, and recorded her findings:

"Humans 382; antelope 76 (species unidentified); kudu cows 28; kudu bulls 4; elephant 18; zebra 8; baboon 11; tsessebe 6; antbear 9; sable 7; duiker 3; reedbuck 5; giraffe 2; rhino 1; jackal 2; monkey 2; pig 2; lion 8; spring hare 1; birds 2." (Winter Cricket)

Residue tests from the paintings indicate they were done about two thousand years ago and, with images from the past in mind, I determined to make a start with my game park. Some people may have questioned my sanity in doing this, what with the bush war intensifying by the day, but the war was the war and I was a farmer and had to get on with farming. I had a strong belief that wildlife would play an economic part in the farming scene and that's why I went ahead.

We weren't the first people to work with game animals of course. The originators were farmers doing game-ranching in the lowveld. For some time they had been combining both game-hunting and photographic safaris as a business. I had been in contact with farmers in the lowveld in the late 1960s and early 1970s and envied their attitude to wildlife. They worked on the principle of 'utilisation' which involved 'correct' culling, selling of the products (meat and skins) and photographic safaris. I wondered why we couldn't do the same in the highveld but on a smaller, more intensive scale and involving smaller acreages.

Because I was in the local Hunting Association and chairman of the Mashonaland Branch for a year or two, I had dealings with various wild-life associations. Other people had also started talking about bringing game onto their farms and I became involved in the formation of the Rhodesia Game Association, which initiated game farming. I went on to become the chairman of the Rhodesia Game Association and we began lobbying government for changes to be made to the legislation so that the animals on your farm belonged to you. We had meetings with a number of senior government officials and these were encouraging; it appeared to me that we were on a strong footing and that it was just a question of time before we would get the legislation changed. In those days, and perhaps because of the preoccupation with the war, I think the government wasn't very involved in what was going on with the wildlife of the country. By 1972 they must have realised that there was big potential in bringing game onto farms and we found significant support from top government officials. We wanted landowners to be entitled to use the game animals on their properties and generate income from them, as long as they stayed within conservation and other regulatory controls. In fact, the legislation which resulted in The Parks and Wild Life Act of 1975 was still a few years ahead but, as more farmers became interested in game-farming, change was inevitable. When it came, it was a turning point and some experts said it was the most enlightened piece of wildlife conservation legislation in Africa. It gave people responsibility for the animals on their land except for a few species of mammals, reptiles, birds and plants, which were classified as Specially Protected Species. Specially protected mammals would include bat-eared fox, cheetah, gemsbok, Lichtenstein's hartebeest, pangolin, black and white rhinoceros and roan antelope. At the time that the legislation was being introduced, Bob Knott was my assistant on Imire and remembers the conversations we used to have:

"Norman was always very conservation conscious and he soon began discussing the idea of integrating game animals with cattle. He said it was imperative that the law be changed to allow farmers to own game animals. Norman's point of view was that if farmers were going to buy game animals then they should belong to the him and not the State. He was adamant that there was no way someone who didn't actually own something was going to take care of it. Norman said that without ownership there was no incentive for farmers to breed or even protect game animals. He said farmers had to be able to utilise their investment: through tourism, or by selling the offspring, or shooting animals for meat. He lobbied for changes in the legislation successfully and this was a fundamental change, which would lead on to the beginnings of the game park

Dung beetle

on Imire and, subsequently, draw people into game-farming all over the country. Norman broke new ground with game. He clarified the thinking, focused attention and provided an example for everyone else."

I felt very confident that, in the long term, the whole plan of bringing game onto farms and turning that game into an economic venture was definitely on. In 1972, prior to the new Parks and Wildlife Act, I was able to start game-farming on Imire thanks to a scheme introduced by National Parks. They had always engaged in culling, as a means of population control in the past, but now they introduced a programme of de-stocking, which involved capturing animals and offering them for sale to farmers. This was a momentous decision, as I wrote in a booklet on wildlife later:

"The Department of National Parks and Wildlife Management, under its director, Dr Graham Child, has been the spark which ignited the enthusiasm of us all. Its enlightened decision to cull animals by live capture, wherever possible, can do nothing but good for wildlife conservation." (Wildlife on Your Farm)

Several farmers and ranchers joined in and we bought animals to stock our farms with. It wasn't a question of what animals I wanted to start with on Imire, or how many males or females, it was a case of what was on offer. The message came that impala were on offer and I accepted.

We had to use our own vehicles to transport the animals when they'd been captured by National Parks. Mine was a five ton truck with home-made wooden sides and canvas roof and we went down to Mana Pools with two or three of the farm staff. We camped overnight and then just sat around waiting until the impala had been captured by National Parks. The animals were chased into a boma with a narrowing funnel and then up a ramp. Our truck was ready and waiting, backed into position at the top of a ramp and the animals were literally run into the vehicle. There were no drugs, no tranquillisers and no handling. We soon learnt that the secret was not to let the animals get too stressed and so we had the engines running. The impala ran onto the truck, the doors were slammed and off we went.

The first wild animals to be introduced to Imire - this small, mixed breeding-herd of twenty impala cost me five dollars each!

I'd built a boma, of poles and pig wire, near the house. On one side was the ramp where we off-loaded new arrivals and, on the other, the gate into the game park. The boma, itself, was small and secure. Twenty yards square, with poles which were two or three yards apart. A low, cement water trough against the back boundary provided clean water and was built in such a way that it could be cleaned and filled from outside the boma. We always tried to have a couple of trees inside a boma in order to provide natural shade and shelter but found that we had to be careful not to leave too much thick bush in there or the animals would hide and then be much more difficult to tame.

On release day we opened the door of the boma into our new three

Impala on Imire

hundred acre game park. The impala took a frightened look and, after a while, dashed out as a group. It didn't take them long to settle down and Gill and I loved to walk out into the park and see the impala. It was always such a thrill. They were not frightened of us and normally stayed around - albeit at a safe distance.

Our farm staff were confused and bemused at first. They regarded wild animals as *nyama* (meat) and couldn't understand why we weren't eating them! I remember discussing it with one of our senior men, Elijah, explaining that we wanted to utilise the animals for breeding, selling and as a tourist attraction. Elijah, at least, said he thought it was a good idea! It wasn't all plain-sailing when it came to other people's opinions of our new venture, as I told author Keith Meadows some time later:

"When I first started game there were a lot of farmers who were dead against the concept. I was told ad nauseam that I was going to ruin the cattle industry, I was going to bring disease in and that I was out of step with reality. There was considerable opposition." (Sometimes when it Rains)

In these early days of game-farming, there was a lot of trial and error but we soon learnt some basics that led to success. We were losing about 10% of the animals that came into the bomas - usually from wounds and injuries received during transportation and, sometimes, from just plain stress. I learnt a way to reduce mortalities and quieten animals in the boma from a chap called Gudo Otto, who was a professional in the game-capture business. Gudo's secret was to have a presence at the boma. He would instruct his staff to move around freely and talk in normal voices - no whispering. Otto said the most important thing was to get the animals accustomed to human voices. As they grew calmer they lost their fear of humans and settled down quickly.

We would keep the animals in the boma for two or three weeks in order to calm them and to teach them what a fence looked like. If released too early they would run straight at a fence, jump it and be gone. As we learnt more about the animals we put droppers into the game fence about three feet apart. If they charged the fence, the droppers held the wires firmly in place (stopping them from parting) thus preventing the animals from rushing off into the bush, or onto neighbouring farms. Then we learnt to use old bits of tin and scrap metal, which we hung on the fence as markers. These showed the animals there was an obstacle, that put the kibosh on their running into the wires and getting caught or
damaging themselves.

With time, the bomas were improved and we learnt to build separate isolation bomas along one side, each with its own access gate, which allowed us to isolate and treat sick or injured animals, if necessary. Our local vet was very helpful in this regard and would supply us penicillin or whatever was appropriate. For the more complicated problems we'd go and chat to the wildlife vets in Salisbury.

Our small herd of impala went on to do extremely well at Imire. Being both browsers and grazers they thrived on our mixed highveld vegetation and their numbers grew very rapidly. In February, the herd would split in two. One herd, the breeding herd, would be ruled by one dominant male who led all the females and youngsters and the second herd, a separate bachelor herd, consisted of all the other males. A few months later, in May, the rutting took place, with occasional challenges to the dominant male from other males in the bachelor herd. Lambing took place shortly after the first rains, seemingly regardless of when the ewes were served by the ram. Some experts were of the opinion that the ewes could hold back their babies until the rains came.

Not long after the impala had settled down, I broached the subject of wildebeest to the family. Barbara remembers the occasion very well and still chuckles about it these forty years later:

"Dad had a wonderful way with animals, a natural aptitude and compassion for them and they responded accordingly. I can remember sitting at the breakfast table not long after he'd got his first animals, which were impala, when Dad said, 'Gilly you're going to just love the wildebeest we're going to get.'

Mum said. 'Oh Norman, they're such ugly, comical looking animals. Can't you get something more beautiful?'

'Oh well, what about gnus then?' Dad asked.

Mum replied, 'Oh that's wonderful darling, I just love gnus.'

We all just cracked up laughing and Dad said, 'Gilly, they're the same thing!'

This was a story told again and again, with much amusement."

Our first wildebeest, or gnus, came from Wankie National Park where de-stocking was underway. National Parks had built a bush boma out of sight of tourists and visitors, a few kilometres inside Main Camp, and there we loaded our first fifteen wildebeest without a problem. After a spell in the boma on Imire, the wildebeest settled down well and, like the impala, seemed to adapt to our highveld environment without any problems. The wildebeest were only grazers and very dependent on water, which was fine in view of the many small dams I'd built over the years. Their calves were also born with the rains, or just before and, so, October and November soon became a busy time for us; watching, recording and monitoring. Wildebeest calving also brought one specific problem in the form of a viral disease called malignant catarrhal fever (*snotsiekte*). Although the wildebeest, themselves, don't get the disease, they are carriers of this herpes-virus, particularly calves under three months of age. The disease can be transmitted to cattle and, once infected, the symptoms appear very soon: fever; prolific, thick discharge from nose and eyes; photophobia (fear of light) and then death. The mortality rate was known to be high, up to 50% of cattle died within three to twelve days of infection. The best thing to do was remove all cattle during the wildebeest calving period, which helped reduce the danger of infection. Being just a simple and rather dim farmer, I learnt much from other people and the tip about wildebeest came from an expert - probably John Condy, who was a great fundi on these things. I did have a disaster many years later when I was sure the cattle had built up a natural immunity to the *snotsiekte* and didn't separate them from the wildebeest herd. It was a catastrophe and we lost thirteen cattle in a single afternoon.

The first attempt at bringing zebra onto Imire was a disaster. When the message came that National Parks were capturing zebra, I couldn't get down to Mana Pools due to other commitments, so my young assistant at the time, Clive Weston, went. With a couple of helpers and my five-ton truck, they loaded the captured zebra at Mana in the usual way: from the boma, along a race, up a ramp and into the truck. By this time we knew that one of the ways to quieten the animals down was that, once you were on the road, you didn't stop the truck again. Our instructions, from the wildlife experts, were that if you had to stop for fuel, or whatever other reason, you should leave the engine running - the vibration kept the animals calm. It didn't work this time! Almost as soon as he left Mana, Clive said the animals in the back of the truck were going berserk - thrashing around, kicking and biting and crashing into each other and the sides of the truck. Before he'd done five or ten kilometres Clive decided that none of the animals were going to survive the eight hour journey from Mana Pools to Wedza, so he found a suitable piece of high ground to back up against and stopped the truck. Opening the back door, Clive saw that some of the zebra had already been trampled to death. He had no choice but to stand aside and watch as the others rapidly jumped out and ran back into the bush, free again! Six weeks later zebra were, once more, on offer. We tried again and, this time, everything worked to plan and soon we had a fine herd on Imire. These very hardy animals soon settled and went on to breed well.

In 1974 we acquired waterbuck from Wankie National Park and both collection and transport went smoothly, without any problems. Even though they were new to Imire, I knew waterbuck had occurred here naturally, from way back, and so wasn't surprised when they settled down easily. Despite being a fairly large antelope they always managed to look in good condition, like the zebra. Later on, however, they did take a liking to going visiting on neighbouring farms. We were never sure why they did this, as the habitat on Imire was quite suitable, but we got used to getting calls from people who suddenly found themselves the proud owner of a waterbuck or two!

This new wildlife venture did so well that within a year, I had increased the size of the area fenced for game to one thousand acres to accommodate all the new arrivals. Rather like stamp-collecting, one can't stop!

Our first giraffe deserve a mention. We bought two giraffe from Ian Henderson, a game rancher in Matabeleland, and went down to West Nicholson in our old three-tonner, which had high wooden sides. Simon and Alastair were still schoolboys and they came along to keep me company. Simon was about fourteen and Alastair eleven and they loved it. They always got very excited at a possible outing and would beg to come along. "Take me Dad, take me," they would plead!

The giraffe were loaded with their heads and necks sticking out over the top of the cab and we set off. Hearing a horrible bump a little later, we stopped

to find that we had collided with an overhead telephone wire, which had been broken by the giraffes' protruding necks! Luckily, there was no harm done to the animals and so we rigged up a pole with a T-bar as a cross-member and Alastair and Simon were delegated to overhead watch. If an obstacle approached they would shout out a warning, 'Telephone wires!' At which point I'd stop and they would hoist the wire up so we could pass underneath, without getting snagged on giraffe necks - and on we'd go!

After we'd been travelling for some hours, on what was a very long journey, suddenly the giraffe lay down and appeared to be in great discomfort. We were on a dirt road that ran through farming lands, from Mvuma to the Sabi Road, which would eventually

Moving the giraffe from Matabeleland

bring us close to the Imire Road. I parked the truck hastily and the boys raced off to a nearby stream, rushing back with buckets of water. The giraffe wouldn't drink at first and I had to push their heads into the bucket. Once they got the hang of it they sucked up gallons and the sick giraffe soon recovered and we were on our way again. This was a great adventure for the boys, which Simon still remembers decades later:

"Dad, Squinks (Alastair) and I went down to West Nick with a truck and a car. It was all very experimental, it was the first time the vet had darted a giraffe and no one really knew how they would react. It was an incredible journey coming back, which took almost three days, and for that whole time we couldn't switch the lorry off because leaving the engine running kept the animals calm. Most of the time Squinks and I were standing on a little wooden bench in the back of the truck. Two or three times the giraffe lay down and we thought they had died and so Dad drove over corrugations at the edge of the road, to get them up, and we ran ahead to get water. The giraffe got so used to us over the three days that they would nudge us and push against us. We drove through Bulawayo early in the morning, during rush-hour traffic, and people were agog at the sight of two giraffe heads sticking out!"

The giraffe adapted to Imire and it wasn't long before they learnt to go walkabout, visiting many farms, some almost thirty kilometres away. I didn't think I had enough browse and, when they started breeding and there were four or five animals, I reckoned that was about the limit we could cope with. The game fence was a good nine feet high and there were grids in a couple of places on the road but these were no obstacle at all to the giraffe, who just stepped right across them and went wandering away. Our neighbours didn't seem to mind, in fact I think they loved it and so, as long as no harm was being done, we would let the giraffe wander. Sometimes they came back of their own volition and other times they needed a bit of persuasion. I did find the giraffe to be very stupid animals and once saw a male straddling a telephone pole, clearly trying to mate with it! The top of the pole had those two spherical porcelain knobs on it and, perhaps, looked like the head and hair tufts of a female to him!

Not long after this, when Simon turned fifteen, he decided that he rather fancied the idea of becoming a professional tennis player and Gill and I gave him a taste of the real world, as he recalls:

"Mum and Dad gave me a trip to Cape Town to go and get some tennis coaching from a famous coach who was touring the country at the time. I rather fancied myself as a tennis player and had thought maybe I could be a professional. Mum and Dad paid my air-fare and gave me a cash allowance for the two weeks as a birthday present. After two weeks I phoned and said I didn't have any money left and wanted to come back by car. Dad said right, you want to be an adult - fine, get on with it! The only problem was that there was no more cash forthcoming and I had to hitchhike back - and I did, on my own, at fifteen!

Dad was quite hard on us kids but, later, I remember an assistant of his, Skip Francis, who had a withered arm, saying, 'I wish someone had taught me the way your Dad has taught you.'

At about this time I began thinking about tourism but, of course, the bush war was raging all around us and so I started up a small venture with wild duck instead. Fritz Meyer put us on the right road to their feeding needs. Fritz was known as the pioneer of wildlife utilisation. He was the outstanding principal of the famous, government-run Mlezu African Agricultural School, near Que Que. He was a brilliant man who we got a lot of our ideas from. We would feed the duck with grain sweepings from the mill, putting the feed on the bank, right at the water's edge. Mostly it was common teal, white-faced duck and knob-nosed geese that were attracted to the feed - it proved so successful that one duck count revealed over a thousand birds on one dam. Before this we had the odd flock, of twenty or so birds, visiting a dam during the rainy season. So many duck came for the feed, that they actually wore a little ledge into the bank of the dam. Of course, it wasn't long before a large snake moved in to take advantage of the very easy pickings. A python took to lying in the shallow water, beneath the ledge, and snacking on the odd duck or two.

We intended to have duck shoots, in season, with friends and once we tried a commercial shoot with four Italian tourists. I didn't agree with shooting on the same dam where the ducks were fed, which was very unsporting and, instead, picked a spot somewhere on the flight line. There were a number of flight lines that the birds might use, as they went to their nightly roosting spots, so it wasn't as easy as it sounds. The birds also passed over fast and high and so had a good chance and, more often than not, they won!

On the day of the shoot I put the Italians on a dam wall in the ducks flight path but, as the birds were flying over, I recognised a gallinule in amongst them. This shy, gangly, deep blue bird, with red beak and feet, is often seen high-stepping and clambering about in reeds and water lilies and was certainly not an intended target.

"No! No!" I shouted but it was too late and disaster struck. One of the sportsmen shot the purple gallinule before I could stop him. That ended our experiment in the commercial duck-hunting field on Imire. Sadly, we also had to give up feeding wild ducks when local villagers found that, by soaking mealie pips in cattle dip, the birds would die and they could then harvest and eat ducks by the dozen.

I wasn't the only person doing game-farming in those early days; Richard Bedford also went in for it in a big way and was very enthusiastic. He was an amazing fellow, one of the characters of the area who seemed to ride over all the problems of life very easily. Determined and hard-working, he was good with his labour, improving their conditions, introducing bonus schemes and the like. He was also a tough-looking bloke, who appeared as fit as anything and was usually dressed in a pair of shorts. Richard's father, JB, had a golf course on his farm (Poltimore) and we'd go and play there quite often. Richard was a keen big-game hunter who, in later years, took people out on hunts, but did no shooting himself. He was always very deaf and I thought it probably due to all his years of shooting. I got to know him well when he took over Poltimore, where he ran the cattle extremely capably and also built up a very nice game-farm with eland, sable, impala, zebra and tsessebe.

12 December 1973 was a momentous day for us when the country's first ever Wildlife Field Day was held on Imire. It was organised by the Rhodesia Game Association whose president at the time was Sir Hugh Beadle, also the Chief Justice of Rhodesia. Speakers included Dr Graham Child, who was then the Director of National Parks and Wildlife Management; Dr John Hanks from the University of Rhodesia and Fritz Meyer from Mlezu. Even the press were there and, the following day, there was a photograph of Sir Hugh Beadle and I, with extracts from some of the speeches made at the event.

Most of the country's wildlife areas were surrounded by Tribal Trust Lands, which by the year 2000 would have an estimated population of nine and a half million. This would create a big demand for land and the future of wildlife would depend more and more on farmers reintroducing game. Farmers stood to benefit from cash returns by the removal of mammals or birds from re-established populations on a sustainable yield basis for meat or sport. These were direct benefits. There were also indirect benefits, such as owls keeping down rodents on the farms.

One day Dave Mirams, who was the district commissioner in Wedza, phoned to say that they had caught a crocodile in the Sabi River. The croc was apparently causing a problem eating goats and calves and Dave asked if we would like the animal. My intention for Imire was to have a game park with a large variety of animals, the more diversity we had the more of a tourist attraction it would become. So, when this chance came, I jumped at it!

The only suitable place we had, at the time, was the swimming pool in our garden. The pool was built on a slab of natural rock and the shallow end was the slope of the rock and the deep end was a depression further down. We had built a concrete wall to surround and enclose the pool and, although it served a very useful purpose, it would be even more useful as a home for the crocodile. Gill was horrified! She was going to lose her beautiful swimming pool but then, she was always very good at looking horrified! Besides, it wasn't going to be for long. Bob Knott, still my assistant at the time, remembers our conversation:

"Norman and Gill had a wonderful relationship and a typical conversation would start with Norman saying something like: 'Gilly, I'm thinking of putting a crocodile in the swimming pool.'

To which Gill would reply. 'Oh Norman, darling, you can't do that! I absolutely refuse. Over my dead body!'

But then, sure enough, two weeks later there would be a man-eating crocodile in the swimming pool!"

The croc had been caught in a trap, lured in with a bit of meat, and when he arrived, his mouth and legs were taped up. The poor creature had obviously had a bit of rough time and wasn't very friendly, hissing at everyone in sight. We lowered the water level in the swimming pool and there the croc stayed, for a month, while we made a permanent pen for him. I announced I could train anything, including the crocodile, as Simon recalls:

"Dad would go out there every day and call him and feed him. He trained the crocodile Pavlov-style by conditioning the animal to associate food with the sound of a human voice. From then on, and for the rest of his time, that croc still came up for meat when called."

Barbara remembers feeding time very well:

"When Dad got his first croc, and it was in our swimming pool, he started off by feeding it from a chair, which he put in the shallow end of the pool. At that time the shallow end was dry and Dad would get in, stand on the chair, call the croc, throw him the meat and then jump out as the reptile approached. As time went on Dad got more and more daring, eventually standing next to the chair and then not putting the chair in at all. Eventually he built the crocodillery and I can't count the number of times I saw him, literally, pole-vault out of there. Dad was a real showman and people just couldn't believe how brave he was, ridiculously brave."

As soon as everything was ready, the crocodile was moved from our swimming pool to its new home. There was a small dam, about forty yards wide, situated on a seasonal stream in a vlei. We built a four foot high brick wall on the two dry sides and used wire netting embedded in concrete across the spillway wall and stream sides, and this became the crocodillery.

Feeding time for the croc became a prime tourist attraction and often caused a bit of a stir. One day, while taking a group of tourists around on the tractor and trailer, we stopped at the croc pen as we always did. This old croc was a good drawcard because he'd often be basking in the sun on a slab of granite and I'd call him over. He'd come across, take the meat, roll over in the water with it, the ways crocs do, and the tourists loved it. On this occasion I jumped over the wall to call the croc, to feed him some meat. He swam over and then, as he came out of the water, instead of his normal sluggish approach , I saw he was on the high walk and coming straight for me. A croc normally slithers along on the ground

Nile crocodile and eggs

on its tummy but, when he needs to move fast on land, he raises himself off the ground with his feet because he can move much faster.

I threw the meat in front of him but, to my horror, he ran straight over it and kept coming. You must remember that a croc's eyes are on the top of his head and I realised straight away that he hadn't seen the meat. I turned to sprint for the wall and gathered, afterwards, that the tourists looking on in horror, expected their guide to be eaten! I reversed so fast that I fell flat, lifting my leg as I went down in order to kick the croc if needed. Luckily, the croc flopped to the ground, a couple of feet away, and started swinging his head from side to side. I knew straight away he was looking for the meat, so I got to my feet and shouted. "You silly bugger, the meat's behind you!"

I'm convinced he just hadn't seen it because, when the croc did find the meat, he went back to his usual routine immediately. Who says you can't be friends with crocs!

Years later we obtained a female crocodile and the pair mated. When she started to lay eggs I put sand in a hollow in the enclosure and, dutifully, the female laid her brood there. We waited until we thought they were almost ready to hatch and then frightened the female into the water before removing the eggs. We put them in a tray of sand and placed the tray on a ledge above the Aga stove in the kitchen.

The warmth from the Aga was sufficient to sustain them and the eggs hatched, coincidentally, on Easter Sunday. Gill was cooking lunch for a group of visitors and the crocodile babies never bothered her at all but she did get fed up with the constant interruptions from the guests, who wanted to see the baby reptiles! I thought we should have taken the babies to bed with us, to keep them warm, but Gill objected very firmly to this. She didn't mind lions, leopards and elephants but drew the line at crocodiles in the bed!

We kept the baby crocs above the stove for a few days - making very sure they couldn't get out, obviously. I moved them into an aviary in the garden, which had a little pond in it, and rigged up an infra-red lamp to keep them warm but, alas, most of them died during the following winter months.

The mother croc eventually escaped and went to a neighbour's dam, where she remained. Some years later a little six foot croc turned up at our dam and we're certain it must have been one of her offspring that had grown up and come looking for Dad!

The father crocodile, which had started out in the swimming pool of our garden, continued to live quite happily in the crocodillery and, almost unbelievably, thirty years later is still with us on Imire. We feed him meat every second day in summer, but less so in winter. Often I wonder if crocs can become pets, like so many other animals and birds? *I* think they can, but many can't imagine it's possible!

Chapter Nine

SUNDOWNERS WITH A HIPPO
Imire ~ Mid-1970s

The mid-1970s were very busy times, as the game park expanded and we procured more animals. It was around this time that Maggie arrived. Maggie was a young female hippo who came from National Parks in Kariba. She had been walking into camp-sites and was, generally, being a nuisance. I don't know how much Maggie weighed but, even as a youngster, she was of considerable size. The experts describe adult females as weighing from 1,000 - 1,700kgs, with bulls growing up to 2,000kgs. Their description is not very attractive, either:

"Large rotund animal with smooth naked skin, short, stocky legs and massive, broad-muzzled head. Mouth equipped with an impressive set of tusk-like canines and incisors. Short flattened tail is tipped with a tuft of black hair. Body colour; greyish-black with pink tinge at the skin folds around eyes and ears." (Field Guide to the Mammals of Southern Africa)

We fenced in a couple of small dams near the house for her but she soon escaped, left the game park altogether and turned up in a neighbour's large dam. We managed to dig in a truck, level with a small earth bank, lure Maggie out with pumpkins and brought her back to Imire. Feeding her with cubes, by hand, soon tamed her down and I quickly discovered that she loved bread - a loaf lasted thirty seconds! I suppose, like all wild animals, if you want to get to know them really closely, you do it gradually. You don't rush in. With Maggie I started her with cubes and then, bit by bit, she came a little closer until eventually she would come right up to me, open her enormous mouth and I could just drop the cubes right in. It didn't take long to add chunks of bread and then, one day, I found that she also loved beer! I think Maggie thought I was part of her family and she totally trusted me. Often she would have bread and beer at the dam with family and friends looking on. Was it taming or training? Who knows? Simon thought it was training:

"Who can train a hippo to swim across a dam? That conundrum started because we'd go down to the dam, in the evening, to fish and have a sundowner. Dad used

to call Maggie, who could be at the far end of the dam, but straight away she would come, swimming like a porpoise through the water to Dad."

Maggie was a great favourite with everyone. Gill remembers her very fondly:

"Maggie was just gorgeous. She would climb up onto the verandah, open her mouth and make gurgling noises as she waited for her bread, snacks or beer."

Gill's sister, Jane, recalls how Maggie was often the recipient of more than just bread and beer:

"Maggie was remarkable. I remember once Gilly had thrown a kitchen tea party and I was horrified when all the left-over éclairs and other exquisite little delicacies went to Maggie!"

Before we put a security fence around the house, Maggie would often wander up to the front garden in search of a bit of green grass to graze on, particularly at the end of winter when there wasn't much green grazing in the game park. On cold winter nights she would come up to the dairy shed and sleep on the compost heap to keep warm. One dark evening, before we had the security fence, we had some guests for drinks. The dogs started to bark and I guessed that Maggie was in the garden, and told everyone to expect a visitor. "Maggie!" I called out and, to everyone's amazement, up the stairs and onto the verandah walked the hippo - mouth wide open! I gave her half a loaf of bread and a bottle of beer, poured into her cavernous mouth, patted her on her nose and said, "Goodbye Maggie, thank you for coming," and off she went. Who says you can't tame hippo!

Many years later, during a particularly bad drought in the lowveld, we took in a small pod of four hippo from National Parks and put them in a large dam on the game park. As they grew and matured, the herd bull drove off a youngster who promptly moved to the dam on Merryhill Farm, right next door. Our neighbours now had the delights of hippo too, even naming one of them, as they wrote in their book:

"The dam on Merryhill attracted Googly, a hippo that came over the dam wall from Numwa, usually on its own but occasionally with others. He would play hide and seek with the dogs, allowing them to swim out and almost reach him before sinking out of sight, only to re-emerge a few minutes later some way off for the whole diverting game to start again. Googly would also follow Corona's canoe while she was fishing for bream. However, he was not welcome in the garden and Corona once used her beloved .410 to pepper him, and a companion, knowing that the shot would not penetrate their thick hides but hoping that the sting would deter them." (A Fenman in Africa)

Unhappily, there was a tragic end for Googly, as Richard Thornycroft relates:

"One day the big male hippo from Imire came up onto our dam and chased Googly away and he eventually went off to Rob Edgar's dam on Scorror. Unfortunately he was doing a lot of damage to the crops there and was eventually shot."

Maggie - the hippopotamus

Despite Maggie's popularity and her endearing little quirks, we had to always remember that she was a wild animal and could have been very dangerous. Many experts in the field say that there are more human deaths due to hippo than any other animal in Africa. Nigel Thornycroft himself had a very close encounter with a hippo some time later, as he relates in a letter to a friend:

"We were drifting away fairly fast when it happened. Must have crossed a shallower underwater ridge when, crash - the boat tipped just about vertical - all loose stuff flipped straight overboard and we clutched what we could to avoid following suit as she slowly came down on her keel again. My first thought was that we'd hit a rock. But, not so. A bloody great hippo - who had no business to be in that kind of water - had taken a dim view of the boat and charged from below. Cracked the hull right along the keel and left four great tooth marks..." (A Fenman in Africa)

Hippos weren't the only large animals we introduced to Imire because, at some time in the mid-1970s, National Parks were embarking on elephant-culling, while saving the young calves to be hand-reared by willing and suitably-equipped and established game operations. Imire fell into this category and we started out with a young female elephant called Nzou, who was a delight to me as well as being a great character on Imire, but more about her will come later.

When the game had settled in, the problem was to make the whole operation viable. We started by advertising lunches, with game drives, in 1973. Our first vehicle was a tractor-drawn trailer, fitted with an awning overhead for shade and comfortable seats, and this proved very successful. We tried oxen pulling the trailer but it proved to be too slow.

Guests arrived at about ten in the morning and we'd start with tea and scones on the lawn by the house, and then I'd take them out on game drives. Part of the game drive included visiting Castle Kopje, a large granite kopje with only a few bushman paintings but many old graves. This was researched, later, by Corona Thornycroft, an amateur archaeologist, who discovered the grave of a woman adorned with gold beads. Corona's son, David, describes the discovery and how it was then seized upon by the authorities:

"She (Corona) became interested in the granite kopjes that dot the area around Wedza Mountain. They had been much used over the centuries as a place of refuge, first by the Bushmen, who left their distinctive paintings and later by Shona tribes hiding from Matabele raiding parties. Corona undertook a course at the Salisbury Museum and was then tasked by them to find, and trace for their records, Bushmen

paintings throughout the Wedza tribal lands. At first she painted them in their original colours but archaeological practice came to prefer black outlines only, on the grounds that the colours would have changed over the years.

She obtained a permit to dig for pottery on Castle Kopje, which was on Norman Travers' farm at Imire. She chose a site that she thought looked interesting and cleared the ground at the entrance to a cave-like structure between two towering granite columns. Two African helpers dug down, inch by inch, while Corona sieved every particle of soil they dug up. About eighteen inches down she found a hut floor made of baked mud and dung. This was removed and, after a month, when they had got down three feet, she discovered an unmistakable gold bracelet that looked as fresh as though it was displayed on a jeweller's counter. Quickly emptying a bucket of earth over it, to hide it, she raced home and rang the museum to report the discovery of a 'gold burial.' Inevitably, the conduct of the dig was taken over by others but it turned out to be an important find, carbon-dated 1450AD, of a Great Zimbabwean culture. There was more gold in the form of arm and leg bangles and hair decorations. Some of the pottery was even older, being carbon-dated 1260 - 1280AD. The finds are now all in the National Museum in Harare, although they are not credited to Corona, an amateur and a white woman." (David Thornycroft)

The whole area was filled with history and had obviously been a settlement of considerable importance in times past. About four hundred yards from Corona's discovery we found numerous graves on an outcrop of granite. Obviously these were the graves of local people, while their leaders were buried higher up. On the farm road leading from Castle Kopje there was a site, which was cause for much speculation, at the Chenikwa River. Situated on a granite outcrop near the river bank there are a mass of oval hollows in the rock similar to those traditionally used for grinding grain. Instead of the normal one or two hollows, that one would find near a homestead, here there are about a hundred holes. On a rock nearby there are three deeper, circular holes in the granite. Speculation about the purpose of these holes is linked to a gully with a quartz outcrop. Geologists thought it likely that earlier inhabitants had found gold in the quartz and to extract it they had carried the quartz over to the granite where they had crushed the stone in the oval holes. Then they had carried the more likely stones to the deeper circular holes where they had extracted the flakes of gold.

Frank Scott, from whom I had bought Welton Farm, said that the original owner of the farm, before World War One, had come across papers that included a miner's licence for the property and his son later confirmed early evidence of gold:

"Noel Wingfield told Norman that amongst his father's papers he found an assay sheet for gold - this had been located on the Chinekwa River on Numwa. A geologist confirmed there was no doubt that there had been gold workings where gullies occurred in the quartz reef." (Winter Cricket)

Game animals, geology and old history provided great variety for visitors coming on our day-safaris around Imire. Lunch provided another highlight. Towards midday we'd head towards the lunch kopje. This was a granite dome on the Imire side of the game park. I picked this site not only because I knew I could drive up the kopje safely with the tractor and trailer but, also, because it was such an attractive spot. The vehicle, loaded with guests, would drive up the side of the kopje, where the gradient wasn't too steep, alongside trees and shrubs, with lovely views across the rolling bush. When we reached the top, the elephants and buffalo would always be waiting for us. Led there by their handlers, this was a wonderful treat for the guests. After a little while, the elephants would be led away to graze and the guests could walk over the dome of the kopje, for about a hundred metres, to our lunch spot. With a view sloping away from us, sometimes you could see sable or zebra in the park below. Lunch was in a clearing shaded by majestic mountain acacia trees. Tree roots twined over rocks and into crevices with lichen staining the boulders in colours of rust, orange and green - making this the perfect place for lunch.

The old family car, a Toyota, was bought into service for our lofty lunches under the mountain acacias. Mattheus, our maître d', was tasked with driving up to the kopje with the provisions and laying everything out before we arrived with the guests. We had built the lunch-site seats and tables out of granite blocks. Our son, Simon, who worked for a firm that ran a granite quarry, gave us a fine slab for the main table. These natural granite tables were covered with tablecloths and magnificent meals were presented for our guests.

Lunches on the kopje were Gill's domain. She had wooden boxes marked and reserved exclusively for game park lunches and they contained everything that would be needed. All was perfectly packed and accounted for, from cutlery and crockery to tablecloths, glasses and cruets. Whenever she could, Gill prepared meals using game meat. Mostly it would be impala or wildebeest and, sometimes zebra, which wasn't easy as Gill found the meat to be very tough and in need of long, slow cooking. Curry and rice with salad was a favourite, as was game stew, or lasagna made with minced impala. Sometimes we'd have a braai and, on those days, the workers would go up the kopje well ahead of time to prepare and light the fire. Puddings were made with ingredients from the farm whenever possible; fresh fruit salad, trifles, strawberries and thick cream - fresh from the dairy.

Gill had the knack of bringing a touch of class to all our endeavours and nothing was ever too much trouble, as her sister Jane elaborates:

"Gilly was always the best hostess, uncomplaining and thinking of everyone's needs. She used to give Norman wonderful birthday parties with Chinese food, which he loved because of younger days spent in China. She'd go to endless trouble getting things just right for him. Then, because of the game park, Gill went to great lengths

to perfect her cooking skills. Morning teas were laid out in the garden for visitors and always included home-made scones and jam with thick cream. Afternoon teas offered home-made cakes, biscuits, éclairs, meringues and brandy snaps - everything being cooked on an Esse, Gill's wood-burning stove! Gill and her wonderful cook, Mattheus, made a very effective team. I'm sure that some guests came as much for the wonderful meals as for the animals!"

Bob Knott, still with us when we started the day-safaris, remembers the fantastic team they made:

"Gill's right-hand man was Mattheus Shaka, the cook. Mattheus only had one eye and was very much a character. He and Gill did everything together. He was loyal and forthright and, although he and Gill used to spar, they were an excellent team."

For people that were interested (and if we had time) about fifty to a hundred yards from the lunch spot, there was a little pimple of a kopje with an old stone-wall ruin on the top - of unknown origin. There were also some very good cave paintings nearby and one, of a man with a spear in his hand stabbing another man lying on the ground, is very unusual. Many of these ancient paintings left me pondering about days gone by. Another mystery is to be found in the Markwe Caves, on the left-hand side of the main paintings. Here is a drawing of a strange animal with a serrated back like a crocodile, a wolf-like face and four legs. For a long time I wondered if it wasn't, perhaps, a creature from prehistoric times but later was led to believe that it is a mythical animal of the Bushmen.

A day-safari on Imire was concluded with a leisurely drive after lunch, back through the park to afternoon tea at the house, before our guests headed home. Many people, then, began signing and making comments in our guestbook. Reading it later, their comments made everyone's hard work well worthwhile. Because the bush war was raging at the time, most of our early guests were Rhodesians who hailed from areas both near and far. These included Rusape, Filabusi, Gwanda, Darwendale, Karoi, Salisbury, Bulawayo and Mrewa, along with our own neighbours and friends from Wedza and Marandellas. However, some came from further afield and we avidly read names and comments made by visitors from Guernsey, England, South Africa and occasionally a few from Australia, New Zealand and Sweden. In July 1976 the visitor's book records the names of Chief Soswe and Chief Ruzani and a group of headmen who visited, which was very encouraging. Comments from all visitors were heartwarming:

Absolutely super! Seeing is believing! First class! Out of this world!

The first comment on our much-loved hippo came from a Salisbury visitor:

Adored Maggie!

Behind the scenes, and out of tourists' sight, we had plenty of work to do with the game animals and the many new species that continued to be introduced. Management of the animals became necessary when we found that, by concentrating the game in a relatively confined area, parasites became a problem. Game feeding-blocks, similar to those used for cattle, had come on the market and, through these, the animals received the right balance of minerals, salt and natural proteins. Other blocks also became available which contained anti-parasitic medication to control various intestinal worms. Then came the issue of ticks. In this regard, someone called Mike Duncan had invented a drum (with a tube in the centre) that could control ticks on game animals. Salt would be put in the drum and an oily dip smeared on the tube so that, when the animals came to lick the salt, some of the dip would be left on their necks. I was never too keen on this and always felt that once you started using chemicals you would destroy the animals' natural immunity to ticks. Like cattle, once you start dipping you have to continue with it all their lives.

I had heard of a couple of ranchers in the lowveld who'd stopped dipping their cattle altogether and had met with great success. In the first year of this experiment a lot of cattle had died but, afterwards, they never looked back as the animals' natural immunity gradually built up. It was a very contentious issue but reminded me of, years before, when there had been two wild oxen on Welton Farm. I'd asked Frank Scott about them and he said they had never been handled or put near a dip. I thought that they must have been carrying a disease and shot them but, on inspection, found them to be in beautiful condition with no ticks at all and their skins glossy and superb. That was when I formed the opinion that all these anti-tick chemicals destroyed an animal's natural immunity. Regardless of my own ideas, I had to find a way round the tick problem and the answer for the game animals was actually with the cattle, which, by law, had to be dipped.

When I started Imire Game Park, I was only using one thousand acres on the home section of the farm but, as the game section grew and I started fencing in more land, I obviously had to reduce my numbers of cattle and integrate them with the game. This decision was crucial to the economic future of the whole operation. Before I started with game in 1972 I had between fifteen hundred and eighteen hundred cattle, which included a breeding herd of four or five hundred, and all the calves and yearlings. My objective, from the beginning, was to prove that cattle and game could be mixed and that they benefited each other in the control of ticks. Provided you could control the ticks on the cattle and the vegetation, the game seemed to have an in-built immunity - unless they became sick or injured, which was when the ticks climbed on in huge numbers and the animal died.

Included in this problem came the issue of burning - another contentious one! I was a

Eland

great believer in controlled-burning and saw it as an essential part of game management, particularly with the grazers. When we first put in tsessebe I didn't think we'd have any problems because they are true highveld antelope, well-suited to grassland and our climate. I was proved wrong, though, because almost all the calves born that first season died. So, before they calved again the following year (in September and October), we burned a couple of sections of the grassland. The short stubble of new green grass shoots made all the difference and, from then on, we never had a problem with tsessebe calves dying again. Rotational, seasonal burning became an important part of the management plan for Imire.

Despite the concerns of some people over bringing animals from lowveld to highveld areas, I wasn't worried. In retrospect, I wish I'd known more about what nature can do and how animals can cure themselves. For example, I found out about eland tick control, and the use of garlic, only after much trial and error and many headaches. We started out with two females and one bull eland, which came from the Mushandike Eland Sanctuary. John Posselt, a former warden of the Mushandike Recreational Park, had pioneered an eland domestication programme and had built up a herd of eland which could be handled much the same as cattle.

When they first came to Imire, the eland were well-domesticated and were used to eating cubes, being handled and treated for ticks. Unfortunately, they soon developed a tick problem because, needless to say, we weren't treating them anymore. We tried all sorts of remedies, talked to a number of experts and, in the end, thanks to the suggestion of an Afrikaans fellow, we tried using garlic. We chopped the garlic up, mixed it with the cubes and the eland ate it without complaint. It worked extremely well and definitely cleared up the ticks. The domesticated eland obviously had a worse tick problem than the other game but, once we'd cleared their initial problem, they never had much trouble with them again.

The eland were quite docile and quickly became used to vehicles and tourists. However, even though they bred, the herd grew slowly because we only had the two females. As a result, some years later I secured a new bull, also from Posselt, and funnily enough we had exactly the same problem with ticks all over again! I had to go back to employing the garlic remedy once more but, eventually, once the little breeding group got going, they proved to be an excellent herd - only losing some animals when the odd young bulls would get out and move onto neighbouring farms.

Before long it was obvious the game park had become a big hit. So we took the operation one step further and began to include an overnight facility. We converted what had been my brother-in-law Frank Chubb's house into guest accommodation. Sable Lodge, as it became known, had initially been built by Gilly and I for my sister Flip (and Frank) in 1953.

Frank and Flip's old house became Sable Lodge

Intended as an ordinary farm house, it faced Markwe Caves and, consequently, it was the obvious site for guests and tourists to stay. Gilly, with her artistic flair, re-designed the rooms in glorious colours with rosy curtains and bedspreads and created the lovely gardens, giving the whole place a very rustic feel. We ended up with an exclusive get-away destination that, now, also offered accommodation and first-class meals - for eight guests at a time. The four double rooms were all en suite and there was a central dining room, where guests had meals with the host or hostess.

Sable Lodge came into being just before Bob Knott left us to start his own farm and he remembers how it all came together:

"I never doubted that the game farm concept would work because Norman always made things work. He was like a steam-roller and was determined that this was going to succeed. It caused a big upheaval in their lives as there were baby animals that needed feeding day and night, tourists coming and going every day and their home became an open house. At first Gill was very unsure but she soon grew to love it. She was a solid support for Norman and in the background all the time. She was wonderful at organising functions and events and, later on, converted a little L-shaped farmhouse into a beautiful guest house for tourists."

Sable Lodge became the perfect home for our little blue duiker, who had come all the way from Moçambique. A family in Moçambique, who were leaving the country because of the war, wanted someone to take over their animals. Their property was about 50kms across the border and so, once I'd received the message and put the necessary paperwork and permits together, drove down there and collected a pair of blue duiker and a couple of bushbuck from them. The blue duikers were fascinating creatures. Not really blue, but a sort of dark brown, grey colour with a blue sheen. They are about the size of a large rabbit standing just a foot (30cms) high and weighing only 4kgs. The little duiker is very shy and creeps around under cover of thickets and really dense forests. I can remember, once, going down to Moçambique on holiday with the family. Not far across the border, in the mountains, there was a big truck in front of us, which was absolutely full of blue duiker skins. Apparently, once a year, the locals would gather and go into the nearby hills where the blue duiker lived, in thick forests, and they'd do drives through the bush and kill the little duikers in their thousands.

The pair we obtained were partially tame (they were at home with being handled) and they started out in our garden by living amongst the roses and wisteria under our bedroom window. Later, when Sable Lodge became John's domain, they moved there.

As the game park went from strength to strength on Imire, an increasing number of farmers began showing an interest in following our example. So, being chairman of the Rhodesia Game Association, I became involved in the production of a 1975 book called 'Wildlife on Your Farm'. Some of the photographs in the book came from Imire, not very good ones, but they did the job. There were also some pictures taken by Roy Creeth, of cattle and wildebeest grazing together on Imire. Roy was a good friend of ours and a very keen and talented professional photographer.

I also wrote the foreword for the book, which contains topics covering all sorts of things; from game birds, bomas and animals to farm dams and fish production. Even though I've been an avid fisherman all my life, I never did very well with fish-farming. I did try to get it off the ground on Imire, mainly with bream in our dams. In those days fish were worth peanuts but it was a way of utilising farm dams, especially if you managed to get the fish poaching under control. I bought gill nets and all sorts of things to make fish-farming succeed but was never very successful. Unlike Fritz Meyer, who had it down to a fine art.

In the foreword to the book I encouraged other farmers to give game-farming a try:

"Wildlife, whether it is fish, fowl, or four-legged animal, has, in the past, been utilised in only a few instances. This picture is rapidly changing and many farmers now realise that, to achieve greater material benefits from nature's bountiful store, a long-term programme of sensible management is most important.

We in Rhodesia were once blessed with one of the greatest concentrations of totally integrated wildlife in Africa. It is sad that within eighty years that situation should be so totally changed. Now, however, with the increasingly progressive outlooks being shown by landowners, and the realisation of the rewards to be obtained from well managed wildlife farming, I feel confident that Rhodesia can become an example to Africa of total ecological utilisation." (Wildlife on Your Farm)

In the book we also covered the economics of game-farming and, I must admit, there was quite a bit of guesswork in that section! We worked out costings and income but, of course, we never made much from game back then. Zebra were the most lucrative, with the skin alone fetching $448. The poor old duiker, including skin, trophy, meat and all was only worth $5. At the time, fresh game-meat sold for between 30c and 50c per kg and dried game-meat, as biltong, sold for $2.20 per kg. Looking back at the prices we quoted in the book, forty years later (and after a decade of super-hyper-inflation and the collapse of the country's currency and economy), it's hard to imagine how it was worthwhile but, surprisingly, it was! Now, the purchase costs sound absurd but were real expenses to be considered then, particularly in view of the war situation and the growing poaching problem:

"At the present time the availability of wild mammals is limited. The Department of National Parks and Wildlife Management is currently (1975) offering limited numbers of animals at the following prices: eland $80 each; impala $8 each and zebra $20 each. Previous prices (1974) have been: sable $20 each and wildebeest $15 each."

(Wildlife on Your Farm)

A couple of species, not on the National Parks list, caught my attention at this time and I took the plunge, privately, to buy them. One of the species would go on to become very successful on Imire and the other was a disaster, destined only for the breakfast table.

I heard about 'Boss' Lilford, a fellow who ran a gold mine and farmed just outside Salisbury. He had imported blesbok from South Africa and they had bred up so well that he was selling animals to get his numbers down. This chap had high-up contacts in the government, which enabled him to get the necessary permits to import the animals. This was no easy task, at the time, because of the very strict controls on introducing non-indigenous animals into the country. Anyway, because of his connections, I had no problems and so, without much ado, I bought a truckload of blesbok from him.

Blesbok are slightly taller, and about 20kgs heavier than impala and noticeably different in appearance. They are reddish in colour, with a distinct white blaze on their faces with a pale rump. Despite being grazers, indigenous to the Orange Free State, Transvaal and Eastern Cape, the blesbok did very well on Imire. A particularly attractive sight is a line of blesbok mothers walking in single file through the bush with their creamy, fawn-coloured lambs running alongside. They are a perfect example of an exotic animal that has adapted to our habitat, and thrived.

I can't say the same about ostrich - another new arrival to the game park. They are definitely not my favourite species and I don't have any good memories where they are concerned. The ostriches were always the bane of my life and most of my encounters with the birds left me waving a stick and running for my life! I regularly had problems with the cock, who really had it in for me, on one particularly bad day, chasing me up an anthill. I managed to grab a branch for protection and, following a protracted chase from one anthill to another, finally managed to get away, very much the worse for wear. Ungrateful overgrown turkey!

John also had many a bad encounter with the ostriches:

"They were always chasing us. It wasn't a one-off but a common occurrence, and was really frightening. It got so bad that we couldn't even take our clients for walks in the game park because they would come for us. When this happened you had two choices, you either lay flat on the ground or you got behind a tree."

Barbara remembers me returning home battered, bruised and with my pride most definitely dented after being chased by an ostrich:

"He came home very dishevelled, dusty and grazed and had obviously had a serious encounter - he even fell a few times with the bird coming too close for comfort. The very next morning on Dad's breakfast plate: Ostrich liver!"

I was always a firm believer in changing direction, if needs be. The ostrich weren't working on Imire and there was no point in keeping a bird apparently determined to do me harm! Adapting and changing are the only ways to do well in farming. A prime example comes from a chap who flourished after pursuing this truism. Rick Holme had been farming in Kenya and then in South Africa but came to Rhodesia in the mid 1960s and ended up in Wedza thanks to a rather strange coincidence:

"A friend of his, who had been engaged to look out for a place, reported that one was available in the Wedza area and, on a hunch - it had the same telephone number as that of his farm in Natal - he went out to view it. After only twenty minutes it was quite obvious that it was the kind of farm he would like: it was also one he couldn't afford. However, after six months, an arrangement was made whereby he could take it over in conjunction with the owner." (Rhodesian Tobacco Journal, 1969)

When Rick Holme bought Scorror Estate, it had an old but well-established orange orchard on it. Planted in 1906, there were apparently over three and a half thousand trees on the place when Rick took it over. Because storing and selling fresh oranges wasn't profitable, Rick decided to have a go at making wine. Having spent part of his childhood in Malta and Italy, Rick had an Italian recipe that allowed him to come up with a new Rhodesian wine, made from oranges - called *Escorro*. The wine did very well. So well, that soon the orchard was expanded by another two thousand six hundred orange trees and tobacco farming stopped altogether. To me, Rick had exactly the right approach to farming - if one thing doesn't work, try something else.

Another good example of adapting to circumstances (and being taken for a ride by my friends) came my way in connection with a pair of sable bulls, who were continually breaking out of the game park and causing no end of difficulties. Mark Milbank takes up the story:

"I had started a company called Abercrombie South Safaris in 1972 and although we didn't undertake any hunting safaris, we did, occasionally, get enquiries about hunting. One day Norman rang up and said that two sable bulls had escaped from his new game park and he couldn't get them back in. He knew pretty much where they were, so, before they disappeared completely, he had decided to shoot them. He wanted to know whether I had any clients interested in paying to do this.

I said, "No!" Then, the very next day, I received a call from our Johannesburg office saying two hunters from Texas had just walked into their office wanting to know where they could shoot a sable antelope at short notice. Sable are a much-prized trophy and most professional hunting organisations insist on a minimum hunt of about three weeks if their client wants to shoot one. So when I told the Jo'burg office that I would be able to arrange a short hunt for two sable, they were delighted.

Norman knew full well that if foreign hunters wanted to shoot a sable it would cost them a lot of money because they would have to pay for a full three week hunt, as well as the National Parks fee. He also knew that his two sable were fairly tame and that he could find them very easily and, as these particular hunters were not going to shoot anything else, the hunt would be over very quickly. Norman was keen to utilise the facilities of his newly-opened Sable Lodge and keep the hunters and their families there for as long as possible, so we hatched a plan! We told the hunters that we could probably arrange for them to shoot a couple of sable but that they would have to spend a minimum of three nights at the lodge. We quoted them a price for the two sable, which included accommodation, food, transport and professional hunters' and trophy fees. It turned out that they would both be accompanied by their wives and a couple of teenage children, so the total cost was substantial, but they were more than happy to pay - in advance!

I met them all at Salisbury airport and drove them out to Imire. Norman and Gilly greeted them and gave them an excellent dinner at the lodge. Next morning, they would set out at dawn, with a guide, to try and find the sable. Norman knew exactly where they had been for the past couple of weeks, but had no intention of taking the hunters straight to them. (What would he have done with them for the remaining three days if they had procured their trophies in the first hour?) Morning and afternoon for the next three days, scouts reported tracks of the elusive sable at various distant parts of Imire and Norman would hurry there with the expectant hunters. They would gaze at the tracks of some young cattle and, with eyes to the ground, stealthily creep into some thick bush to emerge disappointed just in time to return to the lodge for another meal. On the third afternoon the charade had to end so Norman took them confidently to the place where he knew the sable were hiding. They weren't there! Panic stations!

Meanwhile, Norman's friend and neighbour, Nigel Thornycroft, knew exactly where the sable were - they had wandered onto his farm. Nigel was fully in the picture as to what Norman was up to but decided to let him sweat it out for a bit!

Technically the sable now belonged to Nigel, as the then law of the country decreed - any wild animal was the property of the owner on whose land it happened to be. Eventually Nigel drove over to Imire (no cell phones in those days) and found a very worried Norman and a couple of angry hunters. "Did you find those sable of yours?" asked Nigel innocently. Then added, "I've got some on my place, which I might be prepared to let you have a go at!"

So, with time running out, the two Texans were driven onto Nigel's farm, Merryhill, and easily dispatched the sable without ever being told that they could have done this within an hour of arriving on Imire. But I am sure they enjoyed their hunt and savoured the final triumph all the more for their prolonged stay!"

Sable bull

Chapter Ten

A LION IN THE GARDEN
Imire ~ Late 1970s

A number of different species of antelope, together with giraffe and hippo, provided a good variety for our tourists but the game park needed some examples of the 'Big Five' to really become an attraction. The 'Big Five' comprises lion, elephant, rhino, buffalo and leopard. Buffalo are carriers of foot-and-mouth disease but a breakthrough, led by our old friend, Dr John Condy, revealed that buffalo calves, still suckling from their mothers, are *not* carriers of the disease. So, when buffalo-culling took place, the calves were spared and sent off to people like ourselves. We received our first seven buffalo calves on Imire in the mid-1970s and reared them on a special diet of milk and cubes - a diet designed by the Government Veterinary Department. As soon as the calves were weaned off the milk we put them into the game park and herded them during the day.

We did have a fright one year when foot-and-mouth spread into the cattle herds of neighbouring farms. The disease had come from Matabeleland, right up through Mashonaland, putting the whole Wedza district at risk. Fortunately the vets had found that by inoculating our cattle against foot-and-mouth we could bring the disease under control. The vaccine was a live vaccine so the animals were actually given a dose of the disease. It sounds crazy but it worked. We experienced the death of few cattle but the survivors were over the problem within a few weeks. Because we had a foot-and-mouth free buffalo herd, National Parks became involved. They didn't want to inoculate the buffalo because then it would affect all the game in the Park. So they brought out miles of chicken wire and put it around the perimeter of Imire to control any game movements. That seemed to work well and our herd survived. There were the odd misdemeanours over the years, of course, and Simon remembers one:

"I remember coming out to play golf in Marandellas and, afterwards, went to visit Mum and Dad at Imire and arrived to hear that the buffalo had gone walkabout. They had gone for miles before we finally found them opposite the Grasslands Research Station. We then had to walk them all the way back to Imire."

Sometimes we couldn't walk the buffalo back, for one reason or another, and had to use tranquillizing drugs to knock them out in order to move them. One such occasion involved Tony Mitchell, our manager at the time, who recalls what happened:

"We had these two big buffalo bulls that disappeared one day and we tracked all over but couldn't find them. All the neighbouring farmers were getting very nervous and tense about these buffalo, because of the chance of spreading disease to their cattle, so we had to find them in a hurry. We looked everywhere, to no avail. The Marandellas vet, Bruce Wells, went up in his aircraft to try and spot them but couldn't see them.

I went out in Norman's yellow Landrover, with his faithful tracker Elijah. All the animals were familiar with this vehicle because it always carried milk bottles, cubes and feed and so, everywhere we went, the animals followed us. Eventually, about 15kms away (or 9kms as the crow flies) we found the two buffalo bulls. Using the familiar 'come, come, come' call, the buffalo started to follow the Landrover, eating up the cubes that Elijah threw out in a little trail behind us. We walked them about 4kms in this manner, cutting fences as we went along, until we came to a derelict farm where there was an old dip-paddock. We lured the two buffalo into a pen, closed up the fence and tipped in a whole 50kg bag of cubes to keep them busy. We raced back to Imire to get Norman and Bruce Wells and arrange for them to dart and take the buffalo home.

The buffalo were darted and loaded into two Landrovers - each animal weighed a good tonne. I was driving one Landrover, with Norman alongside, when suddenly our buffalo gave a hefty kick against Norman's back. He had just finished lighting his pipe, which went flying and there was the usual performance of sparks everywhere and parts of his clothes catching fire! Luckily the buffalo didn't come round and we got them back safely with no other problems."

As with all animals on Imire, we had to monitor the breeding and change the bloodlines regularly to prevent inter-breeding - and the buffalo were no exception. Tony, Gill and I went together one year to try and get some new buffalo breeding bulls and Tony, always one for a good laugh, this time at my expense, remembers it well:

"Norman was a terrible driver, very absent-minded. He would forget to change gear or would just put his foot flat and go, his mind miles away.

We had planned a shopping trip to a ranch in Chiredzi and I was going along to help do the deal for him, because Norman couldn't hear the bidding during the auction. Gill and I knew we were in for a long, long adventurous journey so, when Norman asked me to drive, Gill whispered in relief 'thank goodness for that!'

We went to Wally Herbst's ranch in Chiredzi to buy the new buffalo bulls and there were a number of other buyers, in the same business, who were also there. We mostly all knew each other and got pretty inked up after dinner, which was fine because we were staying in lodges on the ranch. When Gill had had enough and said she was going to bed, I showed her to her lodge with a torch, said goodnight and she asked me to make sure Norman didn't stay too long.

I tried to persuade Norman to go to bed, some time later, but he refused. I joked that someone else might get into bed with his wife if he didn't watch out! Everyone laughed and the conversation continued. A little later, I noticed Norman getting up to leave and I furtively raced ahead to their lodge, knocked on the door and quickly debriefed Gill, who was sitting in bed reading, took off my shoes and jumped under the covers with her. We switched the light off and, the next thing, Norman came in. With a very slurry, tipsy voice he said, 'Hello darling,' switched the light on and saw me.

'What the hell are you doing here?' he demanded in apoplectic rage as we collapsed in laughter and I hurried out of there.

Definitely not the sort of thing you can usually do to your boss!"

We did have a very serious incident concerning a buffalo many years later. John remembers the event which left a man dead:

"We had a terrible tragedy in the early 1980s when we lost an African worker to a buffalo. He was employed to watch and follow the buffalo and, from everything we could find out later, we think he fell asleep under a tree. When he woke up, to see the buffalo herd milling all around him, he panicked and ran and, as a result, was horned."

We compensated the family, of course, but the tragedy reminded everyone, including us, that all the animals on Imire weren't pets but wild animals, which could become dangerous at any given moment; something we tended to forget.

Our buffalo herd prospered and over the years we returned several, as non-carriers of foot-and-mouth disease, to National Parks (as they bred they went back because I only wanted to keep a small herd).

Not long after the buffalo had established themselves, there came an opportunity to acquire young elephants and, naturally, I didn't say no! I tried to get elephants that weren't too big, about sixty inches at the shoulder that could fit into a framework, on the truck, built to hold them. The trick was in not getting the holes between the poles too far apart. I used to quite often take kids with me and they helped a lot in taming down the animals, which was important. Drinking was always a bit of a problem because they weren't used to drinking from a bucket and so you had to teach them. You had to try and get their trunk into the water and then they'd suck like crazy! Once I knew what I was doing, I related in the Wedza Gazette some of the do's and don'ts when it came to transporting elephants:

"Firstly ensure that your elephant is of a reasonable size - large ones could give you problems. Assuming you have arranged for a beast of approximately eighteen months old and fifty-four inches at the shoulder - make sure your supplier has previously caught the animal and contained it - we do not recommend you catching your own.

A gang of about fifteen Africans, strongly built and nifty of foot, plus about three farmers equally gifted with additional experience of all-in wrestling and gymnastics, about a hundred foot of strong two-inch

Buffalo bull

manila rope will be all that is required to catch hold of and load your animals. Other small necessities, almost too obvious to mention, are a first-aid box and blood plasma. Splints, too, should be handy. The catching and loading should not take more than an hour. If it does, something is wrong in either your organisational ability or your health.

The crate on the truck should be sturdily made. Ours was of two-inch piping welded together. We, unfortunately, had not taken the width measurement of the elephant's head, so one of our gaps was a trifle too wide. Because of this, our elephant travelled over six-hundred miles with his head and shoulders and trunk out of the top of the crate, on top of the cab, while trumpeting wildly. This method is not advised, firstly because it is unnerving for oncoming traffic, and secondly, if he had forced his way out we would have had some problems reloading. While travelling, talk to your elephant as he is naturally distraught, but remember to keep your arms away from the inside of the crate as he probably misunderstands your attempts at kindness. Drive slowly and take plenty of refreshment yourself, en route - you'll need it!" (Wedza Gazette 1977)

Nzou, a female, was our first elephant and came to us in 1975. Nzou (Shona for elephant) was a two-year old, already weaned from her mother and we built a separate boma for her near the buffalo. Of course it had thicker poles and was much stronger than our normal structures but Nzou soon felt at home and when she did it became obvious, and economical, for her to be herded with the buffalo - one keeper could look after them all. There wasn't a problem with this and the buffalo seemed to adjust to Nzou. Before we knew it she had adopted them and soon took over as the matriarch of their herd!

From then on until now, thirty-five years later, Nzou stays with the buffalo all the time entirely out of choice and guards them jealously. Does she think she's a buffalo, or vice versa!? Whatever, it is an extraordinary relationship. Over the years she sometimes killed male buffalo calves and, given a chance, older males too. The buffalo cows learnt to calve some distance away but would return after a few weeks and introduce their calves. Nzou accepted the calves when they came back, but she never did like the old bull, for some reason.

My nephew, Howard Matthews remembers me telling him of Nzou's close inspection of new arrivals to the buffalo herd:

"Norman recounted how a buffalo cow left the herd for a couple of weeks to calve down. He watched with fascination as the cow eventually took back her month-old calf to the herd where it was immediately given the full treatment. Nzou's trunk gave the calf a thorough 'check-up'!"

The calf had passed with honours and was accepted by Mum! Nzou's story is always linked continuously with the buffalo. On one occasion a young buffalo was killed in a fight and Murambiwa, our main animal-handler, told us the most amazing story. He saw Nzou break a branch off a tree and walk over to the grave of the buffalo and lay the branch on top. Murambiwa had started out on Imire working with the cattle and then, when I asked if he'd like to come across to work with the buffalo and Nzou, he said yes and what a good choice it turned out to be. Murambiwa was a great character and very good with the buffalo but especially loved Nzou. It wasn't always easy finding the right person for different animals. You had to juggle workers around and find the guys with the best temperament. We had a lot of very good workers, and a lot of very bad ones. I remember once having to sack one member of staff who hit the elephants too severely. I wouldn't have it - that was not how we handled any of the animals. Murambiwa, however, was outstanding. A genuine chap who loved his job and loved the animals that he looked after and was a natural with Nzou.

Murambiwa was once attacked by a buffalo bull and knocked over. He yelled and shouted for help until Nzou rushed up, knocked the buffalo down and waited until dear old Murambiwa staggered to his feet. Nzou walked beside him for half a mile until he was safe and had reached help. Who says animals have no hearts?

Nzou really was the most gentle and loving animal and our god-daughter, Gilly Curtis, who would one day marry Richard Thornycroft, laughs as she tells of her early memories of Imire:

"I remember when I was a teenager, Norman used to bring Nzou to the garden to show her off and he'd get us to lie on the ground and this elephant would step over us."

In retrospect this sounds a bit horrifying but I was always very careful, of course, and very confident of Nzou, who wouldn't hurt anyone.

In later years we brought in other young elephants, but they were always male and Nzou never joined up with them, she just wasn't interested. She spent her days with the buffalo. At lunchtimes she came up the lunch kopje, to the delight of the tourists, and at night she returned to her little boma next to the buffalo. Nzou never mated, never had a calf and, thirty-five years later, still looks after the buffalo.

There was only one not so pleasant encounter between Nzou and a tourist at the lunch kopje. I must admit that I don't remember the details but Simon was there and recalls what happened:

"Nzou came up to the lunch kopje, the way she always did, and sauntered over to see the people. Dad used to give the guests a few cubes to feed to her and it was always a very special encounter. Dad and I were there with a number of tourists and, on this occasion, instead of giving Nzou the cubes, this

Nzou with her beloved buffaloes

Ele and hippo play in the dam

foreign man held out his glass of gin and tonic. Before we could do anything, Nzou very gently took the glass, put it in her mouth and started chewing. Of course the glass shattered in her mouth and Nzou ran away screaming, trumpeting and shaking her head. She stood some 300m away, carefully picking pieces of glass out of her mouth with her trunk. After a little while Nzou came back and, despite the fact that there was a group of about twenty people, she headed straight for the man who'd given her the glass. Nzou knew exactly who he was and Dad shouted at the man to get out the way while he and Murambiwa struggled to keep the tourist out of reach of the very agitated elephant."

Strange relationships between elephants and other animal species weren't only limited to Nzou and buffalo, as we discovered with a small pod of hippo. We'd picked up four hippo from National Parks and had put them in a large dam in the game park. As they grew and matured, the herd bull drove off a younger bull who was forced to another dam nearby. One day the elephant staff reported that something unusual was going on and so, I went to the dam to see what was happening. The elephants, who always went to the water to bathe and drink at midday, were met by the male hippo that had been ousted from the pod. The hippo swam towards them and an elephant bull swam out to meet the hippo. The two played together in the water for some twenty minutes; the elephant even putting his trunk into the open mouth of the hippo! It was an amazing sight and went on regularly until the dam was emptied for irrigation purposes.

The young male elephants that we got formed their own herd and were all part of the family. Everyone loved the elephants and Simon remembers a sight he came across one day, in his late teens:

"I was sent to go and find the elephant handler and found him, eventually, on one of the anthills below the airstrip. He was fast asleep, with his hands behind his head and, on either side of him, there was a little elephant also fast asleep, both with their trunks resting on his chest. I remember feeling incredibly proud that Dad had been able to tame these animals. They were friends, part of the family and you could fool around with them and they interacted with you. They were just magnificent."

The male elephants were named Hondo, Shaka and Zulu and, later on, came Makavusi, (shortened to Mac), Lundi and Toto. They were always friendly, always pleased to see us, and would walk up to the trailer to see the tourists. The elephants were also a great attraction for local dignitaries. We tried very hard to maintain good relations with our communal neighbours. We would invite the local chief, village headman and other community leaders to spend the day on Imire, have lunch and a tour and, of course, feed the elephants. Someone took a lovely photograph of Headman Goto feeding an elephant from his hand at a function on Imire. It's one of those pictures where you can almost feel the gentle tip of the elephant's trunk as it carefully picks up the cubes.

The Imire visitor's book in the mid-1970s recorded a visit from fifteen 'Chiefs of the Mashonaland East Provincial Authority, Seke.' Amongst the signatures are Chiefs Seke, Kunaka, Chiota and Nyakuchena. A few lines further down are visitors from the University of Natal, in Durban, and more from New Zealand, Australia, Scotland and England. Imire was also being looked at by government departments and the visitor's book notes day-trips from the Rhodesian Promotion Council and the Natural Resources Board. How we were growing!

Some time after the elephants had settled in, I heard that a friend, Colin Hensman, had tamed two young elephant and people were riding them. He was involved in game capture and also started training elephants. That's where I first learned about training elephants and I took two of our elephant handlers up to Colin's and left them there to learn the ropes. Hensman taught them the basics and three days later, when I went back, our workers were riding his elephants! Hensman taught us the basics, such as how to get the elephant to sit down so you could get on their backs easily. It was very basic training and, because his elephants were about the same size as ours, we were easily able to use the same techniques.

Staff learnt to ride the elephants from when the animals were quite young and then it was obvious that we could also offer this as a great experience for tourists. At first we made basket chairs, but they weren't very satisfactory. In the end we found it was better to just throw a blanket over the elephant's back and then people would hang on to the handler and go for short rides around the game park. A little later on we were to meet an incredible woman who would train

Headman Goto feeds a young elephant

our elephants to do all sorts of other things, but that is still to come.

A game park that was varied enough to attract visitors, became a reality with the elephants and so, around this time, I began to think about predators too. Lions, leopards and hyenas were a must - appealing to me because I wanted to get to know as much as possible about a whole range of animals. I never intended to let them go into the game park - we were far too small to have predators alongside antelope in a park the size of ours. I had also learned that hand-reared animals were very difficult to release, because they'd lost their fear of humans. It didn't worry me that I would have to keep predators in cages - I knew this was the only way I could handle them. I did, however, endeavour to make the enclosures as big and as natural as possible.

Cassius was our first lion, hand-reared from a very young cub. He started out in a box in the house, was fed on bottles of milk (at all hours, day and night) and was adored by us all. He grew up with the children and they loved him - especially when he jumped on John's back and they would wrestle together, with shouts of 'NO CLAWS!' coming from underneath!

To be more accurate, the children weren't children any more at this stage. Barbara had left home already and was nursing in the UK. John had left school and we had sent him out into the world, firstly to England where reports back were hair-raising to say the least! Then to Canada and America where he did some work on cattle ranches. He came back to Rhodesia a grown man, did his army stint and then came to Imire. We had our tiffs, but also many good times, as he was destined to gradually take over the running of the farm. Judy described him as being 'Norman's spanner boy' in his early days working on the farm! John isn't quite so polite about our years working together:

"Dad was an impossible, impossible boss. With me he was unbelievably difficult and there were a number of times when I nearly packed my bags and left. It was only in the latter part of our relationship that we developed and grew together. Initially, Dad just hammered me twenty-four hours a day but eventually we got to understand each other better; maybe I matured or Dad mellowed."

Richard Thornycroft, John's close friend and our neighbour, is even more blunt:

"Norman was terribly hard on John, particularly when he was a young farmer. Norman was always very critical and gave very little praise. When John finally took over he did very well. I was probably very rude to Norman in those days and was very critical of how he treated John. He just didn't recognise the abilities that John had. It was only when Norman stopped farming that he had time to look back and see the fantastic job his son was doing."

Gilly was the peacemaker, however, and Judy describes how tranquillity was always restored:

"At the end of the day, particularly bad days, when it was all over, Norman would

invite us to go and fish with him. But Gilly was always the peacemaker. She would arrive with a bundle of flowers, biscuits and cheese straws - ever the perfect foil to Norman."

Our third child, Simon, academically brighter than his siblings, had done extremely well at school and went off to an engineering college in the UK. Once he qualified he became involved in building aerodromes, and it would be some time before he came back to the country.

The only youngster still at home, when we were involved with lions and hippos and elephants, was Alastair. Alastair was the baby of the family, adored by everyone and particularly close to his Mum. Gill's sister, Jane, remembers a lovely story, which always made us smile:

"Alastair was always a very hungry little boy and I remember when he was about six, he'd gone to church with the family. When Gilly came back from communion, little Alastair asked in an accusing and clearly audible voice: 'What are you eating?'"

Alastair had started out at Ruzawi prep school, where he did well under the headmaster, Brian Curtis, who was an ex-Ireland rugby player. The Curtis family were great friends of ours. Alastair was mad on sports - cricket and rugby particularly - and had represented Rhodesia in under-19 cricket against South Africa. Gilly and I went down to Pretoria to watch the game and, to our dismay, he was knocked silly by a bouncer. A Travers' skull is fairly solid, so he survived! He did his national service in the RLI but eventually injured his knee doing a parachute jump. On completion of his national service he returned to Imire, but farming was not his line. Alastair loved going on hunting trips with me to the Valley. Hunting and the bush were absolutely his passion; as soon as he could he went into partnership with Bill Bedford, running hunting safaris. Whenever he was home Alastair loved romping with Cassius, long after the lion was no longer a cub.

In-between wrestling with the 'kids', when they were on the farm, Cassius was quite at home in the house! He'd lounge on a blue floral armchair with our little dachshund, Axle, or on a big comfortable sofa on the verandah, or siesta in the breakfast room. We also had another little verandah, with doors into the morning room. Cassius would lie on the couch in there and that became his den. He paid no attention to anyone and would lie, looking through the door, purring loudly and quite obviously blissfully happy.

When Cassius was only some fifteen months old, he disturbed a party we were having in our

Cassius and Axle play on the armchair

A young Cassius

house one evening. He'd gone to sleep on our bed, as was his normal practice, and when he awoke, he strode through to the dining room. People were all dancing merrily away until he strolled in amongst them, to their great shock and surprise. You can imagine the looks of horror as this half-grown lion came rubbing his cold nose against their knees - only being friendly of course! Our Judy had her party dress damaged before she could get Cassius back into the bedroom but the party continued! Judy relates another important detail about the occasion:

"I remember borrowing a beautiful long dress for one of Norman and Gill's Christmas parties and, at three o'clock in the morning, Norman let Cassius out and he came dancing in and tore my dress to shreds! I handed it back in tatters!"

Lions grow up very fast so, by the time he was about six months old, Cassius went into his own enclosure in the garden. I'd let him out for walks and exercise, or for other occasions, or just to play. We had to watch him though. I remember once, when he was nearly an adult, I took him for a walk in the game park and caught him eyeing a couple of young African children; I stopped that experiment immediately. He loved the bush but obviously had good memories of his time growing up in our house. Barbara remembers how Cassius clearly pined to be back:

"Cassius would sit and look longingly at the breakfast room and you could just see him desperate to be back on his chair. He got out once, when no one was at home, went to the breakfast room and shredded all the curtains!"

In or out of the house, Cassius always had first-class treatment; Jane recalls:

"Norman and Gill used to have wonderful lunch-parties and, sometimes, Norman would take handfuls of home-made ice-cream and let Cassius lick it off his hand. Gilly used to say, 'Oh Norman, can't you give him shop-bought ice-cream, why does it have to be the home-made ice-cream?'"

Friend and neighbour, Mark Milbank, was bringing tourists to Imire on day-trips and Cassius was a big hit:

"We took photographic clients to Imire and all loved meeting Norman and listening to his stories. Cassius, the lion, was a major attraction in those days, when he used to wander freely around the garden. Then Maggie, the hippo, would wander up to the Imire house verandah, at sundowner time, and Norman would pour a bottle of beer down her throat - much to the delight of my clients."

Imire and Cassius clearly made an impression on a guest from France on a day-safari, who wrote, in green ink, in the visitor's book:

Real life! And what a big cat!

Guests sometimes found encounters with the rapidly-growing Cassius a little daunting, as journalist Peta Thornycroft wrote:

"There is a large lion at the bottom of Norman Travers' garden. A sign warns: 'Beware of the lion' which is suitably backed up by tawny-maned Cassius.

Cassius is really a very friendly lion, perhaps too friendly. It is an unnerving experience to have him charge at you at full speed and jump on you. The Travers' verandah has had to be barred off because Cassius is a house-lover. And when he grabs your leg between his massive jaws, to chew it playfully, it takes a strong and cool head to know that this king of the jungle isn't after human flesh. I tried very hard to be nonchalant, but there is something odd about being followed around a garden by an enormous lion, however tame he is." (Peta Thornycroft in 'Winter Cricket')

Cassius had a religious encounter when he was in the garden, early one morning, at a time when we had the Anglican Bishop of Mashonaland and his wife staying in the cottage nearby. Bishop Burroughs was an amazing chap, big and tall and he had walked all around the tribal areas on his own in the course of his duties. Not long after breakfast, I heard a yell and looked out to see Cassius running straight for the bishop's wife. The lion jumped on her and knocked her down but, luckily, by then I was only a few steps behind him. "Cassius, get off, get off!" I shouted. He did and, although the bishop's wife was fine and I apologised profusely, she'd had one hell of a shock.

It would be wrong not to mention that there were problems between Cassius and some people, one of whom was Richard Thornycroft, the son of our neighbours who farmed Merryhill. Richard had grown up with, and was a great friend of, our kids but there was a problem with him and Cassius. Simon remembers Richard's visits as times when everyone had to run!

"There were certain people that drove Cassius berserk when they came to the house. For some reason, Cassius hated Richard Thornycroft and, whenever he came round, there would always be a shambles. Someone had to run out with a stick and chase Cassius away. Even when in his cage, if Richard came up to the wire, the lion would try and go for him."

Richard thinks he knows what started the problem with Cassius:

"As teenagers, John and I always played with Cassius when he was a cub, romping around the lawn with him and it was never a problem. In my twenties, however, when Cassius was grown up and living in a cage outside, I came back to the farm with a little border terrier. As soon as

Cassius saw that little dog, his eyes just fixated on the animal and that I knew there was a problem.

After this had happened a few times, Norman said that he thought I shouldn't come round with the dog anymore, and I didn't - or I'd leave it in the car. But, that wasn't really the end of the problem. Cassius had, by then, associated me with the dog and would mock-charge, or run at the fence, when I approached. At first Norman pooh-poohed it but, one day, Cassius started climbing over the wire, actually trying to get over the top, in order to get at me. Norman then agreed that there was a problem and later put a double-wire fence around the lion's enclosure. On another occasion my brother visited Imire and Cassius wasn't happy with him either - obviously the sound of his voice was like mine and so the association extended to him."

Cassius became as sly and devious as any cat when it came to getting out of his enclosure and, before long, we all found ourselves in situations with an escaped lion - especially our workers, who were in the front-line. Initially, the workers were scared but, when they saw that we could handle the lion, they were also fine with him. Some were better at handling cats than others; Mushupec and Mattheus, particularly. Mushupec worked in the garden with Gill and did a fantastic job - it was magnificent and her sister, Jane, always commented on it:

"Gill was a fabulous gardener. Amongst the rocks she made wonderful little walks where she planted daffodils and all sorts of gorgeous colourful flowers. The garden had superb roses and indigenous plants, too."

Because Mushupec was so close at hand in the garden, he often got called on to help with the lions and was fantastic; quite fearless and very good with them.

Mattheus was Gill's right-hand man on the cooking and catering front and, if Cassius escaped, then Mattheus was the one who could get him back in, luring him with meat. Mattheus was the biggest old rogue you've ever met. In fact I think he spent five or six months in jail once because the police found he was growing dagga (marijuana) on his plot. Jane said that Mattheus was so much a part of the family that Gill even visited him in prison and would take him cakes and biscuits! Mattheus had many encounters with the escaped lion, two of which he recounts here, in his own words:

"One time I remember when Mr and Mrs Travers was out and Cassius the lion got out his cage. Mushupec hadn't closed the door properly after he fed him and I saw the lion come round the garden and run into the house and go straight to the morning room. Mushupec came back to the kitchen and I said to him. 'Oh! My uncle, what have you done, Cassius is out.'

Mushupec jump in fright. 'Hah? Ow! Cassius is out? Why? I am sure I am not closing the gate properly. What can I do?'

First we agree 'there is nothing to do' but then I said to Mushupec. 'No, Cassius must get out of house! And if Cassius comes near me, or touch me, or try to taste me, you mustn't play with him. You just kill him, straight! No waiting, no playing. Just kill him straight.'

Mushupec say, 'Alright my uncle!'

I say everyone in the house must get out; no cleaners must be there, just Mushupec and me. Then I went outside and try my best to get Cassius to get out of the house, calling him and calling him and I was going to run and shut the door, but Cassius wouldn't move. Then I tell to Mushupec he must take some meat to the cage and call Cassius. I will stay at the house and when Cassius go outside I will shut the door of the house. Mushupec took some meat and went round the house calling, 'Cassius, Cassius!'

Cassius sat up and was looking and said, 'Oh! Meat!' Cassius start running. I start running. I shut the door of the house. Bang! Straight away! Cassius run to catch the meat. Mushupec throw the meat in the cage. Cassius get the meat and Mushupec close the cage tight, straight away!"

The second encounter, also when I wasn't there, was rather more serious, however nonchalantly Mattheus tells it all these years later:

"Cassius got out and was patrolling round the garden. The problem was Cassius used to like to eat Mrs Travers' bantam chickens, which were closed on the verandah when the lion was out. That day Cassius ran from my side and went straight to the verandah. 'Oh, meat!' Cassius said and tried to catch a chicken.

'No, Cassius!' I shouting at him. 'Don't eat that chicken.'

Cassius come straight at me! Running at me he knock me down and bite me. I got up and hit Cassius once, hard, with a stick and shout. 'Hey, Cassius, no! Get into your cage.' Cassius went to his cage , I close the door and then looking at the place where he bite me. John came and saw what happen and straight away took me to the hospital.

The Doctor say, 'What's wrong? What happened here?' I told him a lion have bitten me so he give me an injection and six stitches and then I went back to the farm and to work. John said I should go home and rest but I told him its only my leg, not my whole body, no problem to work and I went to the kitchen and start cooking!"

Dear old Matt, what a time he had with us people and animals on Imire!

Luckily Simon was around when Cassius escaped, another time, for a trip down memory lane:

"Cassius had a favourite old blanket which he used to get wrapped in and sleep on when he was a cub. He adored this little blanket and would drag it around with him everywhere. Mum and Dad had an old wardrobe in their bedroom and this little lion blanket must have been shoved on top of the wardrobe when Cassius moved into

Cassius and Norman host an Imire open day

131

the garden. The blanket must have slipped down between the wardrobe and the wall and, years later, as a full-grown lion, he escaped one day and managed to get into the bedroom. He must have smelled his baby blanket because he knocked the wardrobe over and picked it up. Getting him out the house, after that, was the usual mission."

When he was about two or three years old, Cassius was mated with a lioness, Cindy, who came to us from Bally Vaughan Sanctuary. We received Cindy as a cub, hand-reared her and she and Cassius successfully reared their own cubs, one of which was Induna, a male, who also became a great character around the place. We extended the lions' enclosure so that it included a small stone hideaway where they could lie out of sight of visitors and passers-by. The lions' cages were about 40m square, had rocks and lots of trees but, because they didn't climb like leopards, we didn't have to close the top off. Generally the lions were 'scaredy-cats' when it came to tree climbing. But Induna learned to climb a Jacaranda tree. He would climb right up and sit on a very high branch where he could look down on us all. However, he wasn't so brave when it came to coming down and would reverse very gingerly, using his claws, all the way to the bottom.

One day, while showing some visitors our lions, I decided to go into the pen with Induna. My rule was 'never turn your back' but when I was asked a question by one of the guests, being deaf (a little!), I broke the rule and turned round. Induna, who was then fully-grown, jumped on my back, landing on top of me. I tried hitting him with my elbows but I think he just laughed at this! Gill was outside, surrounded by guests and didn't know how to help.

"Call Mushupec," I called to her, which she did immediately. Mushupec came running and, as soon as he saw this huge lion on top of me, he started to laugh! Getting into the pen straight away, Mushupec rushed over to where I was underneath the lion.

"Get off the Boss," he said to Induna in an authoritative voice and Induna obeyed, much to my relief!

Bill Bedford happened to be watching this particular event and had a slightly different interpretation of what the lion was really up to. It was a story that did the rounds and, inevitably, became an urban myth, particularly after a few drinks at the local golf club:

"Norman had a large audience of guests, so took it upon himself to get into the enclosure to play with the lion. After a short while Norman made to leave the enclosure and the lion playfully knocked him over. He tried to crawl to the gate but the lion mounted him and he was left on all fours staring at his goggle-eyed guests, none of whom offered to rescue him until the lion had finished his business."

A game park full of animals - hippos, elephants and lions - we had much to keep us busy, and just as much to be proud of, late in the 1970s. Comments from visitors gave humorous recognition to our ever-growing diversity of species. A guest from Bromley wrote: *"WOT, NO YETI?"*

I was never really concerned with making money, provided I made enough to make a project successful, and the game park did just this. The visitors and game drives covered our costs and we were very proud of the fact that we had proven you could run a game park on a commercial farm. Putting the whole idea over to school-children, from a conservation point of view, was terribly important and we started day-trips for school groups. Schools came from all over the area - from Marandellas and Wedza and even from rural government schools. When the African schools came we would send a Shona-speaking guide with them on the game drives and it was a thrill to see their excitement. Many of them had never seen these kinds of animals before, except as pictures in books.

In February 1978, our visitor's book detailed a group of seventeen head masters visiting Imire from farm schools all over the area, including St Anne's, Mount St Mary's, Numwa, Southlawn, Lustleigh and Fair Adventure.

Eventually, we built a bush camp in the game park, which was mainly used by schools and school children. Situated next to Castle Kopje and Numwa Farm, the bush camp overlooked a dam about fifty yards above the Chenyikwa River. There was a lot of thick bush and acacia trees in the area and it was an ideal location for a camp. It was a simple camp with a series of thatched rondavels, which served as accommodation, a separate ablution area and one larger open rondavel, which was the dining and meeting area. We built an open braai under the trees and kept everything as natural as possible. Slabs of stone were used for seating around an open fireplace that was perfect for lunch-time braais and ghost stories at night! In the early days we would take a water cart up to the camp but later we sank a borehole and used a small diesel engine to provide water. Groups of about twenty children at a time would come and stay at the bush camp. They always had a teacher with them and there were walks, rock climbing and even abseiling. We provided a game guide and David Hamilton gave talks on all sorts of subjects, from birds and animals to trees and tracks.

David and Pat provided marvellous support in all our endeavours, not the least of which was the bush camp. David loved sharing his knowledge and enthusiasm with the youngsters. I don't know if he ever told them, or showed them, his little chip of buffalo horn. I don't think David was really a hunter but he enjoyed the bush, the birds and the game. I remember once we were after a buffalo and the whole herd charged us. David opened up and when the dust settled our tracker came back with a broken bit of buffalo horn, which David proudly kept for many years! Another occasion left David

Youngsters abseiling at Imire

with a photograph, rather than a trophy, an event he remembers - although perhaps he doesn't share this one with school-kids around the camp fire either!

"On one hunt with Norman we found a lone elephant bull. 'Your elephant, David,' Norman announced. I took aim, a bit shaky I admit, and then said, 'Norman, I can't,' and put the rifle down. Norman said, 'Okay, cover me while I get as close as I can so you can take a photograph.' He slung his rifle and approached silently to within 10m of the bull. I aimed my camera lens at the second wrinkle on the trunk and my sights were as steady as a rock. Bless Norman for having such confidence in me. The result was an excellent photograph."

A small excursion to the Valley occurred at around this time and was remembered because of my sudden desire to have a dugout canoe. I thought it would add a bit of colour for guests wanting the real African adventure, but it turned out to be a bit of a nightmare, as Simon remembers:

"Dad, Squinks, Gilly Curtis (later Thornycroft) and I and a couple of others went on a hunting camp and Dad bought a dugout canoe from an African on the Zambian side of the Zambezi River. Dad said he wanted an authentic dugout canoe so that tourists could paddle around and do a bit of fishing on the dams at Imire. He paid for the canoe with a bag of old tobacco scrap sweepings, which is what Dad did all his bartering with.

Dad hid the canoe under all the animal skins and equipment in the truck but when we got to Marongora and filled in all the forms, somehow National Parks knew about the boat and said that it was illegal for Dad to have the canoe.

Initially Dad was put in a cell in Sinoia but was released about an hour later and had to appear in the Magistrates Court the following day. He was fined for illegally importing a dugout canoe from Zambia and it was confiscated, ending Dad's desire for a bit of local colour!"

A great favourite in the late 1970s on Imire, for everyone, from school-children staying at the bush camp to foreign tourists going on day-safaris around the game park, was Dudley. Dudley was a baby warthog, which arrived on our doorstep from a long-forgotten place and we took him in and reared him from a piglet. We, of course, started him off in the house, in a box and on a bottle filled with warm milk where feeding was almost on demand, day and night. This turned into slurping from a bowl under the table and, before we knew it, Dudley would eat anything - a bowl of sadza, fruit, vegetables, monkey nuts, you name it! As he got older, he too had to move out of the house and so we built him a little run in the garden and we'd let him out often; he loved playing with the dogs or anyone willing to have a game. Simon remembered a time when we had a little vervet monkey which used to hop on Dudley's back and ride around on top of him. Dudley's fun-loving nature often got him in trouble, particularly with me during the tobacco season, as Simon remembers:

"Dudley's favourite place to lie in the rainy season was on Dad's tobacco bulks where it was nice and warm. He used to burrow in and make a huge mess and destroy stacks of tobacco in the process, much to Dad's extreme annoyance."

From time to time we found ourselves with little orphaned monkeys or baboons on Imire, one of which was reported in the Wedza Gazette, in 1976:

"A troop of some fifty odd baboons in the Numwa area of north Wedza took up residence in Castle Kopje. It must be twenty to thirty years since a troop of this size attempted to settle so far west in the area. Their reception was rather hostile and after ten days of desultory maize-raiding, the survivors packed up and departed. One babe, whose mother came to a sticky end, is now the sole district representative of the troop and has been adopted by the Imire household." (Nigel Thornycroft in 'Winter Cricket')

Baby baboons and monkeys were always great fun but Dudley was a star attraction! The first comment in the visitor's book concerning the fun-loving warthog was in June 1977 from a South African guest:

Adored the farm. Amused by Dudley. Good luck with the baby giraffe!

Dudley really was a lovely animal and would come for walks with us at every possible opportunity or follow Gill around the garden. Like Cassius before him, and all manner of other babies we had hand-reared, Dudley loved being in the house but, naturally, he was banned once he became a fully-grown warthog. There was the inevitable occasion when he escaped and got into the house and the first I knew about it was when I heard Mattheus shouting from the kitchen. I went to see what was wrong and there was Dudley... Mattheus said, "Ah, this pig is *shuparing* me."

In my most commanding voice I said to Dudley, "Get out!" The warthog, of course, ignored me completely, so I gave him a nudge under the jaw with my foot and repeated the command. "Get Out!"

Dudley trotted off indignantly and, when he was gone, Mattheus asked what was wrong with my leg. I looked down and there was blood pouring down my calf. I realised that Dudley had given me a little quick slash from a razor-sharp tusk, which I'd never even felt. I am sure that, if he'd wanted to, Dudley could have done me some serious harm and it reminded me of something that often crossed my mind as we introduced more animals to Imire... The trouble with wild animals is that you develop this wonderful relationship with them, but there's always this fear in the back of your mind, that the animal may attack - not you necessarily, but someone else. Luckily, it was me on the end of Dudley's tusk, and this wasn't so much an attack as an indication of his annoyance!

Dudley the warthog

Chapter Eleven

CHUIE ~ THE THREE LEGGED LEOPARD
Early 1980s

On 8 January 1980 a VIP signed the visitor's book at Imire. Our friend, Lady Mary Soames, wife of the Governor of the country, wrote her address as 'Government House' and her name gave reality to the independence that was shortly to come. In May, barely a month after war-torn Rhodesia became Zimbabwe, other officials began to visit Imire. They included people from the Zimbabwean Senate, the Ministry of Information and the Tourist Board. Our decade-long effort in building up the game park was being recognised and I was delighted to promote it, along with our country. Mark Milbank gave us a lot of publicity, putting Imire on the American map particularly:

"With the advent of independence, my company had changed a bit and we dealt almost exclusively with agents, rather than directly with the client. This meant that the agents, who in our case came exclusively from America, insisted on seeing what they would be offering their clients. They wanted to come to the newly-independent Zimbabwe to see what the attractions were. We therefore arranged for various groups of agents to visit us, to show them the highlights of the country - Vic Falls, Wankie, Kariba, Mana Pools etc... and always included a visit to the thriving Imire. Norman was as always the charming host and did an enormous amount to promote Zimbabwe as a whole and Imire in particular."

Confidence in the country was growing and developments, long on the back burner, began to take shape. A number of farmers were interested in buying game and starting their own game parks. Mike and Di Bartlett, who had opened up a farm bordering the Wedza communal lands, became

interested in game. Mike was a successful farmer and started up a little game park on his farm - although more for his own interest than for tourists. People soon discovered that a lot of capital had to be invested beforehand - what with game fences, bomas, purchase of animals, transport costs, feeding costs and so on. One needed a friendly bank manager, as well as the ability to grow successful crops of tobacco and maize! Sometimes our efforts at new ventures were frustrated by bureaucracy, greed and jealousy in our new government. A case in point was the project we conceived for Wedza Mountain.

You can see Wedza Mountain from Marondera (Marandellas), if you look from the right place. From the top of the mountain, on a clear day, you can see Birchenough Bridge, which is at least 220kms away. I don't think I've ever seen that myself, maybe I was never there on a clear day! Wedza Mountain, physically, is an upheaval from millions of years ago and is linked geologically with Birchenough Bridge, Beitbridge and a mining area up near Mutoko. There was originally a gold mine on Wedza Mountain and, when it came to an end, was taken over by a man called Jock Cummings. He then mined Scheelite, a tungsten ore, used for light bulb filaments, among other things.

Wedza Mountain contains a conglomerate of minerals and there is even talk of chrome being there, but not in workable quantities. The goldmine is still there but I would be a bit leery of going into it - you might meet a leopard, or the roof could fall in on you. My memories of it date back to when I first started with Frank Scott and we'd go on picnics with Mrs Anne Scorror. It was a lovely spot and, if you could get to the peak, the views were magnificent. The bush used to be quite thick and there were plenty of baboons. If you were lucky, you might see a leopard or kudu.

In 1981 David Hamilton, Mike Bartlett and I went to Wedza Mountain with some members of the Natural Resources Board and the Conservation Council. I had placed an idea before the local Wedza DA (District Administrator), suggesting that we raise money to turn the mountain into a proper conservation area. I said I was sure we could raise the money to do the fencing, which would be a big outlay. Then, through my connections with National Parks and others, and with some animals from Imire, we could stock Wedza Mountain with game and develop it as a tourist area, for the benefit of locals. At that time there were a lot people living right at the base of the mountain, including my dear old cook Mattheus. I suggested we organise the fence in

Wedza Mountain

such a way as to allow the project to work as it did on Imire. At night the cattle would be kraaled, which they were anyway (because of the leopards), and in the day they would be released to graze on the mountain with the game. There was a lot of enthusiasm and everyone said it was a good idea and we should get on with it. The planning chugged along for a while and we had hopeful nudges from overseas about finance but nothing happened, at an official level, for several months. Finally I went to the DA to find out what was happening and he said that he'd put the idea to the local council at Wedza. The council themselves, said they liked the plan but they weren't happy with the placement of the fence right at the base of the mountain. They said they would rather move all the people and put the fence a few hundred metres further into the flat land. This meant the people would lose all their maize fields and arable land at the base of the mountain. The council thought there were about a thousand people living at the foot of the mountain, well over a hundred families, and the best thing would be to move them. I thought that was crazy and asked where they would move all the people to. They didn't have an answer to that but said the government would have to be consulted and *they* would move the people. At that point I knew it had all gone wrong. The whole concept of benefit for local communities was lost.

Wedza Mountain Resort would have been wonderful and made Imire look stupid. People would've flocked there. With management by National Parks, a couple of lodges, the wildlife and natural beauty - the whole district would have benefited. Shamefully, it was not to be. The council wanted control of the entire project. Their idea was to get rid of the local people so that the council could have it all. It was pure greed and, soon after, the whole proposal collapsed and nothing more was done.

Another project, which fell apart at this time, was that of having game in the Wedza ICA (Intensive Conservation Area). In the mid-1970s, when we first started holding wildlife field days and encouraging farmers to stock game animals on their land, the Wedza ICA decided to get involved. I think we might have given them a bit of a prod and said, "Look! Why don't you try this? It might even take hold in other areas."

They had a bit of cash available and, in those days, impala and other small game were very cheap - $5 each! Nigel Thornycroft relates how impala, from Mana Pools, were introduced into the Wedza ICA:

"Finally the date for catching was fixed. Gerry von Memerty and Richard Bedford went down by car, as escorts and general trouble-shooters. We had hoped to get about one hundred and fifty but in fact ninety-seven were loaded. An interesting point of the journey was that, after every two hours driving, they had to stop for quarter of an hour to allow the impala to urinate, which they will not do if in motion. If not, it would result in burst bladders.

When they arrived food was the immediate and vital issue. Branches from any available leaf-bearing tree were strung around the boma. Bamboo, hay, love grass, a munga mixture, greenish tips of Napier fodder, fallen acacia beans, 15% dairy cubes and a block of salt was the menu offered. Water was supplied from a half tractor tyre buried to ground level and fed by hose from a drum outside.

The most delightful thing about these impala is the unbelievably short time they took to recover their nerve. Within forty-eight hours of arrival, I could sit on the ground in the boma with them, talk to them and have them unconcernedly nibbling food within five yards of me." (Winter Cricket)

The impala were released from the bomas to roam freely and, mostly, they stayed together in a small herd. Within a short time we started getting reports of new-born impala being seen. The animals bred well and spread rapidly but, without game-fencing, it was tricky. This was before independence when the area was still virgin bush. However, after 1980, things changed when poaching started and there was a general ecological deterioration. Without game-fencing the ICA idea of free-roaming game was just too difficult to control - the animals moved on when the grass dried off, or there was a fire. You can't farm game this way and unfortunately, although the idea was sound and it encouraged people to think along the lines of game preservation, practically it was not sustainable. But at least it achieved the objective of making people think more in terms of conservation and utilisation. Before this, quite a few farmers would see a kudu, or the like, and go and shoot it for biltong. To me, the objective of having game wasn't to have a herd just to look at but to be able to utilise the animals. It's a matter of seeing what the environment can take and, with the money you make, you then either buy different species of animals, or new bulls or simply sell the surplus.

In 1981, I celebrated my sixtieth birthday and, of course, Gilly put on a fantastic spread and did me proud. As always there was a party and a wonderful dinner and, later, there were games. I was amazed, many years afterwards, to read a book by Phil Gray, a friend of Nigel Thornycroft, who wrote about that very evening:

"We were called to supper at Imire for the occasion of Norman Travers' sixtieth birthday; it was a 'black tie' affair and there were several other guests. The ladies were escorted in until there were sixteen of us seated at the table in a room hung with magnificent skins of zebra, sable, kudu and the like. A massive elephant tusk ornamented one end of the room with buffalo heads along the porch.

Towards the end of the evening came the 'one for the road' game, where everyone joined one of two teams to collect items on a list drawn up by the host. The winner would be the first team to gather all the listed items. The list, from what I remember, included a left-hand silk stocking, a hair from the elephants' tail, a bristle from a bush pig, a pair of silk panties, a hair from Cassius (lion), a tick from Chuie (leopard), etc... Everyone dashed out into the darkness of the garden. Barbie Travers went to Cassius' enclosure and this great fully-grown, thickly-maned African lion, who had known Barbie since she was a child, ambled over and rubbed along the chain-link fence purring like an old tomcat. This purr, however, sounded more like a pneumatic drill. I stroked his back and stole some of his hair as he passed but I made sure I was on the other side of the wire. The drink wasn't that strong!" (A Fenman in Africa)

Not long after this the reality of lions that purred like tomcats was bought home to my birthday guest Phil Gray and, really, to all of us. We heard of a very close encounter that Gerry von Memerty had with a wild lion whilst on a trip to Marongora with Nigel and Corona Thornycroft, and a couple of other friends. Phil Gray included the account in his book, in the form of a letter he'd received from Nigel:

"The tragedy came last Saturday. I was woken at 5.00am by a voice calling. 'Nigel, Gerry has been badly bitten.' I went over - he was sleeping twenty yards away - to find him still conscious but with half his face torn away - slight exaggeration - cheek bone laid bare, one eyelid hanging across his nose, the bridge of which appeared to be missing and a bone-deep cut clear across his forehead and, more or less, lying in a deep pool of blood.

We wrapped him in blankets and put him into the back of a truck and off we drove for the four hour trip to Kariba, where we found a doctor and nurse who sedated him and generally tidied him up before he was dispatched, by ambulance, to Salisbury three hundred and fifty miles away.

The doctor there did a truly remarkable job of sewing him up - sixty-six stitches worth! Of course, we all thought - hyaena - so did the Parks blokes at Marongora, but dawn told a different tale. Definite lion tracks through the camp and you could see where the animal had turned off towards Gerry's bed…" (A Fenman in Africa)

In the early 1980s, despite increased poaching, I was still interested in getting more species of game onto Imire. Next in line were nyala - a species seldom heard of in Zimbabwe. I'd visited a nephew of mine, who was managing a sugar farm in Malawi. They were also running a small game park and supplying meat for the local labour force. The animal they were using was nyala. At that time nyala was a rare animal in Zimbabwe, thought to have only been found near the south-eastern border of the country, with none in the Mana Pools area.

I can remember once, years ago, being on a hunt with Gerry in the Mana Pools area and we were after kudu. Nyala are similar to kudu at a glance but, on closer inspection, are smaller, the males being much hairier and they have two or three distinct white spots on their cheeks. We were stalking through the bush and suddenly there were a couple of buck in front of us. I lifted my rifle but Gerry said, "No, wait! Those are nyala!"

Gerry knew nyala from when he'd been in Moçambique and knew how rare they were in Zimbabwe. Anyway we reported the sighting to National Parks but they just derided us, saying: "Nonsense, you guys don't know the difference between kudu and nyala!"

Funnily enough, six months later, Parks suddenly announced they'd found a herd of nyala at Mana Pools!

The nyala became John's project, as he explains:

"I exchanged a couple of zebra and giraffe for twenty-one nyala. Brought them back, fenced off a little paddock of about a hundred acres around Castle Kopje and they were very successful."

Being browsers, we had specifically fenced off that area just for them because of the thick bush and abundance of desirable foliage. They were pretty shy but all survived and bred well, although at first, not as well as we'd hoped. After a while, a couple of kudu jumped into what had became known as 'Nyala Park', stayed there and also bred, which caused some concern. I was worried that the kudu, being taller, would compete better for the browsing and not leave enough for the nyala. Gill and I had a lookout spot right near the nyala fence where we'd go and sit and have sundowners in the evening. Often I'd put cubes down and we'd watch the nyala and, sometimes, the kudu come down and feed - a wonderful sight.

As time went by it wasn't only poaching that caused a problem for the nyala, but also python, as John found out:

"The nyala are very easy to poach and lately we've had a massive influx of python which has decimated the nyala even more - their babies being taken by the snakes. I think this influx is because all the commercial farmers have gone and everything has been poached, from rabbits to duikers and steenbuck and now there's nothing left. So the python have come onto Imire because of the food supply. On game drives we did with Dad on Imire, in the past, we've seen impala with their back legs sticking out of a python's mouth but now it's become a very regular occurrence, with sightings once or twice every year. Of course we can't kill these python because they are royal game, so we catch them if we can, and move them further away but I'm pretty sure they come straight back!"

A few months after independence in April 1980, to our great joy, John married Judy, the daughter of our long-time friends Pat and David Hamilton. Judy clearly remembers their first home at Sable Lodge on Imire:

"John and I were married in August 1980 and we were living in one single rondavel, which John had built for us at Sable Lodge. This was not only our bedroom but also the place where we looked after and cared for all sorts of little hand-reared and orphaned animals, including the blue duiker and bushbuck that started out in Gilly's garden."

John remembers one incident with the bushbuck that could so easily have ended in disaster:

"We had the pair of blue duiker and a bushbuck in a pen at Sable Lodge for the guests to be able to look at and I'll never forget what happened when we had a sales rep visiting us. His name was Chris Falconberg and, for some reason, the bushbuck literally took a running leap, head down and ran full-speed into the fence.

Nyala

I'll never know how Chris didn't get hurt because the bushbuck hit the fence, horns out, at exactly the place where Chris was standing.

The blue duiker also had needle-sharp horns and were more than capable of standing up for themselves. One occasion, when a blue duiker and bushbuck had a fight, we were all amazed when the tiny duiker, with one inch long horns, slashed the bushbuck (which stood about four foot tall) and come out the victor. The blue duiker did breed and have babies, which were tiny, the size of rats, but one day they all got out and we never saw them again."

A much friendlier little animal was the klipspringer and this fascinating little antelope became a great favourite. It bears mentioning that these little animals, which stand about two feet tall, have amazing hair that almost resembles quills. The experts say:

"The hairs are hollow, flattened and spiny; a unique feature among African antelope. They are springy in texture and adhere very loosely to the skin. In days gone by this hair was prized as a stuffing for saddles." (RHN Smithers)

Klipspringers are usually found around the Bulawayo and Matabeleland area but we'd seen them up on the boulders and in the kopjes around Wedza, so John and Judy's little animal wasn't in unfamiliar territory, although they weren't sure where it originally came from. John remembers what a wonderful little pet it was:

"Someone gave us a klipspringer that used to live in our house and jump from chair to chair and onto the bar counter to eat peanuts. It was the most wonderful pet and in the evenings, whilst sitting outside around the fire with clients, the klipspringer would jump over the fire and nuzzle up to us."

There were always many little, and not so little, animals around Sable Lodge, which Judy remembers fondly and with many smiles:

"'The Menagerie' or 'The Gang' as we called them, consisted of all sorts of found or orphaned animals which were all hand-reared at roughly the same time.

At one time 'The Gang' consisted of an eland called Albert, three buffalo, an impala called Bumble, a monkey, klipspringer, wild pig and an ostrich called Harriet. All these animals came with us for walks in the evenings making the most incredible gathering! At breakfast, Harriet the ostrich used to stretch her neck over your head and literally take the scrambled egg or porridge off your plate and was an absolute menace!"

There was even a giraffe once, a baby that had been born on Imire but had a problem. John and Judy took it in but, sadly, it only lasted a month. When John did a post-mortem he found that the giraffe had a hole in its heart.

As the situation in our newly-independent country stabilised, Imire went from strength to strength and soon we had a great system going, as Judy explains:

"In the Lodge itself Gilly was running the food and John and I would help Norman take the clients out on day-trips. Cooking was often done at the main house on Imire, put in the back of a dusty old truck and brought to the lodge. Gilly and Norman

always entertained the clients with the most fantastic service. The food was always five-star, Gilly was always immaculately turned out and the clients just loved her personal attention. Then Norman would waft in with his pipe, looking scruffy as he always did and he'd entertain the clients, offer wine and drinks and tell stories of animals and all sorts of other adventures. They were a wonderful combination."

Closer to home I started with more cats on Imire, this time leopards. Chuie was our first leopard and came to us when she was a cub, in 1981. Like other babies before her, Chuie started off in a box in the house, was bottle-fed day and night and the dark brown, fluffy little cat was adored by everyone. She was a wonderful pet, very playful but with very sharp claws, which we kept short with nail clippers. She wasn't a fussy eater and ate everything from insects to eggs, lizards and small rodents. Later on she supplemented this diet with great big chunks of game meat. The command 'No Claws!' was used again (as it had been with the lions) and was thankfully obeyed, both when she was a cub and an adult. She loved company and she and our dogs were great friends, often playing together, once being caught on camera by a Herald photographer alongside one of the dogs in the garden on Imire. When she became too big for the house Chuie, like others before her, was moved out to her own enclosure.

Later I was given a male leopard from a chap in Moçambique, who had to shut down because of the war. Because I wanted a mate for Chuie, I took Ingwe (Ndebele for leopard) on. Ingwe wasn't a cub when he came to us but was a youngster and had been kept in a cage. I had found that it was very difficult to form a relationship with animals someone else had reared - and Ingwe was a classic case. He was a nasty-tempered leopard and I never could tame him and so we agreed to disagree!

We built enclosures for the leopards, making them as attractive and natural as possible, with lots of hiding places. They had a big rock formation with overhangs and boulders in an area of about 25m by 15m. There were trees all around and the 7m fence meant the leopards had plenty of climbing space.

Chuie and one of the dogs photographed by The Herald

Some years later Chuie and Ingwe had a terrible fight one morning. After we'd forced Ingwe into his pen, I phoned Bruce Wells, our local vet, who came straight out. Chuie was in a very bad way and Bruce said there were only two options. One was to put Chuie down and the other to amputate her badly wounded leg. I chose the second option and, after giving her a tranquilliser and with the help of Mattheus and Tony, who was the manager at the time, we put Chuie on the kitchen table and Bruce took off her right front leg. He then bandaged it up and I sat with her until sundown.

The next morning, to our horror, we saw that during the night, Chuie had bitten off most of the bandages. Out came Bruce once more and, having tranquillized her again, he cut off the rest of the bandages. It was a very large injury, the size of a dessert plate, but we decided no more bandages. I spent as much time as I could, over the following few weeks, sitting with Chuie while she licked the huge amputation clean. It slowly healed over, with hardly a scar. Eventually she recovered and became a lively, healthy, three-legged leopard who adapted incredibly quickly to her new circumstances.

In those weeks I developed a very special relationship with Chuie. She was a very gentle and loving cat; so trusting and good-tempered - despite the fight and subsequent loss of her leg. Chuie gave us not only anxiety but also great pleasure. Barbara comments on the relationship that built up between the leopard and myself:

"Chuie was the most wonderful leopard and she absolutely adored Dad - and he, her. To me, the relationship he had with the leopard is the epitome of everything that is Dad. Dad's lonely time, when he wanted to be by himself, was spent with the animals and, particularly, with Chuie."

After seeing how Chuie healed, and from that time on, whenever I was scratched or bitten, instead of the usual anti-tetanus and rabies injections from doctors, I would let the leopards lick my wounds and they always healed quickly. I suppose doctors wouldn't approve, but it worked! While on the subject of primitive cures, here's one I tried on the advice of an old friend, Ethel Connolly. Use your own (important, this!) urine on skin cancer. I started this treatment when I was eighty-five years old and it works! Gilly, also, had a nasty blotch on her nose - she tried the cure and succeeded in removing it!

Chuie and Ingwe, despite the fight, went on to produce two cubs, Lulu and William, who we reared successfully and both went on to become great characters on Imire. Chuie's son was a lovely leopard and I got on very well with him. I used to sit in his cage and stroke and play with him and often have my gin and tonic with him at the end of the day. Like others before him William became an expert escape-artist and kept us on our toes.

He escaped from his enclosure once when I wasn't immediately around, so the staff called my assistant. He came at the run carrying a shotgun. By the time I arrived William was wandering around the garden. "Put that gun away," I told my assistant. "That's not the way to handle William. Leave this to me, I'll go and talk to him."

The leopard went towards the fence, found a hole in the bottom and headed straight for the workers compound. There was no time to run for the gate so I crawled through the hole after him, calling urgently for him to stop. At last, thankfully, William heeded my calls. He stopped, turned round, glanced my way and then, reluctantly, slid back under the fence and headed for home. We followed and lured him, finally, into his enclosure with a lump of meat.

Mattheus was, of course, involved in getting William back into his enclosure. However, in his old age, as memories grow dim, he remembers what I think is the same story but is a very different version of it, although I confess my memory is equally vague! This is how Mattheus remembers it, in his own words:

"We got big trouble another day when we saw the leopard was out. Madala call to me: 'Mattheus! Mattheus! Leopard is out!'

I said: 'Leopard is out?'

He say: 'Sure!'

I went there to see, and John was there and Madala (Shona term for old man, referring to Norman) say: 'I will stand guard, Mattheus. You and John come slowly, slowly. One, two, one two, from behind. We see if we can get the leopard back to cage.'

I run everywhere, looking for something like a stick and Madala said we must be very careful and quiet and, if anything go wrong, he will kill him straight away. So, Madala calling the leopard and John and I move slowly, slowly. Bichana, bichana. One, one, two, two, but the leopard don't want to come back to cage.

John say: 'We must fight the leopard, or shoot him.'

But I said: 'No, no, let me run to the farm and get mbudzi (goat).'

John say: 'No, Mattheus. It's too late.'

I say: 'Wait, let me get a tsuro (rabbit), wait, wait.' I run very fast to the cage, got one rabbit and run back. I throw the rabbit straight in the leopard's cage.

The leopard come, look and say: 'Oh! Rabbit meat here!' And he run in, straight! I close door, straight!

Madala said: 'Oh, Mattheus. Very well done!' and everyone laughs."

Dear old Matt. I think he's muddled up because we've never kept goats or rabbits, but he was involved in so many rescues that have been the source of many stories around the fire in the compound - and they have been embellished in their re-telling!

Chuie's daughter, Lulu, was also the most wonderful leopard and a great favourite with guests. Particularly younger ones, who wrote various comments in our visitor's book:

I liked playing with Lulu who was very playful.

And perhaps when her claws were out: *Lulu was painful!*

Simon also had an affinity for the leopards, especially Chuie and her daughter:

Gill takes Ingwe, Chuie and the dog for a walk

145

"Chuie was always my mate and I often went into the enclosure with her. Even after she lost her leg we were still big mates and got on very well. Chuie had produced two litters but none of the babies survived, as the male always used to eat them. Dad decided he was going to take a cub away and so, when her daughter Lulu was born, she was raised in the house and garden until she was a year or eighteen months old. It was always Mum that did most of the feeding every three or four hours, day and night. Dad organised it all but Mum did the majority of the feeding with all the baby animals. But she didn't approve of the animals in the bed - she was far too prim and proper. Mum used to complain about the mess and the torn sheets and the like but Dad just loved it. The leopards, particularly, used to drive Mum mad because they'd chew the blankets, rip the sheets, climb up the curtains!"

Despite the leopard's beguiling spots, our lions weren't forgotten and continued to draw comments from guests:

The lion has terrible indigestion!

Cassius is terrific.

And, in amongst the page after page of compliments and praise-singers, were the people who were just never happy. Like this man from Baines Avenue in Harare:

Tea too strong. Lots of bone in the chicken. Orange juice weak, otherwise excellent!

Despite our refreshments, apparently, being too strong or too weak and our food too bony, visitors streamed into Imire. These included many guests from diplomatic missions. The British High Commission; GDR Embassy; Swedish Embassy and Foreign and Commonwealth Office. We had a number of guests from BMATT (British Military Attachment) who were in the country to help train the newly-integrated armed forces and we also started getting more media attention, with visits from BBC TV and Radio. The efforts of Mark Milbank's Abercrombie and Kent agent tours bore fruit as many Americans signed our visitor's book in the early 1980s. They came from Texas, Chicago, Miami, Illinois, New York, Rhode Island, Wyoming and elsewhere and their comments were glowing:

Wonderful… terrific… superb… beautiful… fantastic!

We were obviously getting things right and diversified a little more. I secured a pair of young cheetah, from someone in the lowveld, built enclosures for them similar to those for the lions and leopards - with plenty of room, trees, rocks and hiding places. Unfortunately, they never did very well. I'd hoped that they would breed but they never did. They weren't terribly tame and obviously weren't used to being handled. Cheetahs have a relatively short life-span, usually only living to be about twelve. It was only years later I found out that the male and female cheetahs should be kept in separate cages, next to each other, and only be put together for mating when the female comes on heat.

With hyaena I did better. In 1981 we received a baby spotted hyaena, that we named Beri (adapted from the Shona *bere*, for hyaena), and reared her from a cub. She started off in the house, sleeping in a box in our bedroom at night. We fed her milk from a bottle and she settled down very well and, like our other hand-reared animals, when she grew a little too big for the house she went into a pen of her own in the garden. Beri was quite delightful and would walk around the garden with Gill and rub herself against our legs. She loved to splash and bathe in a water feature in our garden and was always very friendly, playing with both us and the dogs and, sometimes, with rather nervous visitors!

Later on, I suppose, I was the only one that really felt comfortable with the hyaena. There was a relationship between Beri and I that no one else seemed to have, as Simon recognises:

"The hyaena was a baby in the house and brought up with the family and our two golden labs. When it got older things changed: the hyaena would come up and, although it wouldn't bite us, it really was Dad's animal. No one else could ever really control Beri. It only ever listened to Dad, it would only tolerate us and I remember being frightened of it."

When Beri was mature, Gill had an encounter with her one day, as she drove up to the house in the car. I was playing with Beri in the garden and, for some unknown reason, had a nervous feeling and called out to Gill to stay in the car. Gill naturally saw nothing wrong so she got out of the car. In a flash Beri ran to her and bit her badly in the leg, actually cracking the bone. I rushed up, hauled Beri off and immediately took Gill to hospital. This was another lesson learned the hard way. Beri was a female and as we should have known, hyaena packs are led by females who are known to kill other dominant females in the pack. Beri was jealous of Gilly and showed her!

Gill was, as always, totally uncomplaining. Her sister describes this as a typical reaction:

"Gill reared whatever it was Norman brought in. Lions, leopards, otters, hyaenas - and she was bitten by them all. Once, when the leopard got out, she and Norman slept outside under a rock, waiting to try and lure the leopard back if it returned to its cage for food. Gill just slotted in without any problem, she loved animals so it all worked extremely well. She was always totally selfless, sometimes even

Jeff Keightley, Beri, Gill and Norman

too much so, but she had given her life to Norman 100% and they were totally devoted to each other."

Our growing number of carnivores had special needs, one of which was a steady supply of meat, and so we built a cold-room. We would cull an impala or wildebeest and the meat was hung in the cold-room before it was used - in lunches for tourists on day-safaris and for dinner guests staying at Sable Lodge, as well as to feed the carnivores. There was always meat on hand and, in the event of an emergency (such as an escaped animal), this could be provided quickly to lure an animal back in. We were feeding meat to lions, leopards, cheetahs, hyaenas, crocodiles and even to birds of prey later on. I always had a bag of bonemeal and would sprinkle a handful of this on top of the meat and rub it in. The bonemeal didn't worry the carnivores and helped keep their nutrients on track, particularly calcium. I wasn't a believer in live prey so we always tried to make sure the meat had bones with it, so they had something to chew on. We'd feed some of the carnivores every day and others every second day and, because they were in cages and totally dependent on us, we kept them on a regular diet.

Occasionally, if a carnivore developed an abscess, we would have to inject it with a shot of penicillin to clear up the infection. Sometimes we would do this ourselves, after a chat with a vet, but mostly we could handle the animals without too much trouble. It wasn't an easy job, as they didn't like the needle, so bribes and distractions were necessary. There weren't any guidelines to go by and we had to learn by experience. I used to talk to various people, who were also rearing carnivores, and get tips and ideas from them about food, diet, exercise and so on. From time to time, we'd meet and exchange notes on what to do and what not to do. It wasn't always that easy, though, as some people preferred not to share their knowledge. This is something I later told author Keith Meadows about, when he was looking at our successes and failures on Imire:

"One of the main problems, with us whites, is that we are too many individualists, all pulling in different directions. We've never consolidated. Though I was never a supporter of his party, or him, the only time we've ever pulled together was under Smith."
(Sometimes when it Rains)

We did make mistakes along the way and didn't seem to get it right with some species. Sometimes I looked for carnivores that I wanted, like a lion cub, or a female lion for mating, but many others just arrived, unasked for, in boxes. We had a pair of honey badgers for a little while, which came to us half-grown and I put them in a small enclosure that had a little pool in it. It didn't work out, in any case, as I could never tame them. Sadly, their time on Imire was short-lived as, one day, a swarm of bees attacked and killed them both. When we had the honey badgers (and other animals) in small cages I felt I was going down the wrong path. I don't think tourists want to see animals in small cages and so, when some animal or other died, I didn't replace them. Without a doubt our experiences in handling wild animals - lion, elephant, leopard, hyaena - led, more and more, to my greater respect for them and fuelled my desire to try and conserve them for future generations.

However, looking back on those days, I don't regret having the carnivores in their larger cages. Those lovely animals taught me an awful lot. One of the most important things I learnt was that if you can get in cahoots with a wild animal, you're winning! You've started a relationship, which will go on for both of your lives. It's a wonderful feeling to have that relationship. It helps you in your life and with the outlook on your surroundings and, hopefully, it helps the animal too.

The elephants continued to teach and amaze us every day and Judy remembers a couple of fascinating incidents concerning Nzou. One episode involves her and three other baby elephant, which we had at the time:

"We had three new little elephant calves, which came from Gonarezhou, and we had them in a boma while they calmed down. Nzou absolutely loved these little babies and actually started lactating for them. Then suddenly, one of the babies died and when we did a post-mortem we found that it had, literally, been bashed and battered to death.

We gave Nzou a second baby to look after and, one wintery day, it suddenly grew very ill. The Marondera vet, Bruce Wells, came out and put saline drips into the ears of the baby elephant, to try and get some fluid into the animal and rehydrate it.

The next day we were still trying to decide whether to put the baby in the sun, to get warm, or in the shade, to stop further dehydration, when suddenly Nzou came charging at us, sending us all flying. We watched in disbelief as she pulled all the drips out of the baby's ears and proceeded to urinate all over the little creature - absolutely amazing!"

Another story, equally unbelievable but absolutely true, concerned Nzou and the death of a neighbour, Bill Swanson on Markwe farm. Bill had been a native commissioner, in his earlier days, and one of his duties had been animal control. When he retired from the service he turned to farming and became our neighbour. Judy takes up the story:

"There was an incredible incident that concerned Nzou, one other elephant and neighbour, Bill Swanson. Bill had been involved in conservation in the Gokwe area and, over the years, had shot many elephants - a huge number, without doubt. He ended up with Alzheimer's disease and, when he died on his farm, was buried beneath a jacaranda tree. Our elephants had never had anything to do with the Swansons. They'd never seen them, or come in contact with Bill, but, when he died, something very, very strange happened. Until that time our elephants had never, ever broken out of the Imire game fence but, the night after Bill Swanson was buried, Nzou and another elephant broke out. Trampling fences as they went, they broke through the Swanson's security fence, went over to where Bill had just been buried and proceeded to stomp all over his grave. It was the most unbelievable behaviour - extraordinary and something we could never explain."

Less than a decade after we'd started introducing game onto the farm, Imire had grown into a major under-taking. Visitors were coming every day, Sable Lodge was proving more and more popular for overnight guests and John and Judy were working with us full time. They did a wonderful job managing the game park from 1978 to 1982 and there was plenty of work to keep us all busy. We had a short period when a chap called Bruce Thackwell came to work in the game park, but he didn't stay very long. Some of our assistants settled in quickly and happily - but I know I was a hard task master - so others left quite rapidly! Keeping staff happy was always very important and, at around this time, we added a small butchery to the facilities available for our workers.

Over twenty years before, around 1961, we had started out in this direction when we decided that we wanted a store for our workers and had erected a building near the main road. Aside from providing a service for them, we hoped to also attract some passing trade, and turn a profit. We started out trading as a branch of the very successful Bath Stores, which were run by Peter Hudson, who owned Bath farm.

Bath Stores sold everything from postage stamps to flea powder, from wine to de-worming powders and healing oil. Peter Hudson even put out a circular every month or so, which went to customers and farms all over the district. In Circular No 42 dated 20 October 1962, he wrote:

"Bottle Store - We are gradually enlarging our stocks. Apart from some stuff called Don Juan Old Brown Sherry, which looks like brake fluid and tastes like floor polish, we stock nothing that the writer could not drink himself. We have so far three white whines - la Gratitude 8s 6d per bottle, Lanzerac 7s 9d and Grunberg Stein, which is cheap at 12s 6d. We also have the highly recommended Cherry Heering (put it in the fridge at 5.00pm and serve half a sherry glass to your guests after dinner - dee-licious)."
(Winter Cricket)

Peter Hudson ran the Imire Store for a long time, and very successfully too, but eventually we went on our own and stocked basics like tinned fish and beans, mealie meal and kapenta (a dried Kariba sardine). Bread was delivered by Proton Bakery. We'd to get a bulk-delivery of twenty or forty gallons of Chibuku beer and this was dispensed to people who brought their own containers. In the early 1980s we built the butchery next to the store, where we sold our own meat - beef and, occasionally, game meat. Usually the game meat was kept for the guests at the lodge, but any surplus went to the butchery.

Despite my desire to have as many animal species as possible, for guests to see when they came to Imire, it didn't run to snakes! That's not to say we didn't have our fair share of snake encounters. I discovered a little walk, along the north-west side of our lunch kopje, where there was a little over-hang and found a female python living on a ledge below it. I knew she was a female because of her colouring and size. The females are always fat and big and slate-coloured whilst the males are thinner and have a smaller head and much brighter markings. Guests were enthralled at the chance to see a snake so close up and, one day when we went there, we had a real treat. The female python wasn't on the ledge but was, instead, in a groove in the rock - and she wasn't alone! There were a lot of other pythons also there, all tangled up in a ball. There must have been six or seven males all squirming around on top of the female. What a rare sight this was. Some time later she just disappeared and was never seen again.

I'd seen a mass of pythons once before, many years previously, but they were youngsters and probably quite recently hatched. We were reaping tobacco when suddenly all of the workers took off in a scramble, shouting '*nyoka!*' (snake). On closer inspection I discovered dozens of pythons curled in amongst the tobacco plants. They were about fifteen inches long and must have been the offspring of a big python somewhere in the area. These young snakes normally have quite a tough time of it because, once they leave the nest, they are easy prey for hawks, eagles, mongoose and all sorts of other predators.

Then there is the python story, that happened after Simon and Lorna's wedding. Simon takes up of the story:

"Our wedding was at Peterhouse and the reception was in the garden of Founders House. Everything about the wedding was a catastrophe. Firstly, Mum had invited the world, as usual, and I didn't know half the people who were there. The night before I'd had a bachelor party in Harare, at Wombles in Borrowdale. Driving home later, Squinks and John drove into a ditch and they both arrived at the wedding with black eyes, bandages and plaster casts."

Barbara remembers what happened afterwards, on the way back to Imire:

"We had been to Simon and Lorna's wedding in Marondera, and I was with Mum and Dad, who were going back to the farm. Dad was driving and a bit tipsy, singing all his old favourite Vera Lynne songs, which he knew all the words to. It was sunset, it had been raining and there were a lot of frogs on the road and Dad was singing 'Hang out the Washing on the Siegfried Line'.

All of a sudden we came upon this enormous python stretched out across the road and Dad stopped. We could see the python had been feasting on frogs because he had this big bulge in his belly and Dad decided he was going to rescue it, take it back to Imire and let it go in the bush. I said I would drive. Mum got into the back seat and we watched, in hysterics, as Dad proceeded to pick up the python. He staggered over to the car with the snake, climbed into the passenger seat and held the python on his lap. Mum and I were screaming with a mixture of delight and fear as Dad twirled the python round his legs and held its head.

'Stop being silly girls,' Dad said. 'He's got a full stomach and won't harm you.'

African Rock Python

Eventually I started the car and off we went but before long, the snake started spreading out and curled its tail around the gear lever and then between my legs.

'Dad, stop it!' I exclaimed and Dad pulled the snake back onto his lap.

When we arrived home Dad announced that he was going to frighten Jane (who was also on the way back from the wedding) and so he sat in his chair with this huge python in his lap and its head in his hand. He then, of course, proceeded to fall asleep!"

There is some confusion, in the family, about what happened next. Barbs thinks Jane walked in and screamed at the sight of the snake in my lap, while I did a swaying, snake charming act - but I don't remember that! I think the python simply slipped out of my hands, while I dozed off for a minute, and was later rescued from under the couch. Either way, no one was hurt and the snake was released unharmed into the bush on the farm, where he hopefully lived a long and productive life!

Norman wearing his perennial hat!

Norman and Gilly share a joke

Chapter Twelve

BLACK RHINO RESCUE
mid-1980s

When 'Quills' first arrived on Imire, in a very bad state, we weren't quite sure how to handle him. Brought in by a villager, the enormous black-and-white secretary bird had a broken leg and was very thin and weak, with some sort of bone deficiency. We bound the leg with a splint and then hauled out the bird book to see what it is that these very tall and majestic birds eat. 'Quills' was the obvious choice of name because of his crest and we had an old aviary in the garden, which we fixed up and let him use while he recovered his strength. Insects, snakes and rodents are, apparently, the most important components in the diet of a secretary bird, particularly grasshoppers; but hares and young birds are also eaten. Anyhow, we started Quills off on little pieces of raw meat, which we covered in bonemeal to try and help strengthen his bones. Within a very short space of time he began to improve in condition and his leg healed up very well, although it remained slightly crooked. Quills soon became a great attraction and a very friendly pet. He would spend his days wandering about the garden, catching grasshoppers and other insects, and basically kept Gilly's garden pest-free. At night he was closed into the aviary, which he didn't seem to mind at all.

The bird was a great favourite with tourists and family alike, as Simon remembers:

"Quills was a wonderful pet and he just loved to interact with people and would always come when you called him. He would stride across the garden, play with us or the dogs and even lie on the lawn with the dogs. He was one of the few animals that, even after he had gone wild, would be spotted again and again on the vleis of Welton. Even three or four years after he'd gone wild we could call him and he'd strut over, all gangly, to check us out, before going back to the bush."

Many years later I was delighted to see a pair of secretary birds in the game park. I called out his name and the one bird came a little closer. I was convinced it was Quills and watched as he walked off to join his mate before the two of them flew off the nest they'd built in a flat-topped acacia tree.

Another strange little incident, involving rescued animals returning to the wild, occurred. This time it concerned a pair of side-striped jackals. Simon was particularly fond of the little dogs and remembers the circumstances well:

"We had two beautiful silver-backed jackals, which we hand-reared from tiny puppies. They were bottle-fed by Mum and, like so many before, lived in the garden. They loved playing with us and rushing around but, eventually, they went wild. At first we'd see them often and they'd come into the garden and play with the dogs, but they became increasingly shy and eventually went off altogether.

A couple of years later the two jackals came back, very pregnant, around Christmas time, and gave birth in the barn complex. We caught two of the puppies and put them in an old kennel, but they escaped by chewing their way out! We saw the pups again, fleetingly, some time later when we were hunting pigs in Dad's vlei maize and they were completely black in colour. They had much longer legs than usual and we were positive they had bred with Tim Swanson's alsatian dogs, from the next-door farm."

Then came the big birds! We collected three large birds of prey from a chap in Harare, who had them in cages and said they'd all been injured one way or another and couldn't fly. The raptors stood between two and four feet high and were very imposing birds. There was a big bateleur eagle with a distinctive red beak and feet; a large black eagle with a clear, white Y on its back, and an enormous whitebacked vulture. The three raptors went into Quills' old aviary near the main house and were fed on raw meat, with the occasional sprinkling of bonemeal, and were a great attraction. The vulture was christened Harold and his mealtimes, were a particular highlight, as Simon remembers:

"Only the vulture ever had a name. He became a real character, hopping around in the cage which was right outside our dining room window. Dad named him after Harold Wilson because he said the bird was so ugly and Harold Wilson was the

Gilly feeding Quills

154

ugliest thing he could think of at the time. At lunchtime the vulture used to sit on the windowsill and peck at the glass, literally drooling as Dad carved the roast. Lines of saliva would run down the window pane! Of course, Dad always cheated and would give Harold little tit-bits but then the vulture would continue to sit and watch us while we ate!"

On another occasion a visitor, from the Philadelphia Zoo, was having lunch with us and witnessed this same imposing, hunched-over vulture staring, with hooked beak and baleful gaze, at every mouthful. Our guest wrote in the visitor's book:

Tremendous day, absolutely superb. Never had lunch with a vulture before!

There was a big dead tree in the aviary, which the vulture and eagles perched upon and they all gradually whitewashed the back wall over the years! One night we were having a dinner party when the vulture came in through the window that had foolishly been left open, between the aviary and the dining room. Harold jumped on the table, negotiated himself around our best crystal glasses and started helping himself to our meal, tearing bits off the roast quite calmly!

One day Harold escaped from the aviary and was hopping around in the garden. I went outside, wondering how I was going to lure him back in, when, all of a sudden he took two or three hops, a couple of long running steps, lifted off and up he went. He circled overhead a few times, and then was gone. We were all absolutely amazed because we thought he couldn't fly! We'd had him for nearly fifteen years and he'd never shown any signs of wanting - or even being able - to fly. A few days later we spotted a large flock of vultures circling above a dead cow and I thought Harold Wilson must have joined them.

Harold Wilson - the vulture

A barn owl chick

These hand-reared birds and animals, who were often in our house or garden or rolling around on the lawn with our dogs, were always very popular with visitors. We had plenty of guests to keep entertained and, as peace took hold in Zimbabwe, many important foreign guests came on day-safaris. Our proximity to Harare was, undoubtedly, an advantage for diplomats who could only spare a day in the wild. Guests regularly came from the British High Commission, followed by the Embassies of Yugoslavia, France, China, Spain, Italy, Sweden and Egypt. The Australian High Commissioner came on a day-safari - as did an official from the USSR Embassy and the Ambassador of the People's Republic of Bulgaria. The High Commissioners from New Zealand and Bangladesh signed the visitor's book, as well as an official from the Polish Trade Mission. We had also started getting group tours and clubs, including a ladies tennis and hockey club from Bietgheimer in West Germany, a Chinese medical team, Chinese Embroidery group and airline staff on stopovers with British Airways and Quantas. People began comparing us to other game-viewing areas and it was with pride that we read their comments:

Better than Hwange…

We learned more today than in three weeks in Kenya (and eaten more!)

As Imire's reputation and popularity grew we had to find full-time managers to assist in the running of the game park. John and Judy were at the forefront and were helped by Andy and Kelly Bone from 1983 to 1985. They were a very nice couple and Andy was starting up as an artist, following in the footsteps of his brother, Craig, a famous wildlife artist. Tony and Marje Mitchell, who were to become good friends of ours, came and worked on Imire from 1989 to 1994. Tony had a very good sense of humour and he and I got on very well and, between us, kept the wheels turning. Tony remembers his interview for the job on Imire:

"There was an ad in the press for a game park manager and the position was for a couple - the husband to work in the game park and wife to run the overnight lodge. Marje and I applied, our two sons were both in boarding school at the time, and we went to Imire for an interview. It was a typical Norman interview, wherein you were made to jump in the Landrover, with guests in tow, and off you went for a look around the game park. Norman's driving was something else: pulling away in fourth gear, bumping and juddering along! After our interview, Marje and I were invited to stay the weekend and run the bush camp for children that was taking place. The bush camp actually went on for a week, so we had a week-long interview! Everything went very well. Marje and I both love kids and we knew about the bush so there were no problems there. When the bush camp was over, we were invited to John and Judy's house and met them (and Alastair and Anne Marie) and, I realised then, we were being checked out by the whole family! We were offered the job and that's where this amazing adventure started."

It wasn't long before Tony and Marje got to know the various characters and personalities, of both people and animals, better. One particular encounter, between the vulture and a visitor, left a lasting memory with Tony:

"Young English graduate teachers used to come out to teach at the school on Numwa Farm, on an overseas development or exchange programme. There was a Dutch chap, called Jan, who became very friendly with the Travers family and would often come over for meals. He was invited to a fondue dinner one evening and after the meal, there were bits and pieces left on the table. Norman opened the curtains and then the window. Harold suddenly jumped through the window and straight onto the dining room table. Norman picked up a piece of left-over meat and threw it onto Jan's lap. Of course the vulture went for it instantly! Jan shrieked as the bird pecked at his groin and we all collapsed with laughter."

Tony's memories of Ollie are less dramatic:

"There was a barn owl, called Ollie, that Norman and Gill had reared from a baby. We could call and Ollie would glide down and take meat from our hands. This would happen even in the daytime, much to the delight of the tourists, and was fantastic because most people never get a chance to see an owl close-up."

Tony and Marje Mitchell arrived at a time when we had just embarked on our biggest, and perhaps most important, project yet.

There were thought to be fewer than two thousand black rhinoceros left in the wild by the mid 1980s. Poaching, however, was whittling this number down almost daily and it became obvious that intervention was essential if the animals were to be saved from extinction. Poaching of the rhinos was for their horns, which are used for their medicinal properties in Asia and as ornamental handles for ceremonial daggers in Yemen. Rhino horn was selling for up to $45,000 per kilo and, as there could be 4-5kgs of horn on an adult rhino, the incentive to poach was worthwhile. Despite black rhino being listed as an endangered species worldwide and the trade in their products illegal, they were proving extremely difficult to protect in the wild, due to their solitary nature and preference for remote areas where they could be easily hunted.

In order to try and save the species, National Parks teams began darting adult rhinos and moving them to big conservancies, such as Bubiana and Save in the lowveld. Black rhino calves were being allocated to approved game farms where they could be hand-reared and protected from poachers. The idea was that the calves would remain state-owned animals but would be reared in safety, hopefully breeding so that their offspring could be released back into National Parks in the years ahead.

I went and saw Parks, told them I was very interested in being a part of this project and received a lot of advice from George Pangetti, Willie Nduku and Rowan Martin. The rhino story was a different one, for Imire, in that I wanted to prove that it was a feasible project for a private game park. Parks were talking about the ecology of the thing but I told them that Imire was

different because we would always be feeding and supplementing the animals. Judy remembers the early struggles I had in convincing National Parks that the plan was viable:

> *"Norman struggled with Dr David Cummings at National Parks, about getting rhino, because Cummings said they were solitary animals, that the highveld was not the right habitat for them and that you had to have fifty square kilometres for each breeding pair. Norman fought vigorously to get black rhino calves to Imire, finally won and the first seven arrived in May 1987. They were all orphans, being held at Rukomechi, after their mothers had been slaughtered by poachers."*

The seven black rhino calves that I collected were between four and six months old and had already been named by Parks staff. There were three males *viz.* Noddy, Sprinter and Fumbi and four females *viz.* Cuckoo, DJ, Amber and Mvu. Mvu had no ears, as they had been bitten off by a hyaena. All seven calves were put into a boma, near the main homestead, and we began bottle-feeding them immediately. We had a lot of help from our good friend the government vet, Dr Chris Foggin. He was a real fundi on hand-rearing black rhino calves and specified all the necessary dried milk powder and concentrates that they needed and, along with his other useful advice, we found that they tamed down remarkably quickly. Milk was given three or four times a day - a two-litre bottle for each calf - and the bottles were fitted with large rubber calf teats. Gill and her faithful assistant Mattheus took the new catering needs in their stride. Judy remembers how the kitchen adjusted:

> *"We fed those rhino, with help from a few sponsors, from the time they were six months old until they were about five years old. You've got to imagine what hard work that was. Gilly's kitchen was just this massive mixing-machine. Not only was she making these lovely ice-cream cakes, meringues and soufflés for guests and tourists but, on the other side of the kitchen, were seven bottles and mixing bowls for the animals along with glucose and Pronutro (porridge), milk and lactate. This whole bottle-feeding affair went on for five long years - until the rhino were huge great animals!"*

Mattheus was very possessive of his position in the kitchen:

> *"Nkoskas she had a very nice kitchen, very big. One side was for people and the other side was for animals. Mrs Travers taught me everything from when I first came to Imire forty-seven years ago. She is my number-one teacher and trainer! I could cook everything like Christmas cake, chocolate cake, pies, venison, roasts, stews, curries, spare ribs, marmalade, chutney - so many things. At six in the morning and five in the afternoon the workers for the rhinos and elephants came. They had their own place in the kitchen with bottles, teats, milk, Pronutro and they worked on their side mixing for animals. But my place was by the stove, cooking for people!"*

Alongside their milk and porridge diet, we soon introduced the rhinos to game cubes and thorn-bush branches (to teach them how to browse) and, after a very short time, they were ready to go on walks with a handler. First, their handlers would lead them out into the garden and then, after a week or so, on even longer walks into the paddock below our house. They grew incredibly quickly but, despite their size, were kept on the routine, which started first thing in the morning. Tony Mitchell recalls the job:

"You would go to the pen and they would all be milling around waiting for their bottles, which they loved. They didn't need the bottles, by then, but this was our method of controlling them while giving human contact at the same time. They were chest high and each was given a five-litre bottle, with a big teat on it, which contained Nestlé milk powder. Because the milk was routine and a pacifier, more than a necessity at this stage, the mixture wasn't as critical as it had been when they were little. Often it was powder that had been rejected, for one reason or another, such as lumps - but the rhino didn't mind. Sometimes it was straight milk and other times it was flavoured with chocolate. The rhino weren't fussy they would suck it down as quick as anything! If any of the rhino were sick and we needed to add medication of any kind, it would be added to the milk, which made things very easy. The rhino would do anything for their bottle and, once they were sucking, you could do anything to them - check them over or treat them for sores, ticks or wounds. Norman had obviously thought it all through and believed, above all, that human contact with the animals was critical. There were visitors and tourists on Imire all the time and being able to touch and handle the rhinos was very important. Once they had finished their bottles, they went out with the guards who, at prearranged times, would meet up with us on the game drives so the tourists could see them in the bush."

Right from the beginning we had rhino guards. With the help of National Parks some of our staff were trained, issued with FN rifles and they were with the rhinos all the time - protecting them from poachers. The guards had houses right alongside the rhinos' boma and so their protection was twenty-four hours, day and night. The rhino handlers were excellent and soon learnt how to deal with the occasional tantrum. They always carried a little bag of cubes and the rhino calves would happily follow them wherever they went! We had to remember, however, that the rhino were wild animals, even if we had reared them from when they were very small. Simon says that I gave firm instructions:

A fully-horned adult rhino

"I remember Dad being incredibly stern with us about the rhino, saying we had to be firm with them and not get hurt, because they were always charging and knocking us over."

Having the rhino wasn't a cheap undertaking and, although they would never belong to an individual farmer, the benefit was the attraction for visitors and tourists and, of course, the enormous educational value. As a game park, Imire wanted to be involved in doing whatever it could to help conserve the species. I always felt it very important to keep in close communication with National Parks because this was the only way game-farming was going to work. I knew there had to be a governing body and hoped that we could influence some of their decisions in the conservation of black rhino. National Parks knew how we were caring for the rhino and regularly came out to monitor their progress.

Of course, other people - such as Nicholas Duncan of the SAVE Foundation of Australia - were also fantastic supporters and were passionate about rhino conservation right from the very beginning.

Over the years - including the farming side but more so when we started with the game animals and, later, the elephants and rhino - there had been a lot of interest shown in various aspects of research. As mentioned, we had a lot of support from National Parks, which at that time was headed by Graham Childs. I always had the greatest respect for these men and women who were usually working for low wages but were totally professional and utterly committed to the environment. John Condy was a dedicated wildlife vet who was always a great help concerning dosages, broken bones and all manner of issues. A good-looking man, John had an excellent sense of humour and later became a good friend of mine. He was one of the heroes of conservation in those early days. Another vet, who helped us in countless ways, was Chris Foggin. Chris was our government vet on wildlife and the head of the Veterinary Services Department. He also was a super man, very concerned with wildlife and always the first to come out whenever we had a problem.

We had people, from numerous different government, university and research departments, who carried out vegetation surveys, browse and graze utilisation and the control of internal and external parasites. From the University of Zimbabwe, students and researchers would come from the Animal Science, Agriculture and Veterinary Departments. Sometimes they found things not visible to the naked eye, including parasites in the water. Once I had to treat a wet vlei and pools in a streambed with copper sulphate in order to kill snails causing an infestation of liver fluke in the animals. We also got to know Peter Ginn, a well-known ornithologist and author of numerous bird books. He taught at Peterhouse School and was very dedicated to conservation, often visiting Imire, where he escorted bird-watching groups.

Specialists came from further afield too, including one visitor from the Wildlife Institute of India. His words in the visitor's book were high praise indeed for our endeavours:

I consider I would have missed an important wildlife management area had we not visited Imire. This seems to be the best way to manage our marginal lands. I express my thanks to the Travers family for all that they have done.

Back at home there were two men who we worked closely with when it came to animal capture and relocation. Their services were invaluable to Imire and Mike La Grange was involved right from the early days. He was an expert at capture and we saw a lot of him because we often employed him to dart and transport animals. Tim Paulett was another very nice fellow who was with National Parks at first but later went independent. Tim became a professional at game-capture and animal movement and was indispensable in those days.

In the mid-1980s, game-farming, animal-capture and movement and the small-scale safari businesses were still in their infancy, and often experimental. We were all learning as we went along. Who could have guessed that rhino calves loved rubbing themselves against you, rather like a cat does? Some of them became quite friendly with certain people. We had one young fellow come out to stay at Imire, as he was studying rhino. One day, out walking with them, the rhino all lay down in the grass and fell asleep, this young fellow followed their cue and settled down for forty winks. He awoke with a start - one of the rhino had nudged up and was resting her head in his lap! The rhino were very popular with school-children, including those from African schools in the Tribal Trust Lands. Most of these children had never seen rhino, elephant, lions and leopards before.

The visitor's book was full of compliments:

Wonderful day, especially the rhino…
Please can we take the rhino home with us…
Can we have the rhino with no ears…
Quite an experience to feed rhino…

Judy feeds Tatenda

Our rhino fitted in very well with the elephants. To economise we had a group of staff who looked after both rhino and elephant. Occasionally there were barneys between the elephants and rhino - pushing and shoving - but nothing serious. We usually didn't let people go right up to the rhino when they were feeding - to avoid an accident. Rhino are always bad-tempered; they can be very docile but sometimes they get angry and, on those occasions, we would discipline them. The main thing, with all the animals, was to get their respect. In the wild a young animal's mother looks after and plays with its baby, but she also disciplines it. You can't bend a rhino over and smack his bottom and I wouldn't allow the use of thick sticks for discipline. Instead, the staff used long, thin whippy sticks with leaves on the end. Just flicking the leafy end in front of a rhino's nose was quite adequate.

Our rhino-workers were generally very good but we had the occasional mischief. I used to go fishing down at the dam and once found the rhino-workers there, also partaking in a little angling. I didn't have much success and when I was leaving one of the rhino guys gave me a fish to take home, which I thought was very generous of him. However, when I gutted the fish, I found it was full of cubes - rhino cubes! Then I cottoned on! Next time I went to the dam, I sat next to the same chap who, as might be expected, started catching bream immediately. Shortly the whole story came out: he was using rhino cubes to feed the fish - but worse, he was then selling his illicit catch. We put a stop to this practice very quickly!

As the rhino poaching problems in the country escalated and spread into conservancies and game parks, National Parks decided that our rhino must be dehorned. The theory being that if they didn't have a horn then they wouldn't be killed. When Parks hadn't come for a couple of months I decided to saw off about five inches of their horns myself, using a hacksaw. With the help of a couple of workers and plenty of cubes to keep them quiet, we steadily cut away at the horn using a hacksaw. When the rhino started fidgeting we would stop for a break, calm him down and then carry on again. Each animal took about twenty or thirty minutes to do and it was a bit like sawing wood. I had initially decided to take only the tip of the horn off, which turned out to be idiotic because there was another ten to twelve inches of horn left behind, which was more than enough to attract a poacher.

When I delivered the sackful of rhino horns to National Parks, they were furious! They started accusing me of profiteering.

"Well someone had to do it, so we did it ourselves," I said, but they weren't amused. As each piece of horn was being recorded and weighed, one of the Parks men decided that I must have kept some for myself - as there wasn't enough horn, in his opinion! After a while things calmed down and our relationship with them returned to an even keel.

About a year later, Parks came out to Imire and did the dehorning again, this time cutting the horns off at the base, filing the stump round with a file and leaving a small neat lump. The whole thing was quick and painless and didn't seem to make any impact on the rhino's behaviour or lifestyle at all. If anything, the dehorned rhino were now a bit safer for us to handle: mind you, being charged by a rhino, horn or not, is a bit uncomfortable!

The seven rhino calves stayed together as a herd and, despite all the criticism about Imire's apparently unsuitable highveld vegetation, the animals thrived. Even though they are largely solitary animals in the wild, mating and breeding did not seem to be a problem for our 'Magnificent Seven' either. They reached sexual maturity in 1993 and, following a gestation of seventeen months, the first calf, a female, was born to Cuckoo on 26 July 1994. Two years later Cuckoo gave birth to her second calf, which we named *Umgofu* and, when he was six months old, we introduced him to the press:

"Bustling six-month-old Umgofu is already proving popular with visitors at the game park. In fact, when he was released from the boma, baby Umgofu decided to show his strength, determination and stubbornness by charging in full ceremonial speed at eight humans, who took refuge up trees! On realising his victory he trotted back to an irate and aggressive mother, Cuckoo, who immediately decided her son needed a night of experience out in the bush. It, however, turned out to be a night of horrors as all guides spent a restless night wondering where they were. To the relief of all, they both sauntered back to the boma for their breakfast of cubes the next morning.

Where once, only twenty years ago, sixty thousand rhinos roamed, today less than two thousand remain; a decline of about 97%. But, on a happy note, there has been no rhino poaching for over a year now, thanks to the intensive protection accorded the rhinos by both private ranchers and the Department of National Parks and Wildlife Management. At Imire there are eight armed guards guarding seven rhinos."

(Sunday Mail)

Eleven black rhino calves were born on Imire over the next seven years, tragically one died after falling into a water pit. The remaining ten calves - five male and five female - were successfully reared to weaning age and returned to National Parks, going to Tashinga, in the Matusadona National Park, on the shores of Lake Kariba.

The names of some of the rhino calves born on Imire were Madonna, Chibaki, Mvura, Tsotsi, Mapranka and Bumper. As some rhino left, others arrived and this programme of breeding and returning animals to the wild continues today on Imire. More recently there have been rhino called Gomo and Cumchasa, who have caused their fair share of worries and amusement. On one occasion a South African television crew came out to Imire to make a documentary on the rhino. Hardly had the rhino and their handlers been located when Gomo charged the television crew, who sprinted for their truck. John dodged behind a tree and he and the rhino played ring o'ring o' roses for a while, until Gomo calmed down!

Another time, Gomo and Cumchasa broke out of the game park and went on a 20km walk towards the Save (Sabi River). After a couple of days tracking they were located, but the only way to get them to come home was by using the elephant bulls, who they followed - this took another half a day! We also had four rhino who ate excessive amounts of the milk-bearing cactus, Euphorbia, which sent them completely mad for a day; rushing around uncontrollably. We knew they could eat small amounts of Euphorbia, which apparently helps scour their intestines but, in sizeable quantities, it is poisonous - causing skin irritation, burning and diarrhoea. There was nothing we could do except wait and, after a day, they returned to normal and peace reigned again!

When I think about the future for rhino, I hope that when things return to normal in Zimbabwe, tourism will start again. Farms may be able to start up with game again but they'll have to drag themselves up from where they are now. Maybe in the years to come some of the things done on Imire will be used as a model for the future.

There were always some animals that stood out from the rest and one frequent visitor, Gareth Hassall, remembers a few, including a famous little rhino:

"For many years, while I was at school, I used to spend holidays on Shaka Farm, in Wedza, and regularly used to visit the Travers family on Imire. They had a sign on the gate saying: 'Never mind the dog, beware of the cat!' This was when they had a pet lion called Cassius. I used to play with Cassius when he was a cub (so was I!) until he grew too big. One day he jumped up, put his paws on my shoulders and knocked me flat. Do you have any idea how bad a lion's breath is?

Another time, I went on a horseback safari and one of the rhinos had a youngster she was protecting. We didn't see her until she came charging out of a thicket and my horse bolted. One rein snapped, and I was taken on a roller-coaster ride until the horse jumped a donga that the rhino couldn't negotiate. It took me two hours to find my way back as I was terrified of meeting the rhino again! Not only that, but the one person who could've helped was a Canadian woman in a 4x4. Did she drive to my rescue? No! Did she try to help? No! She filmed the whole thing on her video camera (remember those huge bulky things, which took a full-size VCR tape and a separate battery the size of a small handbag?). When I saw the video later, with me white-faced and clutching the horse's mane, the clearest sound was the woman's commentary. 'Oh my Gawd! Wouldya look at that. Amaaaaaazing!'

However, other memories followed. After a terrible bush fire in the Zambezi Valley had orphaned some very young rhino, causing severe burns, I remember going to Imire over a few weekends to rub oil onto them and help feed them. One of the rhinos was called 'Big Ears' - ironically his ears had been partially burnt off in the fire. I had a five-litre Mazoe bottle filled with milk formula, with a custom-fitted teat, and the baby rhino would drain the whole thing in about five minutes flat. I remember the cream teas in the Imire garden, the little blue duiker that used to putter around the tables, the playful otters and a warthog named Dudley. He would roll on his back so you could scratch his tummy, whereupon he'd grunt happily and lie blissed-out! Those times live on in my memory, a part of my childhood forever."

It was always very satisfying to know what happy memories our visitors to Imire had and that we made a difference in people's lives.

Despite the perilous state of the black rhino population in the wild and the seriousness of the work we were doing, with rearing and breeding them on Imire, there was always time for relaxation, friends and social events in the district. My life-long friend David Hamilton remembers how important Gill was in keeping me under control:

"Norman was very much involved in the Wedza area as a whole and the welfare of the district and of course Gill was also completely involved in the district community. Gill played an enormous part in moderating Norman's often impetuous approach to very many issues that possibly required a more gentle approach, which Norman was inclined to overlook. He was very much a man of action and often missed the niceties of a situation.

On the negative side, Norman was never a particularly good committee-man. The general humdrum of an everyday agenda bored him to tears and he never excelled as a committee chairman. But, having said that, give him something or, more likely, allow him to create something on the agenda that required 'action' - and Norman was in his element.

*He was once a bored-stiff member of the Marondera road
council, until he found that he could browbeat a stereotypical,
unimaginative committee into tarring some of the dirt roads.
Norman was in his element and, almost personally, supervised
the tarring of the Bridge Road right up to the Imire turning -
after which he retired from the council!"*

It's true that I liked to be active most of the time but, as Simon
recalls, I always found time for half an hour on the bed after lunch every day:

*"Every afternoon Dad would have a rest on his bed. He'd read his book for half an
hour and sleep for ten minutes and he always had to have one of those baby animals
on the bed with him - an otter or a lion, leopard or hyaena or whatever it was that was
being hand-reared at the time.*

*And then there was the box of sweets - Dad's other fetish! Mum had a sweetie box
kept in her cupboard and we were only allowed two sweets each after lunch. Dad can't
live without his two sweets - so he'd lie on the bed with his book, his animal and his
two sweeties and be completely content!"*

That half hour was a good time to think over events and problems and, sometimes, to even contemplate bigger issues. I am basically Church of England
but was never a very good Anglican, though my mother did her best. I suppose
I believe in a life in the hereafter but, when my daughter-in-law told me that
all animals have souls, it sounded to me that heaven would be over-crowded!
My philosophy is to live one's life to the best of one's ability, following the
standards taught to us.

I always tried to make time to read a little in the afternoon. In my early
days I liked Boys Magazines and adventure stories and, for a time, I enjoyed
classical books. I didn't read much as a young man but, when I did, it was
adventure stories like Robert Louis Stevenson's Treasure Island and so on.
I'm a big reader now, thrillers and the odd historical war books.

Family get-togethers and social gatherings were always very important at
Christmas time. I sometimes struggled with these occasions, because of my
hearing, but mostly people just learned to shout! My hearing problem started
after the Second World War and deafness was a problem all of my life, getting
worse as I grew older, of course. A doctor friend of mine checked my ears
once and said, "You must give up smoking your pipe, or it'll make you deaf!"
Despite my bad hearing I enjoy music - especially if dancing with my wife.
Gilly says that she likes dancing with me too and that I have very good rhythm!
I like country music, jazz and martial music but was never much good with
classical! Later in life I enjoyed dance music and always enjoyed sing-songs
in our local pub. My favourite songs are Irish ballads i.e. 'South of the Border'
and suchlike.

Christmas in Wedza was the time our friend, Mike Hill, played a very
important role and he is remembered fondly by many hundreds of children.

When Mike acquired his farm in Wedza, in the 1950s, he was surrounded by military people; colonels, captains, generals, admirals and so on. Mike put up his signboard, which read: 'Corporal Hill!'

He was a good cricketer, playing for Wedza as wicket keeper for many years. Mike and Jean and their children became good friends of ours, even though they lived some distance from us, their farm being on the western side of the district. Mike was a good farmer; they had a small dairy, beef cattle, tobacco, maize and pigs at one stage. Mike was what I call an efficient farmer - doing a number of different things, which all brought in an income. Mike also enjoyed fishing and playing snooker but his most well-known job in Wedza, apart from propping up the bar on most social occasions, was being Father Christmas at the annual Wedza Club Christmas party. Mike did this for many years and, in those days, there were a lot of children in the district who would all line up to get their presents from him. He made an excellent Father Christmas and had a great ability to remember all the children's names!

Every year our family carried on the tradition we had started after the war in the early 1950s, of having a big family and friends' get-together on Christmas Eve. Richard Thornycroft remembers the annual occasion very well:

"Christmas Eve was always a Travers, Seagers, Curtis and Thornycroft bash. They were held on Imire at one long, long table - with the adults at the top and the kids at the bottom - arranged by age; as you grew up you moved up the table!

It was a very formal affair and we all wore our glad rags - dinner jackets for the boys, long dresses for the girls. The meal was always enormous and I'm sure Gilly and Mattheus slaved over it for four or five days beforehand.

During dinner there were always formal toasts for absent friends and the Queen and, after dinner, the men stayed behind for cigars and port - all very British. Later on, we used to play games and Norman was the organiser. There was one game where we were all given a number and had to stand in a big circle. Norman had a big brass tray and he'd spin it and call a number; if it was your number you had to catch the tray before it fell to the ground - failure resulted in a penalty, such as kissing a girl or some other desperately embarrassing thing. Norman always had this very wicked look and he'd stand there in his DJ and cummerbund and look at us with this glint in his eye and we knew we were for it. There were other games, like 'Moriarty says stand on one leg' etc... and, of course, Norman always

A young, de-horned rhino

167

got us into such ghastly contorted positions, we were bound to fall over. The Christmas
dinners were great fun and carried on until after we'd left school and were in our twenties.

Mattheus had such a life and put up with so much in his years with that family and all
those animals. He really was an amazing guy and Gilly's right-hand man. We always
said that Gilly could have done without Norman but not without Mattheus!

Gilly and Mattheus certainly always did us very proud and presented the
most magnificent spreads. Simon remembers another Christmas Eve dinner
in particular; it was his turn to say grace:

"Traditionally, Mum and Dad had a big Christmas Eve dinner every year with
probably twenty five or thirty people sitting around the table. All the adults were at
one end and the kids were at the bottom - we used to sneak cigarettes under the table.
We had a pair of barn owls as pets once. They bred and nested in the Musike barns
and these two chicks somehow ended up coming into the house. Mum fed them with
a pipette and as they grew up they stuck around. They used to come at breakfast time
and would look down on us from the rafters while we ate, lovely to see. One Christmas
Eve, Mum had, as usual, laid the table beautifully with all her best crystal and silver-
ware. I remember exactly when it was because, that year, I had been nominated to say
grace and was highly embarrassed by the whole affair. The atmosphere was considerably
lightened when, in the middle of my attempt at grace, the barn owls flitted down and
knocked silver and glasses all over the place and Mum went berserk. My effort, happily,
came to an abrupt end!"

Chapter Thirteen

POTTER THE OTTER
Late 1980s - 1990s

Going for a walk at the end of the day was a routine that Gill and I kept to whenever we could. A sundowner at the dam, fishing line in the water and, needless to say, the followers who invariably tagged along - what could be better? Simon remembers the sight of that daily procession:

"Mum used to take the dogs, otters and all sorts of other followers for a walk every evening. It was common to see Mum walking along with an otter, hyaena, lion, leopard and a couple of dogs - an amazing sight! Dad would walk with Mum, if he was around, or he'd meet up with her after he'd finished work."

Potter the otter was Gilly's friend and was a great character. Potter and Edwina were Cape clawless otters who came to us, as babies, from National Parks. Like all the other little animals before them, the otters started out in our bedroom - and in the bed, whenever I could get away with it! Simon remembers this as being one of the few things that Gill objected to:

"I remember when they were tiny, the two otters used to live in a dog basket at the bottom of Mum and Dad's bed. Mum used to feed them every three hours, twenty-four hours a day, with a mixture of milk and Calsuba from a little pipette. When they were about six weeks old, Dad let the otters get right into the bed where they would run down to the bottom and lie next to his feet. Dad always had cold feet and said the otters were the finest hot-water bottles ever. Mum didn't like this at all because of the mess they made of the sheets. She didn't mind them on top of the covers, but not underneath!"

When they became too big to be in the house, Potter and Edwina were put out in the garden and had the run of our old swimming pool, where the crocodile had lived. Edwina never tamed down much but Potter became a firm friend. She was a handsome specimen with a glossy dark-brown coat, silvery white throat and neck and long brown tail. Potter used to love diving into the swimming pool and was delightful to watch as she swam and played in the water. In the late afternoons she would stand and look over the wall, waiting for us. Her natural diet would have been crabs, snails,

Gill with Potter

fish and frogs but she was happy with raw meat, which we fed her every day, and she loved to come with us when we went fishing at the dam. We'd open the gate to head for the dam and she'd come scampering along with the dogs, and whatever other orphans we had at the time. If we caught a fish we'd give it to Potter and she would take it under a tree and clearly enjoy every bit of it.

Not all had such happy encounters with the otters. Our manager, Tony, recalled that they had a bad habit of going up ladies dresses and nipping them in the groin. On one occasion Gill had been away for a month and when she got back her first thought was of Potter. We went down to the old swimming pool and Potter came dashing out to go for her walk. Potter wouldn't leave Gill alone and would swim for a short time and then run straight back to her. After a while we realised that she was jealous of any attention Gill paid me. Suddenly she came out of the water, ran at Gill and gave her a vicious bite on her leg. I grabbed Potter by her neck and told Gilly to get back to the house - by now she was bleeding badly. Potter was squealing and crying and clearly upset at what had happened. When Gill was out of sight I put the otter down and we walked home quietly together. Animal behaviour is so difficult to understand. Potter surely only intended a gentle love-bite!

Animal behaviour and human tragedy were two things that were much a part of our lives in the 1990s. Before these trials, however, I had the unexpected chance to go hunting again. I won a raffle at our annual Hunters' Association AGM. It was for a shoot that allowed one bull-elephant, one buffalo cow, a hyaena and some antelope. I had stopped hunting by then but, much to my son's dismay, I accepted the opportunity. I think he'd hoped I'd say I was too old, almost seventy by then! I asked my old friend Gerry to be my co-hunter. He agreed and so Gill and I set off early to set up camp until Gerry could join us a little later. The first morning, after Gerry arrived, he and I - and our tracker, Elijah - set out. Elijah had been with me on several hunts before and was an African gentleman of the finest kind. Gill said she wanted to finish chores, so she didn't come.

About an hour out of camp we spotted an elephant bull walking rapidly through the bush. We drove ahead for a mile or two then walked into the bush and, to our amazement, the bull elephant came into sight.

"Shoot!" Gerry whispered.

"What? On the first day?" I asked, plaintively.

Nonetheless, when the bull was thirty yards away, I fired. Gerry also fired and the elephant dropped stone dead. Two shots though his heart. When we returned to camp to collect the men to do the skinning and cutting up, Gill couldn't believe it.

"Why are you back so early?" she asked.

"I've just shot my elephant!" I replied.

The tusks weighed 33kgs each - my best ever! Then, a couple of days later, I got my buffalo cow; also with one shot. Both my elephant and buffalo were, ultimately, the winners of the best-of-year prize at the Hunters' Association that year.

After that hung up my trusty .458 rifle and concentrated on wildlife conservation. Some might say 'about time!' and you may well ask why I call myself a conservationist! However, I do believe that controlled-hunting is a conservation tool (provided that it is ethical in every respect). It helps to keep wildlife areas intact, with wildlife preserved for future generations, by giving that area an income. This 'good vs bad' dilemma provides for many arguments with other conservationists, over sundowners!

After I'd hunted my last elephant, I asked Larry Norton if he would paint me a picture of it. Larry was a renowned artist and I've been lucky enough to buy several of his wildlife paintings over the years. Larry was the son of Ben Norton, a keen pasture man from Umvukwes who was also a stalwart in the hunting world from earlier days. Because I hadn't taken a photograph at the time, Larry invited Gill and I to join him for a weekend in the Zambezi Valley. There we found a site, with very similar scenery and vegetation to that from the hunt, and Larry painted me a wonderful picture of a lone elephant bull walking through the bush. Thinking back on it now, I wonder why I enjoyed hunting so much and yet, today, love our elephant and buffalo with an equal passion. It's no good asking a psychologist unless he, too, has been on a hunt in the Zambezi Valley. Only then might I listen to him!

How fortunate I was to have had that last hunt with Gerry because, not long afterwards, he went on what was to be his last trip to the Valley. Gerry and I had many hunting and fishing excursions together and, even after he'd given up hunting, he still loved going into the bush as a guide, which he did with a farmer from the Burma Valley on this fateful occasion. David Hamilton relates the events that followed:

"Before dawn on their first morning, Gerry, the African tracker and the farmer set off in the Landrover. As the sun emerged over the distant hills the vehicle was parked not far from the Nyamumba airstrip. The long morning march began. Eventually the spoor of a herd of buf- falo was found, tracking ensued and it was midday

before the herd had been overtaken and studied. No shots were fired and the trip back to the Landrover began.

Hot and tired, their concentration flagged as they neared the vehicle. Suddenly, within three hundred metres of the truck, the party found themselves in the midst of a herd of elephant cows with calves.

Gerry was found the next morning. He had dragged himself to a tree and died with a whimsical smile on his face. On a tamarind tree overlooking the Zambezi River a plaque was erected bearing his name, the date of his death and these words: The Zambezi Valley was his spiritual home." (Winter Cricket)

It was a sad ending for Gerry but, from his point of view, probably exactly how he wanted it.

In July 1992, our last-born and much-loved son, Alastair, met with a similar tragic fate. The baby of the family, doted on by his brothers and sister, Gilly nicknamed him Squinks, a name which everyone used, but Gilly couldn't remember how or why it had started. After finishing school and army, he had followed his passion in life and started a bow-hunting company with Bill Bedford. Bill remembers his partner's skills and their early publicity:

"Having gone through junior and senior school with Alastair whose sporting ability was outstanding, it came as no surprise that his natural talent as a professional hunter was of a very high standard. He had amazing confidence in his own ability to handle difficult situations with dangerous game without being over-confident.

Alastair did the bow-hunting trials for National Parks on elephant and buffalo. The elephant trial was extremely successful, he killed it with one arrow and it lived for less than a minute. He then took off to the USA to promote our newly formed company 'Ingwe Bowhunting Safaris'. Alastair was rushed from JFK airport straight to an 'Outdoor TV Show' where he was interviewed live about his experiences and the future of bow-hunting in Zimbabwe. Whether it was the long flight without a shower or just nerves - I am not sure, but he developed a severe itch in his groin, which he proceeded to scratch throughout the interview while being transmitted to millions of viewers!

We only discovered after the successful elephant-hunt with a bow, that if we had sought sponsorship from the big bow manufacturers in the USA, we would have been able to sell the video footage for a fortune. Pity we were not up to speed on international marketing!

Probably the funniest incident in our very early days as supposed safari operators, was taking two South African couples hunting, illegally, in the Charara area which was only for Zimbabweans. We allowed them to shoot the animals on our quota but the Parks guys figured out the deal and arrested the two prominent South African businessmen. The guilty parties (Bedford and Travers) were able to spend the night in a very comfortable Kariba Hotel consoling the wives, whilst the South Africans spent the night in jail with no shoes, or belts etc... Fortunately, we were all great friends and remained so after the event."

Despite their awkward beginning Alastair and Bill were doing very well.

Apparently Alastair had some other peculiar habits - as I found out from Bill many years later:

"He had a bad habit of not wearing underpants and, on one safari, I came across him sitting on the side of the road opposite his client's wife having a well-deserved cold drink with everything hanging out. She didn't appear to be perturbed - in fact quite fascinated! Maybe a case of khaki fever!

Alastair's standard kit for a fortnight safari was one spare pair of boxer shorts, one spare shirt (no underwear), one toothbrush and no toothpaste - as someone in camp would usually have. His hunting equipment was found wanting on one occasion when his Maglite ran out of light while he was following a wounded leopard. He resorted to a mini flashlight being shone over his shoulder by his tracker following the blood. With the little flashlight fading he almost trod on the leopard - fired both barrels from his shotgun, clean missing with both, and fell over backwards on top of his tracker. Once they realised they weren't being eaten they regained some composure, found the little torch and dispatched the leopard!"

Alastair met and married Anne-Marie Ingham and there was one hunt that Alastair and Anne-Marie went on together which got Bill and his colleagues talking, and then laughing:

"One hunting trip we did with him and Anne-Marie, they arrived with a full-on double bed mattress strapped to the back of the Landrover. This prompted a lot of banter and a certain amount of envy from the rest of us as they selected a honeymoon suite overlooking the Zambezi! Two weeks later when it came time to leave, they lifted the mattress and the whole bottom fell out having been completely eaten by white ants!"

Alastair did like his comforts, as Bill found out on one long and very cold journey:

"He caught me beautifully once on a very early departure from West Nicholson in mid-winter. Alastair had the old faithful farm Landrover, with no doors, and it was freezing. I, fortunately, had a vehicle with doors and a heater. We had only just reached the main tar road to Bulawayo when he pulled over and asked if he could drive my vehicle for a short while as he was falling asleep. Without a second thought, I agreed and that was the last I saw of him until we arrived in Bulawayo for breakfast, where he advised me he had not been falling asleep at all. He just found the Landrover a little slow and very cold!"

When he was at home on Imire, Alastair would share his passion for bow-hunting with visiting school-children. Tony Mitchell remembers how impressed the children were:

"Alastair would come to the bush camps with his bow and give demonstrations for the children. He would put up a target of a little red Madison 20s cigarette box, which has a crest in the middle of it. Alastair would put the box 20m away and put his arrow straight through that crest and the children were always very impressed."

Alastair and Anne-Marie had two daughters, first Tara, then Sam but tragedy struck when Anne-Marie died while giving birth to Sam - leaving us all heartbroken. It was a very sad time for all of us, especially Alastair. Then, in July 1992, Alastair was killed by a buffalo which had been wounded by his client, who also died. Tragically, Alastair died after being flown to hospital in Harare. John and Judy adopted Tara and Sam and were a tower of strength during this sad period. Bill Bedford has also been a great support over the years, paying for the girls' education and much more.

John and Judy and their extended family had become more and more involved in the daily running of Imire over the years and, in the early 1990s, we also took on Ian du Preez, an eighteen-year-old, as an assistant who could help on both the farm and the game park. Ian stayed with us for a decade during which time he gained a lot of knowledge and experience handling animals. He left Imire for Shearwater, in Victoria Falls, where he is one of the top elephant handlers and runs the Shearwater game park. By the time I was in my early seventies and partly retired from the daily affairs of Imire, I felt greatly contented to know that John and Judy would carry on where Gill and I left off. We may have looked at some things differently but they were full of praise for what we had achieved. Judy couldn't praise Gill highly enough:

"Gilly and Norman were always in control of the game park. Gilly's food and hospitality was known throughout Zimbabwe. Their home was everyone's home - the doors were always open. The garden was always immaculate, the best rose garden in Zimbabwe. Gilly's winter garden was a stunning sight. The house was always filled with flowers from bundles of sweet peas to arum lilies. Food was always in abundance. Guests were met with scones, cream and home-made jam. Lunch on the kopje included home-made venison pies. Mattheus the cook would help load a barn with tobacco and then run back and knock up a pavlova and choccie cake - still with unwashed hands! Gilly always looked immaculate, her dress sense was perfect - a hostess beyond words. Norman too, was the perfect host and his knowledge much valued. Norman was fearless and always had the last word on fireguards, burning and animal behaviour."

With John and Judy handling so many of the day-to-day issues and with Tony, Marje and Ian all working together, Gill and I took the time to visit England where we met up with Dr Marthe Kiley-Worthington, a noted animal behavioural expert, trainer and lecturer at Exeter University. On a visit to her farm in Devon, Gill and I were invited to tea and, to our merriment, Marthe called out to one of her girl helpers, "Call Suzie in please, there's no milk."

In walked a Jersey cow, which Marthe promptly milked straight into the jug!

This impressed me a great deal, especially when we went round the farm and saw that she had tamed all the animals, including a bull that was with the cows. Marthe was a great horsewoman and undertook long treks on horse-back through Wales. When she heard about what we were doing on Imire she said she wanted to come out and work with our elephants. I told her we couldn't pay her very much but Marthe didn't mind about the money - she just wanted to work with our elephants. She was a very strong character and had a real love of her job. She had trained Indian elephants and other animals for game parks in many parts of the world. Marthe did what she wanted, went where she wanted and was a very outgoing person. She seemed to be able to understand what animals were thinking.

Marthe came out to Imire with her partner, Chris, and just took over! They didn't want to stay in our house, Marthe said they wanted to be near the elephants and so they stayed in the bush camp which we used for school-children. Every day for a couple of weeks, Marthe would go out and train the elephants.

Marthe was a wonderful trainer, always so patient and encouraging and would use cubes to reward achievements. She was far more restrained than I was when it came to giving rewards and would admonish an elephant: "You can't expect a reward every time you do it!" She stressed how important it was to teach the elephants tricks and, when I protested, saying they weren't circus animals, she said it was to stop them getting bored. In the wild animals would roam for miles so when you keep them in comparatively confined areas you have to occupy them. The elephant handlers used to ride the animals up to our farm store - it gave the elephants a good walk, and enabled the handlers to buy their cigarettes and be seen by other customers and passers-by. Another great boredom breaker was a bath in the dam. The handlers would strip down to their shorts and sit astride the elephants as they waded into the water. They were issued with scrubbing brushes and the elephants loved it. Another diversion for the elephants was to have them go out and fetch browse for the rhinos; thorn branches were cut from trees in the bush, loaded onto a cart and the elephants would pull the cart back to the night enclosures.

Marthe taught the elephants to kick a football and watching was terribly entertaining.

"Lift your left leg," she would say to the elephant. "No, not your right, your left."

The elephant then lifted his left leg. I often wondered if there was a wink in the elephant's eye!

One of my party tricks, which went down very well with guests, was to throw my hat into the grass. An elephant would lumber over, retrieve the hat and then bring it back and put it on my head! Of the many people who witnessed this lovely little interaction, Keith Meadows describes what he saw, and the little game we played:

"There is no doubt of his love for them. Watching Norman amongst his six elephants, talking to them, patting them, his gaze quartering each animal for signs of anything amiss. At the risk of being anthropomorphic, it looked as if the feeling was reciprocated…

As we stand amidst the elephants, enjoying their company, a breeze lifts Norman's worn old bush hat from his head, tumbles it into the grass at his feet. Out of nowhere a sinuous grey trunk inserts itself between us as one of the bulls retrieves it and places it gently back on the farmer's head. Norman strokes the trunk affectionately whilst I search the animals face for any kind of expression.

There is communion. Dare I say there is an elephantine twinkle there? One that matches the sparkle that is seldom far from the eyes of my bespectacled host."

(Sometimes When it Rains)

Marthe was a great tonic, who, spending hours with them, ultimately produced trained elephants, which have given hundreds of adults and children some very exciting moments. The elephant rides became a great draw for visitors and, at first, we started out with bare-back riding. The guest would get on the elephant, with the handler, and sit on a cushion - close to its head. After a while we modified this and had special baskets made, which were strapped onto their backs, and people then sat in a little more comfort. The elephant handler had a little stick which he used to prod the elephant's ear - left ear to turn left, right ear to turn right. A little tap on the elephant's head would bring the animal to a stop and a tap on its knee was the signal it needed to sit down.

Marthe came out to Imire in 1991, 1993 and 1996 and worked with the elephants. She made follow-up visits and wrote papers on what she was doing because, before then, it had only ever been Indian elephants that had been trained and this was all very much groundbreaking work. I would say that Marthe gave us the first true insight into how to handle a big and so-called dangerous animal like an elephant. I'm sure she had a huge effect on us and how we were doing things.

For Marthe, animal-training is about respect, compassion and understanding as she explained in an article, in the local Farmer magazine, which covered a demonstration that we held to show the elephants' skills to villagers from nearby communal areas:

"Dr Kiley-Worthington and her partner Chris Rendle have been training elephant trainers at Imire Game Park, Wedza, on how the elephants can be used for agricultural production purposes as a means of conserving them.

'People could have more to do with elephants. They are an industry which everyone can have something to do with.' She emphasised that elephants need to be trained with compassion and that people involved with them should desist from using punishment and inflicting pain as a way of teaching, as this makes them violent and dangerous."

Trained elephants, inevitably, attract attention from the press. Our local newspaper highlighted our twenty-year-old bull elephant, Nyasha. He and Mac, the country's first and oldest trained elephant were trained by Marthe and were mainly used for pulling wagons, ploughs, discs and tandem discs - and they were very successful. Mac and I seemed to be in cahoots, he always seemed to know me when I went to find the elephants:

Untamed African Elephants Learn To Help Speed The Plough

Every day, Nyasha the bull elephant plods through the fields to trample on one of Africa's last great myths. For generations, Africans believed that the powerful beasts could not be trained for work. But a small game ranch in Zimbabwe is proving the sceptics wrong.

Nyasha is one of two elephants working in the maize fields of Imire Game Ranch, sixty miles east of Harare, confounding years of myth that the beasts are useless to man.

Peter Musavaya, 22, a game ranger, said. 'I think the first white settlers were fond of shooting elephants for their tusks and didn't realise that elephants live in family units and this stress was passed on to future generations, making them aggressive to humans.'

At this 11,500 acre ranch the sins of the past have been buried with the help of an animal psychologist, Dr Marthe Kiley-Worthington, of Exeter University, who wanted to prove, through training, the intelligence of the African elephant. Three weeks of schooling was enough to put the elephants into harness to till the ranch's maize fields.

Barbara Travers, 45, said. 'The elephants love it. They need to use their highly developed brains and this is the best way of doing it.'

Three tons of pulling power means the elephants draw a deeper furrow at greater speed. Farmers estimate an elephant can do the work of six cattle. Game rangers want to

The author, Cathy, chats with Norman

train more elephants and establish a training school at the ranch. It is also hoped that training elephants for useful work may reduce bush and crop destruction caused by overcrowding among the growing herds.

After their day's work, the elephants play their favourite game, also taught them by the psychologist: kicking a football, thrown by their laughing drovers. Another sign that, once taught, an elephant never forgets. (Christopher Bishop in 'The Herald')

Training the elephants on Imire was an important management aspect and something that John and Judy would continue to develop:

"While Dad was the initiator of elephant-training in the country, he and Rory Hensman were on a par. They used to swap notes regularly, share knowledge and training methods and techniques. Dad was the first person to get Marthe Kyle-Worthington to come out here and, once that training had been initiated, everyone wanted her. Rory is now onto the most amazing project with his elephants, working on a spooring and tracking programme with them. He tracked his gardener for 28kms through the bush. It was difficult terrain with thick bush, small kopjes and other obstacles and, occasionally, the gardener would drop a small piece of clothing to be followed. These days Rory is taking his elephants to Angola to sniff out landmines. This spooring and tracking programme is the direction we're going with Dad's elephants. It's going to be a long process and we've got in-depth reports from Rory on how to begin. If we'd had tracking elephants when all our rhino were slaughtered, we could have achieved success in finding the perpetrators immediately."

By the time we could offer visitors rides on the backs of our trained elephants, the Imire Game Park had become a full-time enterprise in its own right. Elephant rides became hugely popular but, in the early days, there were occasions when things went very wrong. Judy remembers one such incident, concerning Mac and knitting:

"Mac is the most handsome elephant God has ever put together. He is out of this world with a massive great head, gentle by nature, a real gentleman and a perfect specimen. But did once get out of hand!

The elephant loading platform

We had sixteen missionaries from America who were in the country working at a youth camp on a Doma orphanage and were loving it. They all arrived full of praise and passionate about what they'd done and the cherry on the cake for them was Imire and the elephants.

That afternoon I asked who would like to ride an elephant and of course sixteen hands went up and I knew we'd have to do elephant rides in the afternoon and again the next morning. So we put the first lot onto the elephants in the afternoon and that went smoothly. The second lot was getting organised and climbing up the stands

A rare photo of Norman riding Mac

to get on the elephants and there was one woman who was passionate about wool and knitting. She had a sheep farm in Hanover and was knitting socks with four needles. She was being photographed sitting on the back of her elephant, knitting her socks, when suddenly Mac decided he was fed up. Toto was in front of him at the loading ramp, his client had been loaded and Mac, also carrying his client, just came straight at him. Mac literally lifted Toto up off the ground and sent him flying - that's how strong Mac was. The client, by now, was underneath the elephant and Mac came at him again, scrabbling to do another hoofing of Toto. There was screaming, clouds of dust everywhere and then the third elephant dumped its knitting client and took off. We actually found the client's half-finished knitting the next day, about a kilometre away. Meanwhile, the guide managed to rescue the clients who had been thrown off; one had a broken ankle, the other had hurt her back. Meanwhile Mac proceeded to chase all the elephants and behave really badly.

We found out later that it was all about one of the female elephants that had just come into oestrus and Mac wanted her, badly! Luckily no serious harm was done and, to prevent this ever happening again, we started injecting the elephants with hormones to control the musth and it's never been a problem again."

As the elephants and other animals began to attract an increasing number of visitors it was just as well that Gill had mastered the art of catering for very large numbers of people. She had become famous for her hospitality - and for cooking underground. Mattheus describes exactly how they did this:

"If you want to cook meat underground first you make a very big hole. When you have finished digging you find very big stones and you put them in the bottom and on the sides. Then you go and find firewood from Msasa trees, a lot of wood. It must be

msasa or other 'real' trees, not gum trees, and you make a very big pile next to the hole.

If you want to start cooking the meat at six in the morning, you must start the fire at six o'clock the night before. Then you must stay there all night; keep putting wood on the fire until four o'clock next morning, when you take everything out of the hole. All the wood, coal, ashes - everything comes out and you leave only the stones.

You first pour on the beer, wine, chutney, onions, garlic, salt and pepper and you rub this over the whole meat. Then you make a thick paste with mealie meal, flour and water and you cover the whole meat with this and then you wrap it all in silver paper and put it in a half drum (cut lengthways). You put the drum in the hole, put a flat simbi (tin sheet) on top of the drum and then you put another sheet of simbi, with hot coals in it, on top of everything. Then you cover the hole with soil. Don't leave even a very small place for the air to come from outside, you must fill the hole full, full, full so that if you put your hand on top you can't even feel the hot.

Then you leave the meat for twelve hours. You can easily do two back legs of nyathi (buffalo) or mombe (beef) together at the same time. This is underground meat and when you take it out everyone is very happy and says, 'Where is this cook, who cooked such good meat like this, where is he!?'

I cooked like this many time with Nkoskas. One time I remember I cooked two back legs of mombe underground for Miss Francis' (Simon and Lorna's daughter) birthday party, when two hundred people came and everyone was very happy."

Mattheus was correct, everyone did ask where the cook was that made such good meat. It was delicious and cause for many compliments. You would

The view across Imire from the lunch kopje

break off the mealie meal shell and then carve this succulent, moist meat which was done to perfection. The mealie meal shell was good too, cooked, browned and suffused with the flavours of the meat and marinade.

For her exquisite garden and home, the big functions we hosted, and for her great cooking, Gill received many compliments in our visitor's book. Perhaps, those from Zimbabweans said the most, albeit in fairly basic language!:

Sadza relish was superb - and animals too!

Good Nosh!

And, from Kerry Kay and her son Clive:

A fantastic day and what a meal - Yum!

The Kay family were esteemed in the district and surrounds. Jock Kay was a farmer in the Ruzawi River area, so we weren't really neighbours, but I knew him well mostly because he was a prominent politician. Jock was what I'd call one of the better politicians. He was forward-thinking, with sound ideas and knew how to handle people. He was a very honest and trustworthy man (and politician) and not an extremist of any sort. Jock was what I would call a sensible liberal! Jock's son was Iain Kay, who I got to know because he and his wife Kerry have played a big part in politics in these later years.

I admire Iain tremendously although, sometimes, I wonder whether we whites should get involved in politics. It's always been a question mark for me because we are such a very small minority. We are 'allowed' to live here by whatever black government is in power. I wonder if Mugabe's views changed in the 1990s because the whites were getting involved in the opposition. I wonder if we were wise, but I won't argue because some people feel strongly that they must stand up for what's right and, perhaps, getting involved in politics is the only way to do that. I think there is a future for white people in Africa but they have to learn to adapt.

Iain is a very admirable man and he and his family went through a very difficult time, particularly in recent years. Because of their beliefs they were targeted, threatened, beaten, put in jail but Iain and his family are very brave people who continue to be involved.

The catering on Imire was so admired, that we began offering our game meat to interested guests. This wasn't from random slaughtering but through a carefully monitored and managed programme, so that we would not become over-populated and have more animals than the environment could cater for. We used to work on a take-off of 10%, which did not cause the herds to deteriorate but, later on when the herds built up, we had to take off much more - up to 30% or even 40%. Mostly we slaughtered impala, tsessebe and wildebeest and the meat was used for guests at the lodge. A wildebeest would last as long as a month in the lodge, a tsessebe didn't last so long and impala about a week. Excess meat was available to customers and big asterisks in the visitor's book told the story:

Venison? When ready, phone…
Wildebeest leg, phone…
NB Zebra meat…

Of course we didn't offer raw game meat to the many VIP's who visited - but they did enjoy the delights of game stew, venison pies, wildebeest curries and impala casseroles. Around the late 1980s and early 1990s Esther Rantzen "and BBC friends" signed her name in the visitor's book. Another entry, alongside eight signatures, reads:

The Royal Air Force crew that brought the Prime Minster Mrs Margaret Thatcher to Zimbabwe.

I suppose Imire reached the height of its achievement when we had our first game auction. Apart from game-viewing we had tried hunts for trophy animals in order to get their numbers down, as we were becoming over-stocked. These attracted the odd hunters from America and Germany and, naturally, we tried to make the hunting difficult, which wasn't easy as the area was small - by then some ten thousand acres. It worked, to a certain extent, but then we graduated to holding annual game sales, which solved the problem of over-stocking.

The game we wanted to de-stock was captured by professionals like Tim Paulett and Mike La Grange and the auctions conducted by Robbie Isaacson from Shapiro and Co. At the early game sales it was touch and go because you didn't know if it was going to work, whether buyers would come or if it was going to be economic. The auctioneers were very good. They were quite happy to come out and operate, just like at a cattle auction.

Tony and Marje Mitchell were still with us when we had the first-ever game auction. It was a lot of work for Tony but he remembers it as being a great achievement:

"The game auctions were the ultimate pinnacle of Norman's concept: proving that the whole game and cattle venture was sustainable, all the way from buying and breeding the animals, to incorporating them with the cattle and then rearing and selling their offspring. The preparations were huge, setting it all up in advance, arranging the water and shade and bomas. We had to catch the animals at least a month in advance so that they would tame down enough to be able to cope with the stress and the changes. The game-capture team would come in, Tim and Doug, and Mike La Grange was there, with his helicopter, to do the transporting."

We built a sale pen consisting of some dozen or so bomas, each 20m square. There was a central passage leading to the loading ramp and plenty of shade trees everywhere. There were little peepholes for people to inspect the animals, catalogues were printed and then we moved across to an area of big flat rocks, where we'd laid out hay bales, and conducted the auction.

At that first sale we were biting our lips all the time wondering how it was all going to go. When the people arrived, and there were streams of cars, we thought they'd all just come for the drinks and a bit of lunch but then the auction started and the bidding went well. Impala that we'd paid $5 for in 1974, sold for $300; sable which had cost $60 to $100 fifteen years before went under the hammer for $16,000 and buffalo were sold for $20,000. Once a sale was made, the burden was on the buyer to arrange for the transport of the animals. The animals, meanwhile, stayed in the bomas and I'd feed them until they were moved.

There was criticism, of course, and some people said that wildlife should be just wildlife but, in today's world, can it be? Is it possible? If people don't utilise the animals then what will happen to them all? The elephants, for example, would have to be shot. The most terrifying thing today is the standard of the culling. In the early days, when the culling was done on a pretty professional basis, an elephant herd was pinned down and experts, like Paulett, would go in at 5m range and boom, boom, boom the animals would be dead. Today they spray them from helicopters and you have wounded animals and it's a shambles. So, which do you want?

John played a leading role in the first game sale and would soon take them over completely:

"Games sales initiated in the 1990s and soon became an annual event and were a great success. Game sales enabled us to take off our surplus animals and we could then replenish blood-lines and have a rotational system, introducing new blood and keeping very healthy herds.

The game sales were absolutely the ultimate. The farm i.e. tobacco, maize and crops - had subsidised the game park from the beginning. Although it never made any real money, luckily, Dad was an excellent tobacco and maize farmer, whose passion was game, and he didn't mind which part of the farm the money came from. Dad never divided the enterprises on Imire; it was all one farm and when he needed a hundred dollars he'd take it out of the kitty and go and buy five impala or whatever it was. But when we got to the game sales it made a significant difference. Suddenly, the whole concept made sense. The income from the game sales provided 60% to 70% of the running costs of the whole park. Until then the day-trips and safaris had only paid 40% of the running costs. The game sales were the pinnacle because they finally allowed the game park to stand on its own. I have a different business approach to that of Dad, which has made my life much easier!"

At one game sale, held a couple of years later in 1996, there were ninety-six impala in the pens and we sold them all at an average price of $900 dollars each. We sold the impala in viable units of one adult ram with five or six adult ewes and a couple of youngsters. This was so that the impala could be introduced as an

imire

wildlife auction 1996

at imire bomas, wedza

FRIDAY 2nd August 1996

VIEWING 9.00am – LUNCH 12 Noon
SALE 1.00pm

SALE MANAGER – JOHN TRAVERS
Imire Central Booking Office
Telefax Harare 731856, Wedza 122-354

AUCTIONEER–TIM COUGHLAN
Harare 736881/7

established herd when they were released. It was a very successful sale conducted by Tim Coughlan of CC Sales on a clear, warm day in early August. Viewing started at nine in the morning and we had cold drinks, a huge buffet and braai and the sale was to start at 1.00pm, by which time everyone would have had a chance to walk around the boma pens and decide which animals they wanted to bid on. A huge crowd of people turned up and the atmosphere was fantastic. We had put hay bales under trees and around the rocks, which was to be the auction floor. After the impala, we sold ten kudu ($1,200 each), five tsessebe ($3,000 each), ten zebra ($5,500 each), nine blesbok ($5,500 each), seven giraffe ($12,000 each), fifteen eland ($4,000 each), eight nyala ($20,000 each) and four foot-and-mouth-free buffalo ($27,000 each). We also sold two elephants, for $170,000 each, and the pair went together. Regrettably, this fantastic trend, which proved that integrating game and cattle was viable, was interrupted by politics. John was left with a real problem on his hands, as he explains:

"The last game sale we were able to hold was in 1998 or 1999. I haven't been able to have any game sales since the land acquisition scheme began in 2000. I haven't purchased any wildlife for the last nine years, because of the situation, and the results are very apparent. Horn growth and size have been dramatically reduced but, more disturbingly, are the signs of inter-breeding. Recently we've had one giraffe born with a hole in its heart and another with a club foot. Our buffalo herd is now badly interbred and you can see it in the calves."

In the mid-1990s I bid a very sad farewell to my old friend Cassius. What a joy it had been rearing him. The excitement, for those involved in his day-to-day escapades, continued almost to the very end. When Cassius was an old lion, of some twenty years, and living contentedly in his enclosure in the garden, the staff one day weren't quick enough closing his gate and, not unexpectedly, he made his getaway. I was out so they called John, who arrived with a shotgun and immediately tried to arrange the return of Cassius to his enclosure. By then the lion was inspecting his old house - our home in fact: bedroom, kitchen and, of course, his old favourite morning room! John called on Mattheus, the old stalwart, to get some meat and walk Cassius back to his enclosure. After a short charge from the lion, which Mattheus stopped with a shouted "NO CLAWS!" - he walked Cassius quietly to his cage. Quite a man was our friend Matt!

Cassius was about twenty-three, which is very old for a lion, when we had to have him put down. It was something I couldn't bring myself to do and, with a lump in my throat, I asked Tony to do it for me. Which he did with compassion, because he had a good rapport with all the animals and they responded very well to him. His particular favourite among the lions was

Nduna and there was one memorable occasion when this lion let Tony know that the feeling was mutual. It was witnessed by a large number of people and is something that neither they nor Tony would forget for a very long time:

"We had a very big farmers' meeting one day and there were seventy or eighty of us sitting in the garden at Imire. The talk was by some New Zealand chaps, who were telling us all about rearing deer. Nduna was in the garden and walked in amongst all these people, sniffing legs and feet and chairs until he found me, jumped up and settled down on my lap - and went to sleep!"

Tony, naturally, was also involved in rescuing and returning escaped animals. One episode he remembers involved the leopard, William:

"William got out one day and was strolling around the garden when the guests arrived. Everyone was exclaiming in excitement, saying, 'Ooh look, there's a leopard,' completely oblivious to the dangers, while we, meanwhile, were desperately trying to shepherd them out of the way and into the house.

We tried all sorts of things but couldn't get William back into his cage and, when the leopard started getting a bit aggressive, we phoned Norman. It was a Wednesday and Norman was at the Wedza Club. This Wednesday afternoon outing was a ritual for him, as he would meet with his cronies Mike Hill, Jack England, Reg White and Harry Orphanides, to play snooker. They weren't any good but it was a good get-together and they'd take turns to bring something along. If it was Norman's turn he'd take four slices of cake from the kitchen, slap them on a plate and that was it. Sorted! Norman would just get up off his bed, after his afternoon nap, put his hat on, stick his pipe in his mouth, grab the plate and off he'd go. We all knew that, if it was Wednesday afternoon, you didn't get in Norman's way. This Wednesday was different!

We phoned him at the Wedza Club and said there was a problem with William, who had escaped. We told Norman that we had tried and failed to get the leopard back into his cage, there were tourists in the house and that he'd better come home and help.

Norman came back to Imire and, by then, I'd taken out the shotgun - just in case. Norman looked at the shotgun and said: 'What do you want that for?'

I pointed to the bodies of the two black swans in the garden that William had just killed - not eaten - only killed, and told Norman I thought he should watch out because the leopard had the taste of blood now.

Norman had literally not handled William for years but he simply went out in the garden and read the riot act to this great big cat, 'William, William, come on!' Sure enough the leopard came straight on over, rubbed himself against Norman, the way cats do, urinated all over him and then strolled back into his cage!

It was definitely a gift that Norman had with the animals. The contact between him and them was very big in his life and I saw the way they responded positively to him again and again over the years. There was something in his manner and his tone of voice that they responded to."

A great relationship built up over time between ourselves and Tony and Marje Mitchell. Tony certainly knew me better than some of my other managers and saw me when I wasn't always at my best, particularly after lunch on Fridays, as he is fond of relating:

"Norman came back from one of his Friday club sessions, looking distinctly the worse for wear. I took one look at him and shook my head.

'What's the matter?' Norman asked. He'd a hankie stuffed under his glasses over one eye.

'Did you get in a fight or something?' I asked.

'No,' he replied. 'I was so tipsy that I couldn't see straight, so I stuffed a hanky over one eye and then I was fine! The only problem was that I got stopped at a police road-block. The policeman asked me what the matter was with my eye, so I said an insect or something had blown into it through the window and I was rushing home to get it out.'

'Oh, okay. Proceed,' the cop said.

Norman was also always losing his hearing aid and would come and ask me if I knew where it was. We'd walk around everywhere searching for it and eventually find it when we heard it whistling - in the bathroom, behind the toilet - all over the place!"

Like everyone who constantly works with tourists, Tony knew, only too well, how tiring it was to always be on your best behaviour. We would look at the diary together and banter over who would take which group that day. Tony was once allocated a blind bowling team and remembers what turned out to be a very special safari:

"Norman, of course, got the air crew (and hostesses) and I was relegated to taking the New Zealand Blind Bowling team on safari that day. I wasn't sure how it was going to work because there was only one fully-sighted person in the group and the rest were either completely, or almost completely, blind. I took them on the usual drive, chatting as we went and stopping at the usual places. They were absolutely enthralled to be able to feel an elephant's skin, the gentle softness of the tip of a trunk, the tough hide of the rhino, a lion licking them through the fence. At the end of the day the leader gave a little vote of thanks, on behalf of the group.

'Through you we have seen animals today,' he said and even now his words still choke me up. Days like that made every-thing worthwhile."

When Tony and Marje Mitchell left us, to take over a small game park in the Chinhoyi area, my daughter, Barbara, came and ran Sable Lodge for a few years. She renovated the main lodge and built six rondavels, which meant we could have sixteen guests at a time. Barbs remembers managing Sable Lodge as a difficult time:

Gill, Norman and Barbara at the lunch kopje

The Travers and the Hamiltons - life-long friends

"I came back to Imire to run Sable Lodge and it was a battle of wills because so many dominant people were all in such close proximity. John and Judy were running the farm, Mum and Dad were running the game park and I took over Sable Lodge. At the lodge we had tourists and overnight guests, film crews, photographic safaris and some hunters. The game guides were trained and managed by Dad at first, and then he took on Ian Du Preez, who went on to manage the day-to-day issues with the elephants and rhinos. I ran Sable Lodge for six years but it wasn't an easy time because of the constant battle of wills between me and Dad."

Being in my seventies, and whilst I still could, I embarked on one last fishing trip to Moçambique. David Hamilton was there, as he had been on so many other happy holidays, and relates what happened:

"Norman was an indefatigable under-water hunter for crayfish - not so much the spear fisherman. His very last trip was out to the Moçambique islands, by then in his seventies. He went out goggling, dived on a reef (well out to sea) and, at the end of the day, simply could not get back into the boat.

Solution: tow him back to the island behind the boat, which is the picture Gill was presented with. She saw the boat returning without her husband and only then noticed that the boat was towing something. There was Norman, pipe in mouth, looking very comfortable and being towed gently towards the shore!"

Chapter Fourteen

ROUGH DIAMOND
The Dawn of the New Millennium

As the 1990s drew to a close, it was nearly time for Gill and I to leave Imire. What a wonderful life we'd shared, a great adventure spanning half a century on a very special piece of land. In 1998, when I was seventy-seven, I was extremely honoured to be awarded the Wildlife Oscar by the Conservation Trust. There was a big presentation made at the Cresta Oasis Hotel in Harare and the Minister of Agriculture, Joseph Made, attended. The award was in recognition of all my achievements with game on Imire.

Something else happened in 1998: I met a man in a bank, in Marondera. No big deal, you might think, and it wasn't until twelve years later, in 2010, that I would hear from him again and understand the impact Imire had on his life. Morgan Chokwenda, living in Middlesex, near Heathrow Airport, wrote us an e-mail sharing his memories of Imire:

"I come from Wedza and in 1988 was a boarder at Chemhanza Primary School, which is in the vicinity of Imire Game Park. As you can imagine, my first school trip was to Imire to see giraffe (twiza, in Shona), zebras, elephants (nzou) and the buffalo (nyati) that could pull a plough!

I enjoyed my trip, at that tender age, and it was to be the only time I ever went there but, up to this day, I cherish that moment and am proud that Imire is the only tourist attraction of note in Wedza. What I really want to share is not what was happening at Imire, but the man running Imire! Ten years later (in 1998) after finding a job with the local bank, guess whose account I was looking after? Small world indeed! Imire Game Park and Kurima Farm business accounts, whose signatory was Mr Travers. He is a remarkable man! The people of Chimanimani talk of Roy Bennett being 'Pachedu' - our Shona term for 'one of us'. Well, Mr Travers used to look after us (bank tellers, as we were called then). Remember, I dealt with a lot of farmers, most of whom were horrible to black people, sorry to say, but not Mr Travers. Once I had told him about my visit to his game park, he would not leave the banking hall without shaking my hand. Mr Travers is Pachedu, from Mashonaland East."

A landmark came in 1999 when we held a big gathering to commemorate fifty years on Imire (1949 - 1999). We invited all the managers who had ever worked on the place and they came with their wives and children. Judy remembers the day as being very special:

"Gilly did the most incredible spread of food and there must have been fifty or sixty people. Every person stood up and gave their little review of working with Norman. Every one of them said what a hard task-master he had been to work for, how much they adored Gilly and how, despite everything, they'd all become the firmest of friends with Gilly and Norman thereafter."

Tony and Marje Mitchell were among the guests - Tony remembers the day well:

"David Hamilton had phoned and asked if I would give a speech and I was delighted to do so and be able to talk about a man who really was a legend. Norman had the most amazing ideas and foresight. He could see where wildlife was going to go in the future and made plans to fit his vision. Norman was more like a friend than a boss to me, like a father in fact, and we had become very close in the years that I worked on Imire. When I gave my speech there was much laughter, of course, as we'd all had such similar encounters with Norman and Gill and Imire.

'Norman's been here fifty years,' I announced. 'But there are fifty-seven managers present, so some of you didn't even make a year - will those responsible please stand up!' It was a lovely, lovely day and I think Norman and Gill were both overwhelmed."

One guest was Mupia, who had been an Imire foreman, and I'd sent him to run a farm, on the Bridge Road, called Cheverton. In those days it was unheard of to have a black manager running a tobacco section, but Mupia did very well and stayed on Cheverton for two or three years to grow tobacco. Mupia had eventually retired but John managed to find him for Imire's 50th Anniversary and it was quite a reunion, I hadn't seen him for thirty years! Mupia was dressed in his best suit, complete with hat, and he made a super speech. I can't remember what he said - probably what an old bastard I was!

There had been so many important people in my life. Gill being the first and most important VIP, having put up with me for sixty years, given me a beau-

Gill, Norman and Mupia - an old foreman

tiful daughter and three fine sons - what man is so blessed? Gill put up with so much and supported all my exploits. When we went hunting she would come along just to run the camp, even though she didn't like the hunting herself. She loved the birdlife and the animals and walking in the bush. Gill said that she came on the hunting trips because she didn't want to ever hold me back. She said she was very proud of the way I handled life; just as proud as I, and all the family were, of her. Barbara summed it up so well:

Norman feeds a grandchild

"Mum always showed such courage and bravery and was the strength behind Dad. Little Mum always just took everything on board. It didn't matter what Dad asked her to do or what he arrived with, Mum just accepted it, she always supported him in whatever he did. Mum trusted Dad completely and adored him, unconditionally. She had all these lion cubs and leopard cubs and other little animals which were always just everywhere, in her garden, behind the bushes, jumping out at her. She always carried a stick wherever she went, in order to ward off these animals - a hyaena that was hiding in the bougainvillea, a leopard waiting to pounce from behind her roses, a lion crouching in the shrubbery...

However, Mum was the one in control - she was always there, holding the fort, organising everything, from the meals to the functions and she would put Dad's clothes out for him and make sure he was tidy and that everything was done properly. Dad was a rough diamond and Mum polished him up into a very bright diamond, indeed."

Of course there are many VIPs in our extended family, all of whom we love and cherish. Our only daughter, Barbara, is living in New Zealand where she's had lots of battles bringing up two boys on her own, with little money (a Travers failing!). Barbara is now successfully running a cancer hospital, as manager, and her sons, Mark and Nigel have grown into fine young men who are a great credit to her. Mark is quiet, religious and has lately been teaching skiing. Nigel has inherited hunting instincts and is a very successful fisherman and wild pig and deer hunter. He has grown into a strong young man, was in the 1st rugby team in his last year at school, and is joining the New Zealand Army.

John and Judy produced Kate, Bruce and Riley - grandchildren for us. Kate has grown into a lovely woman, working in the UK with her partner, both highly respected in their work and surprise, surprise, making money! Bruce has grown into a quiet, good-looking young man. He did well in sports at school and now lives in Australia but is coming home soon to farm. Riley is best described as a heart-warming *skellum* - if you know what I mean? He is working for John on Imire and, in spite of the political climate, has started a scheme where young people pay to work with the rhino and elephant.

Norman fishing with Barb's son in New Zealand

This is working well, apart from the odd girl falling in love with him. He is too good-looking for his own good! His latest plan to raise money for the rhino was to canoe, with two friends, from the source of the Zambezi in Angola, to the sea - quite an undertaking and an epic trip.

Alastair and Anne Marie's two daughters - Tara and Sam - were raised by John and Judy, who refer to them as their own children. Tara is a lovely girl, quiet but full of fun and is now planning her life having left school. She hopes to study for an International Hotel School qualification. Sam takes after Alastair and is dedicated to sport - always with a ball in her hand, either rugby, tennis or cricket! She made it into the Zimbabwe under-19 hockey team and did very well, considering she was only seventeen! Her ambition, which she recently achieved, was to get a scholarship to an American University concentrating on hockey. Alastair and Anne Marie must be very proud of their two daughters - we all are!

John and Judy took over the game park and went from strength to strength, making a great success of Imire. In 2009 they brought white rhino successfully into the park. Judy is of the same calibre as Gill; completely devoted to conservation and the rearing of wild animals. Our first baby elephant was born under her care. The game park is in good hands with John and Judy at the helm, and Gill and I are so proud of them both.

Simon and Lorna produced two attractive and clever children, Christopher and Francie. Christopher went to university in the UK, passing his Sports Management degree with honours. He has a girlfriend whose family owns an estate in Scotland where he gets good salmon and trout fishing! Francie, their daughter, is a lovely girl and always has a smile on her face. She moved to Arusha, Tanzania, with her parents and has a handsome boyfriend, Keith Charters - the son of a Wedza farming family. Keith is a very successful big-game hunter and safari operator in Tanzania, Congo and beyond. Keith says that, until he has finished building a house, he and Francie won't get married! Simon and Lorna visit us when they can but are carving out a new life in Tanzania.

What a lucky couple Gill and I are! A wonderful family who, although spread all over the world, give us endless joy and love. It makes life very worthwhile.

Gilly and I left Imire in 2004 and retired to a cottage at Borradaile Trust, in Marondera. Judy describes our leaving:

"When Gilly and Norman left Imire in 2004, after being there for fifty-five years, and

went to live at Borradaile Trust, it was very, very emotional for everyone concerned. The next day Imire had lost its soul with them not there. It was a Friday, the kids were due back in school on Monday but none of that mattered. In distress, we packed up there and then and, taking nothing with us except a few basics like tea and biscuits, went on a week-long walk with the elephants. We walked down the Sengezi River, up into Wedza Mountain, down the other side to the Save (Sabi) confluence and then back home. Mandy Bibby's little son came with us and Mandy wanted me to have a cellphone so that she could phone us, meet us somewhere and get her son back to school. I said, 'Mandy, sorry. I'm not touching a cellphone, he's either in or out,' and so Sam, our daughter, said she'd take the cellphone.

Every night we chained the elephants to trees wherever we stopped, something they were very used to, and, on our second night, Mac stretched out his trunk, grabbed Samantha's rucksack and spent the night going through everything. He eventually got to the cellphone and ate it! It was as if the elephant knew that the cellphone shouldn't have been there! We then spent an entire day following him and checking his droppings to see if we could find the SIM card!

Sometimes the kids rode on the elephants but not much, mostly we all just walked. No-one knew we were coming so you can imagine people suddenly seeing these animals for the first time. A lot of the people had never seen elephants before. It was a very poor area and some people said they thought the elephants were rocks in motion, or animals with all pieces stuck together! A lot of people, in the areas we walked through, had the elephant as their totem and they told us that, now they'd actually seen an elephant, they could die peacefully.

The elephants were fantastic. We went to a funeral, one day, at dawn. It was misty and the people at the gathering said it was the highest honour for them to have the elephants at the burial of their relative. As we travelled onward, other people came out of their huts to meet the elephants and it was absolutely wonderful to see. They would never say thank you to us, but instead would thank the elephants. We had no idea how strong the presence of an elephant was in these rural areas and the villagers would bring huge sackfuls of their pumpkins, that were meant to last them through winter, but they wanted to give them to the elephants as a gift. There was one incident, when we were surrounded by about forty people, and we did our little conservation talk. Toto was always shy and removed but was an elephant of great courage. Blind in one eye he had just never been social. He always left the social occasions to Mac, who was the party animal! Suddenly Toto walked

Relaxing on the banks of the Zambezi

into the crowd and went straight to a young man, of about eighteen, and smelt him closely, from his head to his feet, over and over. We went to the boy who, understandably, was standing there wide-eyed and fearful, and asked him if he was alright, but he didn't reply. Then we learnt that the boy was actually mute and Toto had obviously sensed it, even amongst this huge gathering of people.

It was such a fascinating trip, took six days, covered about 135kms and was life-changing for all of us."

A couple of years later, the family gathered on Imire to spend Christmas 2006 with John and Judy. Gill and I came from our cottage at Borradaile Trust, Barbara and her son Nigel had come over from New Zealand and Simon and Lorna were there from Tanzania. We had arranged that everyone would meet at Alastair's dam to have sundowners and sing Christmas carols. Meanwhile Nigel, my grandson, and I went fishing in an old tin boat on the other farm dam near John and Judy's house. Nigel then was fifteen years old, and I, Grandpa, was eighty-five! We had caught two or three small bass already when I stood up to land a fish on my line. The boat tipped over and everything, including us, landed in the water. Nigel asked, "Shall we swim to the dam wall, it's closer than the bank?"

"I'll never be able to climb up the dam wall," I replied and so we set off for the bank. By now the boat had sunk and disappeared completely, along with fishing rods, tackle and fish! Floating on my back, with pipe in mouth, Nigel pulled me by the shoulders while I tried to help by kicking feebly.

"Grandpa, are you alright?" Nigel kept wanting to know while, puffing and panting, we struggled the eighty or so yards towards dry land.

Meanwhile, at sundown, Judy had come down to the dam to look for us but, when she didn't see the boat, she'd gone back and had set off with John to join the sundowner party. Luckily for us, Judy had a feeling that something was wrong and returned to look for us again. She saw someone waving from the far side of the dam, just as Nigel came running over to tell her what had happened. I was then rescued, given a bottle of whisky and, after a hot bath and a couple more tots, felt as fit as a fiddle.

Five years after Gill and I had left Imire, our old friend Mattheus came to visit and reminisce about the old days. About lions, leopards, warthogs and cooking underground. An old man, and now also retired, he said he had good memories of our years together and didn't hesitate to recall the real meaning of my nickname!

"Oh, my life with Mr and Mrs Travers was very good; it was a number-one life. I worked with them for forty-seven years and Mrs Travers taught me everything. I want Jesus to give them more life. Mr Travers is a very big man and is the chief of Imire. He is a madala (old man) in his body but his brain is still very, very sharp.

I still remember that we workers on Imire used to call Mr Travers 'Umgufu'. In Shona, Umgufu means that you give a shove to someone who is working slowly and you say, 'Come on, wake up!'"

In the year 2010, aged eighty-eight, looking back on it all, what a wonderful life we had on Imire. We built up a farm that I am very proud of. I'm also very proud of everyone involved with Imire, from Gill and all the family members through to all our African staff, who have been superb. Now that we're old and retired it has given us tremendous satisfaction, particularly, to see how well our children are running it. That gives us perhaps more contentment than anything else.

Sad to say, Parkinson's disease has reared its ugly head and Gill is now nearly blind and unable to walk. However, she is still, and long may she remain, my right-hand man. Her support for all my ideas and plans, in both commercial and game-farming, was always there. How she put up with some of the crazy projects, I don't know! Rearing leopards, hyaenas, lions and even young rhino became part of our life together. And what a wonderful life it has been; no-one could have had a more loving companion than Gill - the mother of our four children and foster-mother to a never-ending stream of smelly, naughty little animals. I hope heaven will give her the peace she deserves!

Looking back on my life, the most special place for me - and the place where I'd most love to be right now - is on the kopje where we built our lunch spot. It's a lovely place with tremendous views over several farms and kopjes into the distance, even Wedza Mountain on a clear day. It brings back so many silly little memories. I especially remember, once, finding a rock nightjar (freckled nightjar), which live on the kopjes. I took a group of people over to show them where the nightjar had made its nest. We crept very quietly towards her. A nightjar has very big eyes, which show her up when she's lying down on the bare rock. As we approached her nest, which was just a few twigs in a little crevice, I saw her eyelids slowly close - a means of hiding herself. Those little special things will always stay in my memory; they are the Imire that I love...

Nightjar

When through the woods and forest glades I wander
And hear the birds sing sweetly in the trees,
When I look down from lofty mountain grandeur,
And hear the brook and feel the gentle breeze.

When Christ shall come with shout of acclamation
To take me home, what joy shall fill my heart.
Then I shall bow in humble adoration,
And there proclaim, my God, how great thou art!

POSTSCRIPT

At 4.00am, on Thursday 18 March 2010, Norman Travers passed away peacefully in Marondera. The day before he died I'd stood at his bedside, alongside his son John. Norman had opened his eyes, smiled at us and said, "I know my book is in good hands."

We had finished the final draft just a week earlier and Norman had checked through every chapter and page. Some chapters had to be reprinted, after he lost them, and others had evidence of encounters with his pipe and whisky glass! Norman and I had worked on the book for fifteen months, which entailed me visiting him once or twice a week to record his memories and ask the many thousands of questions that helped to jog his memory. Norman wasn't very good with names and even worse with dates. A hundred times over he would ask, "Gilly, what was the name of that chap who..." and, very often, Gill would remember the name of the person, although it usually took a bit of time! Norman never kept a diary. He said his life was always too busy and, as a result, there are likely to be many unfortunate omissions in this book.

As we worked, I often scrawled little notes to myself on scraps of paper - reminders of other questions I wanted to ask. One of these was. "Which was your favourite animal?"

Every time I asked this question, Norman gave me a different answer! Sometimes he said it was Maggie the hippo; who would career across the dam, at full speed, in answer to his call, and proffer a gaping mouth for half a loaf of bread and a gulp of beer. Cassius the lion was also his favourite; purring loudly, licking his hand with a rasping tongue. Chuie the leopard was Norman's soul mate; rubbing up against him, sleeping contentedly on his lap, never showing any resentment for losing a leg. Dudley the warthog was another favourite; sniffing and snuffling, always looking for a snack or a titbit, always wanting a scratch on his chest or belly. Even the crocodile, Norman told me once, was a favourite because it clearly responded to his call - or was it to the meat held in his hand!

Time and again, however, Norman told me that among his most favourite animals were the elephants; intelligent, clever and so gentle. They had souls, Norman said. He particularly loved Nzou, the elephant cow he'd raised from a baby, alongside the buffalo herd. Nzou, the majestic elephant, who came every day to the lunch kopje to be seen by tourists. The elephant that often killed buffalo bulls but never harmed a hair on Norman's head. The giant of the animal kingdom, so loved by a giant of man.

Norman's funeral was held at Castle Kopje, Wedza, on 24 March 2010. The notice of his death proclaimed: 'Our mountain has left us.' It was a hot and cloudy day and, all along the road to Imire, the grass was tall and golden, heavy with seed, bowing and dipping in the wind. Thousands of pink and white cosmos flowers, scattered in the grass, provided a magnificent avenue of colour. A lilac-breasted roller, sitting on a telephone wire, attested to the beauty of the surroundings although the sign outside Southlawn School stood in stark contrast to this peace of the African bush: 'Beware! Sex thrills and Aids kills!'

Acacia trees, combretums, msasas and munondos threw their shade over the road and I wondered how many hundreds of thousands of times Norman must have travelled along this exact same route. First, seventy years ago as an eighteen-year-old teenager, newly arrived from England and China, driving on these dirt roads past the farms displaying name-plates of majors, colonels and captains. Later, with Gill and their children, on holidays, going fishing and hunting, or with crops and stock feed, carrying giraffe and elephant, buffalo and lion - bringing wild animals back to their ancestral home-ground.

Two hundred people or so were gathered in the field below Castle Kopje. A couple of black rhino were grazing in the newly-cut grass and a pair of huge elephants were flapping their ears and browsing in the trees nearby. Hay bales were arranged in semicircles before a giant acacia tree, while pots and milk churns were filled to overflowing with cosmos.

Dr Kevin Martin led the service, paying tribute to Norman whom he described as a big man in every way, open-hearted and a pioneer of the old stock. David Hamilton spoke about how Norman thrived in challenging situations, always determined and positive. He said that it was only because of Norman's optimism and John's tenacity that we were gathered together in this place, the most glorious of settings. David also paid tribute to Gill saying it was she who introduced Norman to compassion, love and laughter - the things he hadn't had much of in his life before he met her. As David spoke, our eyes couldn't help but be drawn to the two enormous elephants, Mac and Toto, who towered above us, breaking wind unashamedly as they gathered up cubes from the ground.

Norman's nephew, Howard Matthews paid tribute to his uncle whom he described as being like the landscape around us: rugged and dependable. People nodded and smiled when he talked about his uncle's laughter and

humour and his ability to make you feel complete and alive. Howard said that Norman was a titan of the past and would be an inspiration in the future.

Norman was buried beneath the big acacia tree, to the singing of a small African choir. His coffin was covered with hay, pink and white cosmos and sunflowers. The proceedings were watched over by his beloved elephants. They ate some of the flowers, drank the water from a few flower pots and carefully smelled the soil that covered the grave of the man who had reared them.

In my mind's eye I could see Norman smiling at these events. I could smell his pipe and hear his laugh. This, I knew, was exactly how Norman would have wanted to be buried: in the bush, surrounded by his family, his friends and his elephants.

Cathy Buckle
Marondera, Zimbabwe ~ March 2010

Norman Mockliffe Travers
10/10/1921 - 18/03/2010

Lord grant that I may fish until my dying day.
And when it comes to my last cast.

BIBLIOGRAPHY

Bothma, J du P   1989   "Game Ranch Management"   Van Schaik - Pretoria, South Africa

English, P   1995   "Lushington: A Fragment of Time"   Print Holdings - Zimbabwe

Garlake, P   1987   "The Painted Caves"   Modus - Zimbabwe

Gray, P   2006   "A Fenman in Africa"   Reedbush Press - UK

Kenmuir, D   1983   "Fishes of Kariba"   Wilderness Publications - Zimbabwe

Kenmuir, D & Williams, R   1975   "Wild Mammals"   Longman - Zimbabwe

Macartney, P (Ed) 1975   "Wildlife on Your Farm" Longman - Rhodesia

Macdonald, Sheila (Comp) 2003   "Winter Cricket: The Spirit of Wedza"   Sheila Macdonald - Zimbabwe

Maclean, GL   1985   "Roberts' Birds of Southern Africa"   John Voelcker Bird Book Fund
- Cape Town, South Africa

Meadows, K   "Sometimes When it Rains"   Thorntree Press - Bulawayo, Zimbabwe

Sayce, K (Ed)   1987   "Encyclopedia Zimbabwe"   Quest - Zimbabwe

Smith, I   1997   "The Great Betrayal"   Blake - UK

Smithers, RHN   1983   "The Mammals of the Southern African Sub-region"
University of Pretoria - South Africa

Stuart, C & T   1988   "Field Guide to the Mammals of Southern Africa"   Struik - Cape Town, South Africa

Thornycroft, D   2009   "Nigel and Corona"   Verity Thorncroft - South Africa

West, G (Ed)   1985   "Black's Veterinary Dictionary"   Fifteenth Edition, A & C Black - London

Unknown   1974   "The Bundu Book of Geology, Gemmology and Archaeology"   Longman - Rhodesia

The Farmer; The Rhodesia Herald; The Herald; The Wedza Gazette

Wikimedia commons and other photographic and illustrative credits: Chris Eason - Helmeted guinea fowl and chicks;
Paul Rae - Buffalo bull; Paul Maritz - Sable bull; Tigerpython - African rock python; Raeky - Cape clawless otter;
Überraschungsbilder - Orange tree; Newt - Nile crocodile; kevinzim - Crocodile eggs; Lip Kee Yap - Elands; Aaron Logan
- Warthog; MozamPete - Hippo in water; Walter Voigts - Wildebeest; Dewet - Dung beetle; Nature at Your Backyard -
Nightjar; Aluminium - Barn owl chick; Davefoc - Egyptian Geese; Hendrik128 - Tobacco seedling; Duane Raver - Rainbow
Trout; Zimbabwe Association for the Rehabilitation and Prevention of Tuberculosis (RAPT); PTC Zimbabwe; Luis Manso
Preto; Travers and Hamilton family albums; Denise Lues; Imire stock photos.

Cathy Buckle is a well-known Zimbabwean author. She first met
Norman Travers in the 1980s, when she was Estate Manager of the
Mukuvusi Woodlands, in Harare. She was hand-rearing baby elephants
at the time, before they relocated to Imire when they became too
big. It was ten years before Cathy saw the elephants again, and they
immediately recognised her - but Norman didn't! Consequently, with
his memory fading even more in recent years, and having read her
work, in 2009 he asked her to help compile his autobiography.

This is Cathy Buckle's ninth book. Born and raised in Zimbabwe,
she is a dispossessed farmer, has one son and lives in Marondera.
She writes a popular current affairs column 'Letter from Zimbabwe'
for 'The Zimbabwean' newspaper, which broadcasts weekly on www.SWRadioAfrica.com
and is posted on her website www.cathybuckle.com

Recent books by Cathy Buckle include "African Tears", "Beyond Tears" and "Innocent Victims"